The Mental Models Theory of Reasoning

Refinements and Extensions

The Mental Models Theory of Reasoning

Refinements and Extensions

Edited by

Walter Schaeken
André Vandierendonck
Walter Schroyens
Géry d'Ydewalle

LAWRENCE ERLBAUM ASSOCIATES, PUBLISHERS
2007   Mahwah, New Jersey   London

Camera ready copy for this book was provided by the editors.

Lawrence Erlbaum Associates, Inc., Publishers
10 Industrial Avenue
Mahwah, New Jersey 07430
www.erlbaum.com

Cover design by Kathryn Houghtaling Lacey

Library of Congress Cataloging-in-Publication Data

The mental models theory of reasoning : refinements and extensions / edited by Walter Schaeken ... [et al.].
     p. cm.

Includes bibliographical references and index.

ISBN 978-0-8058-4183-1 — ISBN 0-8058-4183-0 (cloth)
1. Reasoning (Psychology). I. Schaeken, Walter.
BF442.M47 2007
153.4'3—dc22   2005040691
                                                       CIP

Printed in the United States of America
10 9 8 7 6 5 4 3 2 1

List of Contributors

Pierre Barrouillet, L.E.A.D. - C.N.R.S. UMR 5022, Pôle AAFE, Esplanade Erasme, BP 26513, 21065 Dijon, France

Ruth Byrne, Department of Psychology, Dublin University, Trinity College, Dublin 2, Ireland

Vicky Dierckx, Department of Experimental Psychology, University of Ghent, Henri Dunantlaan 2, 9000 Gent, Belgium

J. St. B. T. Evans, Department of Psychology, University of Plymouth, Plymouth, Devon PL1 5RR, UK

Aidan Feeney, Psychology Department, Durham University, Department of Psychology, South Road, Durham, DH1 3LE, UK

Vittorio. Girotto, Department of Art and Industrial Design, University of Venice,, Dorsoduor 2206, Convento delle Terese, 30123 Venice, Italy

Michel Gonzalez, CNRS, Université de Provence, 29 Av. R. Schumann, F-13621 Aix-en-Provence Cedex 1, France

Eugenia Goldvarg-Steingold, Infant Cognition Laboratory, Department of Brain and Cognitive Science, MIT, 77 Massachusetts Avenue, Cambridge, MA 02139, USA

David Green, Department of Psychology, Centre for Cognitive Science, University College London, Gower Street, London WC1E 6BT, UK

Nelly Grosset, L.E.A.D. - C.N.R.S. UMR 5022, Pôle AAFE, Esplanade Erasme, BP 26513, 21065 Dijon, France

Simon Handley, Department of Psychology, University of Plymouth, Plymouth, Devon PL1 5RR, UK

Philip N. Johnson-Laird, Department of Psychology, Green Hall, Princeton University, Princeton, NJ 08544, USA

Karl Christoph Klauer, Institut für Psychologie, Albert-Ludwigs-Universität Freiburg, 79085 Freiburg, Germany

Thorsten Meiser, Friedrich-Schiller-Universität Jena, Humboldtstr. 11, D-07743 Jena, Germany

David Over, Business School, University of Sunderland, Reg Vardy Centre, Sir Tom Cowie Campus at St Peter's, St Peters Way, Sunderland, SR6 0DD, UK

Maxwell Roberts, Department of Psychology, University of Essex, Wivenhoe Park, Colchester, Essex, CO4 3SQ, UK

Walter Schaeken, Labo Experimental Psychology, University of Leuven, Tiensestraat 102, B-3000 Leuven, Belgium

Walter Schroyens, HEC Montréal, 3000, chemin de la Côte-Sainte-Catherine, Montréal (Québec) H3T 2A7, Canada

Jean-Baptiste Van der Henst, Institut des Sciences Cognitives, 67, Boulevard Pinel, 69675 Bron cedex, FRANCE

André Vandierendonck, Department of Experimental Psychology, University of Ghent, Henri Dunantlaan 2, 9000 Gent, Belgium

Contents

Preface

This book has proceeded from the Workshop on mental models and deductive reasoning in Brussels. This workshop was sponsored by the Fund for Scientific Research Flanders and the Federal research project IUAP/PAI P4/19.

We hope that this book will serve the purpose of directing the reader attention to various recent opinions about the status of mental models in the psychology of reasoning.

Mental models are representations in the mind of real or imaginary situations. They can be constructed from perception, imagination, or the comprehension of discourse. Each mental model represents a possibility. Cognitive scientists world-wide have studied how models bring about thoughts and inferences. In the domain of deductive reasoning, the mental model theory is very influential, but definitely not without its criticisms.

We hope to show a sample of the diversity of research related to the role of mental models in reasoning: There are chapters about propositional reasoning, about relational reasoning, about statistical reasoning, and some more meta-theoretical chapters. Moreover, the final collection includes the work of scientists from all over the world: Belgium, England, France, Germany, Ireland, Italy, and the United States.

Since many of the contributions do not deal exclusively with one topic, they have not been explicitly placed in sections. However, the ordering of the chapters reflects the main issue addressed by the authors. Reading the first version of the manuscripts for the book raised the question of what we would do with the presentation of the mental model theory. Indeed, many of the authors gave their own introduction to the theory. We decided that it would be best if the authors produced their chapters to stand alone. As a consequence, each chapter is self-contained and can be read on its own. Some repetition of key theoretical issues therefore occurs.

We owe much to Marleen Devijver. Her secretarial work for the workshop was invaluable. Moreover, she made a major contribution in preparing the manuscripts for publication. We gratefully acknowledge those individuals who contributed to planning and conducting the conference: Vicky Dierckx, Kristien Dieussaert, Niki Verschueren, and Wim De Neys.

Finally, we want to thank all contributors for their enthusiastic cooperation in the realization of the workshop and of this book.

1

Memory Retrieval and Content Effects in Conditional Reasoning: A Developmental Mental Models Account

Pierre Barrouillet
Nelly Grosset

The mental models theory assumes that conditional reasoning is mainly constrained by the number of models individuals can hold and process in working memory and the nature and the accessibility of knowledge used to construct these models. Both constraints result from the limitation of the cognitive resources available to activate knowledge from long-term memory and maintain it active for processing. Because the amount of cognitive resources increases with age, the mental models theory allows precise predictions about the way children, adolescents, and adults interpret conditional sentences and reason from them, and about how contents affect reasoning at different ages. These predictions have been tested in two experiments in which adolescents and adults were asked to reason from conditional sentences that involved either familiar or unfamiliar relations between the antecedent and the consequent. The results confirmed the main developmental predictions of the mental models theory and provided evidence that the fleshing-out process is achieved through a process of retrieval from long-term memory. Both developmental and content effects result from the same processes of constructing and manipulating mental models.

INTRODUCTION

Evidence in support of the mental models theory of conditional reasoning (Johnson-Laird, 1999; Johnson-Laird & Byrne, 1991, 2002) has been growing during the last 10 years. According to this theory, understanding an "If p then q" conditional sentence results in the construction of an initial representation of the following form:

(1) p q
    ...

that contains only one explicit model representing a state of affairs in which both p and q propositions are verified. The three dots refer to other possibilities that are

1

kept in an implicit format and in which p would be false. Thus, this initial representation supports only affirmative inferences (i.e,. modus ponens [MP], from p conclude q, and affirmation of consequent [AC], from q conclude p). To draw denial inferences from a negative minor premise (i.e., either not p or not q) requires reasoners to flesh out this initial representation with additional models that explicitly represent negated values ($\neg p$. $\neg q$, and $\neg p$. q).

The mental models theory assumes that this fleshing-out process is demanding and time-consuming. Accordingly, it has been shown that the production of denial inferences that require a fleshing-out process is slower than that of the affirmative inferences supported by the initial model (Barrouillet, Grosset, & Lecas, 2000). In the same way, it has been shown that modus tollens (MT; from not q conclude not p) is more often endorsed when the minor premise not q is presented before rather than after the conditional premise (Girotto, Mazzocco, & Tasso, 1997). Indeed, the preliminary presentation of negative information (i.e., not q) leads reasoners to focus on negative values and thus facilitates the explicit representation of the $\neg p$. $\neg q$ model that supports MT. Furthermore, it has been suggested that the mental models theory provides an account of Wason's selection task (Evans & Handley, 1999; Johnson-Laird & Byrne, 2002), probabilistic reasoning from conditional sentences (Johnson-Laird, Legrenzi, Girotto, Legrenzi, & Caverni, 1999), and the compelling illusory inferences that result from a disjunction of conditional statements (Johnson-Laird & Savary, 1999). Thus, the mental models theory is undoubtedly the most explanatory and heuristic among the available theories of propositional reasoning. However, we would suggest that the standard version of this theory still suffers from two gaps on which this chapter focuses.

First, the theory must account for content effects, which are ubiquitous in conditional reasoning, in a more effective and convincing way than it does. Bonatti (1994a, 1994b) argued that the mental models theory cannot account for content effects in propositional reasoning because this theory relies on a truth-table approach that is formal and ignores both the content and the context. Despite that Bonatti seems to neglect the role of the fleshing-out process in conditional reasoning (see Barrouillet & Lecas, 1998, for a discussion), it should be acknowledged that the standard theory lacks the precise machinery to account for content effects in a predictable way.

Second, the theory must account for the developmental phenomena that have been the focus of past psychological studies on thinking, reasoning, and rationality (Inhelder & Piaget, 1955; Piaget & Inhelder, 1959) because a developmental approach probably constitutes the best way to validate the theory. Indeed, if reasoning is a matter of constructing and manipulating mental models in working memory, these processes should be constrained in three ways. The first of these relates to the limited capacity of the working memory in which mental models are maintained and processed. The second concerns the structure and content of the semantic memory that provides reasoners with knowledge from which mental models are constructed. Finally, the third relates to the relative accessibility of this knowledge in long-term memory. The impact of these constraints on reasoning processes should evolve with age, thus leading to a predictable developmental trend. One of the main developmental changes that could have a direct influence on reasoning skills is the developmental increase in cognitive resources.

It is widely acknowledged that there is an age-related increase in cognitive capacities (Barrouillet & Camos, 2001; Case, 1985; Cowan, 1997; Halford, 1993; Halford, Wilson, & Phillips, 1998; Swanson, 1999). The most recent models of working memory conceive these capacities as a pool of attentional resources available to activate knowledge from long-term memory and to keep it active for processing (Anderson & Lebière, 1998; Cowan, 1995, 2001; Engle, Kane, & Tuholski, 1999; Rosen & Engle, 1997). As a consequence, any increase in cognitive capacities should have an impact both on the number of models that can be processed in working memory and on the accessibility of knowledge from long-term memory (i.e., the two main constraints on reasoning hypothesized by the mental models theory). This theory should thus make it possible to predict the form and content of the representations used at different ages as a function of the amount of available resources and knowledge. Thus, the mental models theory is not only more suited than others to account for content effects, as Johnson-Laird and Byrne (1991) claimed, but it is also developmental in nature.

THE DEVELOPMENT OF CONDITIONAL REASONING: A MODEL

Markovits and Barrouillet (2002) recently proposed a developmental reformulation of the mental models theory of the conditional based on two main assumptions. First, they assume that although advanced reasoners may develop or learn strategies specific to logical reasoning, children and probably many adults use processes that are general and rely on existing cognitive architectures. Second, they suggest that children (and adults) have an understanding of if-then propositions that is inherently relational and involves the application of a rich linguistic and pragmatic knowledge. More precisely, an "if p then q" statement is understood as introducing a directional relation between a variable P, one value of which is specified by the proposition p, and a variable Q, one value of which is specified by the proposition q. Thus, the "if p then q" relation defines a semantic space that depends both on the semantic nature of the terms used and on the reasoner's knowledge about the relationship between them. For example, "if he is a postman, then he has a blue cap" would be understood not only as introducing a mapping between different kinds of people and different kinds of hats, but also as referring to hats of professional uniforms because we assume that mental models for conditionals represent not only specific elements but also how they are related (Thompson, 2000; Thompson & Mann, 1995).

In line with Johnson-Laird and Byrne's (1991) theory, it is assumed that children construct an initial representation that contains only one model in which specific tokens represent both p and q propositions as verified. However, the authors suggest that this model does not represent the mere cooccurrence of p and q but takes the form of a relational schema in which p is understood as a hypothetical state of affairs and q as its resulting outcome:

(2) $p \rightarrow q$

The directionality of this relation, already suggested by Evans (1993), accounts for the fact that forward inferences (MP and denial of the antecedent, i.e., DA) are faster than backward inferences (AC and MT) from "if p then q" forms (Grosset & Barrouillet, 2003).

When a minor premise is given and an inference required, this initial representation could be enriched through a fleshing-out process. Markovits (1993; Markovits & Vachon, 1990) suggested that this fleshing out is the result of an automatic process of the activation and retrieval of knowledge from long-term memory. This process would provide the reasoner with information that makes it possible to construct additional models that represent the values of Q that could result from alternative hypotheses on P that differ from p. In children, at least, these models would then represent specific values of the variables P and Q rather than negated values using propositional-like tags (represented as $\neg$ in the standard theory).

The outcome of this fleshing-out process and the resulting representation depend on several factors, including children's ability to maintain complex representations in working memory, the efficiency of the retrieval process, the semantic structure of the concepts the conditional sentence involves, the nature of the relation between the antecedent and the consequent, the amount of available knowledge in long-term memory concerning both these concepts and this relation and finally, the context of enunciation. Though this theoretical framework might seem rather complex, it permits several precise predictions about the way children understand conditional sentences and draw inferences, how this understanding evolves with age, and how contents affect reasoning at different ages.

A first distinction must be made between familiar and unfamiliar relations between the antecedent and the consequent. Indeed, in the first case, retrieval from long-term memory provides the reasoner with knowledge about cases that link possible values of the two variables. For example, on the basis of the conditional premise "if the petrol tank is empty, then the car breaks down," reasoners can retrieve knowledge about the fact that, usually, cars with full tanks run, or that if the spark plugs are dirty cars also fail to start. Such cases constitute ready-made models in which different possible values of P (i.e., possible causes of cars breaking down or running) are already linked to their resulting outcome (the car either runs or it does not). On the other hand, when unfamiliar relations are presented, the retrieval process can only provide reasoners with values from the variables P and Q that must be combined to form models. For example, from an artificial relation such as "if the piece is a square, then it is red," individuals must combine alternative shapes (circle, triangle, etc.) with possible colors. However, there is no available knowledge about this relationship that could direct this construction and help reasoners to keep the constructed models active for processing. Thus, constructing and maintaining models should be easier from familiar rather than unfamiliar relations. As a consequence, the developmental impact of a limitation in cognitive resources depends on the type of conditional relation that is being investigated.

As far as reasoning from artificial relations is concerned, both the construction and maintenance of mental models should be particularly difficult for young children who have limited working memory capacities. As a consequence, the most primitive level in understanding the conditional should involve the construction of only one explicit model of the form $p . q$, the content of which is directly provided by the conditional sentence. This representation leads to a conjunctive-like interpretation of "if p then q." The developmental increase in cognitive capacities should allow children to construct more complex representations that involve an increasing number of models. Thus, the next step in the development of conditional reasoning should involve the construction of a two-model representation in which a not-p–not-q model is added to the initial model. Indeed, this additional model maximizes the relevance of the conditional statement (i.e., the amount of information it provides; Sperber & Wilson, 1986). This level corresponds to a biconditional interpretation. Finally, adolescents and adults should be able to construct and process three-model representations that correspond to the complete conditional representation hypothesized by Johnson-Laird and Byrne (1991).

This predicted developmental trend from a conjunctive to a biconditional and then to a conditional interpretation of the conditional sentences involving artificial relations has been observed in many experiments (Barrouillet, 1997; Barrouillet et al., 2000; Barrouillet & Lecas, 1998; Lecas & Barrouillet, 1999). It has also been demonstrated that both developmental and individual differences in understanding conditionals rely on differences in working memory capacity (Barrouillet & Lecas, 1999).

However, as we previously stressed, the way children and adults understand and process conditional sentences does not depend solely on their working memory capacities but also on the semantics of the terms and on the context of enunciation.

CONTENT AND CONTEXT EFFECTS IN REASONING WITH ARTIFICIAL CONDITIONAL RELATIONS

We stressed earlier that fleshing out should be the result of a process of retrieval from long-term memory. Thus, even when the conditional sentence that is being considered introduces an artificial relation between the antecedent and the consequent, the nature of the mental models and the resulting interpretation would depend both on the semantics of the terms the conditional statement involves and on its context of enunciation. Indeed, both the semantic and the context determine the possible values that can be combined to construct additional models.

For example, Barrouillet and Lecas (1998) showed that conditional statements that contain binary terms mainly lead to a biconditional interpretation in children. This phenomenon results from the structure of knowledge in long-term memory and can be accounted for by the mental models theory. Suppose reasoners are given a sentence such as "if the light is lit, then the door is open." They should construct an initial model of the following form:

(3)   lit → open

When fleshing-out is needed, the retrieval process is both straightforward and highly constrained because this conditional contains binary terms in both the antecedent and the consequent that offer only one alternative value (the light can be either lit or off, and the door can be either open or closed). These alternative values (i.e., "off" and "closed") should then be highly activated and very easy to retrieve. The resulting mental models would be of the following form:

(4)   lit → open
       off → closed

However, the facility with which this second model is constructed has its own counterpart. Note that this set of models exhausts the possible values on both the antecedent and the consequent, which are linked in a term-by-term correspondence. This type of representation, which Barrouillet and Lecas (1998) referred to as complete, would block any further fleshing-out process because each possible hypothetical value on P results in a different outcome, thus maximising the information the conditional sentence conveys. This representation would lead to a biconditional interpretation.

     In contrast, when a conditional sentence involves nonbinary terms, several alternative values are possible for both the antecedent and the consequent. For example, a conditional such as "if the piece is a square, then it is red" refers to situations in which the color of a given piece depends on its shape. Additional models should then involve combinations of possible alternative shapes (triangle, circle, etc.) and possible colors (red, blue, white, green, etc.). With these NN conditionals (for nonbinary on both the antecedent and the consequent), the large range of possible values within both variables would make it difficult to determine the precise nature of the possible alternative cases. Thus, the content of the mental models to be added should remain undetermined. The resulting set of models should then take the following form:

(5)   square → red
       ind shapes → ind colors

in which *ind* refers to indeterminate values. It should be noted that this additional model admits not p . q cases that lead to a conditional interpretation. Thus, according to our theory, the tendency to interpret "if p then q" sentences as biconditionals should be generally greater with binary than with nonbinary terms.

     Now, the number of possible alternative values depends not only on the semantics of the terms the conditional involves but also on the context of enunciation and, more generally, on any factual knowledge that could direct the retrieval process. Barrouillet and Lecas (1998) reasoned that an NN conditional should primarily induce biconditional interpretations provided that it is inserted in a context that permits only two possible values for the antecedent and the consequent. For example, if you were informed that there are only two possible shapes (e.g., a square or a circle), and two possible colors (red or blue), the NN conditional "if the piece is a square, then it is red" would become a binary conditional (Legrenzi, 1970). Thus, if the predominant biconditional interpretation elicited by the binary conditional results from the characteristics of the fleshing-out process, NN conditionals presented in a restricted context would elicit the same type of interpretation.

We tested this hypothesis in a recent experiment in which we asked 12- and 15-year-old children and adults to perform a pencil-paper inference production task (Barrouillet & Lecas, 2002). The participants were presented with a short scenario that introduced a conditional sentence that involved either binary or nonbinary terms. In the latter case, the scenario either restricted to two the possible values on both the antecedent and the consequent or permitted several possible alternatives. This resulted in three experimental conditions defined by the type of conditional presented, either binary (BB conditionals), nonbinary (NN conditionals), or nonbinary restricted (NNR conditionals). For example, the scenario and the conditional sentence in the NN condition took the following form:

> A company's vehicle pool consists of various makes of car: Peugeot, Citroën, Ford, Fiat, Renault, ..., present in different colors: red, blue, grey, green, ... After looking at all the cars, an observer claims to have found a rule linking the make of car and its color. The rule is "if the car is blue, then it is a Peugeot."

In the NNR condition, the scenario stated that there was only one possible alternative value in both the antecedent and the consequent and took the following form:

> A company's vehicle pool consists of two makes of car: Peugeot and Citroën, present in the colors blue and green. After looking at all the cars, an observer claims to have found a rule linking the make of car and its color. The rule is "if the car is blue, then it is a Peugeot."

In each experimental condition, each conditional was presented with the four canonical forms MP, AC, DA, and MT.

We stressed earlier that the first level of conditional interpretation should be conjunctive in nature and rely on the construction of the initial model only. Thus, younger children should more often produce the affirmative inferences MP and AC on the basis of the initial model than the denial inferences DA and MT that require a fleshing out. Older children should manifest a biconditional interpretation that results in a high production rate of the four canonical inferences. Adults should be able to construct and process three-model representations and thus should manifest a conditional interpretation that corresponds to a high rate of production of the logical inferences MP and MT and a lower production rate of the fallacies AC and DA. We predicted that this developmental trend should be observed with NN conditionals.

However, content and context effects should modulate this developmental trend in a predictable way. Indeed, we hypothesized that conditionals with binary terms should facilitate the construction of a first alternative model of the form not-p .not-q. As a consequence, younger children should overcome the conjunctive interpretation when presented with binary conditionals and should then reach a biconditional interpretation that results in the increased production of both DA and MT inferences. The same phenomenon should be observed with nonbinary conditionals in restricted contexts that explicitly provide alternative values. On the other hand, content and context effects should have a low impact in those participants who are already able to construct and manipulate two-model representations. Their interpretation should be biconditional in nature, whatever the type of conditional sentence presented. Finally, we expected adults to manifest a conditional interpretation with nonbinary conditionals. However, if binary and nonbinary conditionals in a restricted context impede a complete fleshing-out process, both types of conditionals should induce more biconditional interpretations than nonbinary conditionals, thus resulting in more frequent AC and DA fallacies. In an earlier experiment (Barrouillet & Lecas, 1998), we failed to demonstrate the biconditional interpretation that should result from binary conditionals in adults. Thus, the present experiment used larger samples of participants who were presented with a larger number of conditional syllogisms to solve. Moreover, we had never previously tested the predictions concerning the restricted contexts.

As we predicted, the nonbinary conditionals led to the standard developmental trend described previously. As far as 12-year-old children were concerned, we observed a main conjunctive interpretation, the affirmative inferences MP and AC being produced more often than the denial inferences DA and MT (85% and 47% for affirmative and denial inferences, respectively). The performances in 15-year-old children corresponded to a predominant biconditional interpretation. The production rate of denial inferences was higher than in the 12-year-old children (63% vs. 47% in 15- and 12-year-old children, respectively), whereas the production rates of the affirmative inferences MP and AC remained unchanged. As we predicted, adults manifested the pattern of inferences that should result from a conditional understanding. Indeed, they more often produced the correct inferences MP and MT (98% and 74%, respectively) than the fallacies AC and DA (57% and 44%, see Figure 1.1a and 1.1b).

In line with our theory, the effect of age was reduced with binary conditionals that elicited a predominantly biconditional interpretation in all the age groups. The production rate of denial inferences increased from 47% to 77% in the younger participant, whereas adults more often endorsed the fallacies AC and DA (from 51% to 72%). Thus, contrary to what Barrouillet and Lecas (1998) observed, binary terms induced biconditional interpretations in adults as well as in children. However, it should be noted that even with binary conditionals adults obtained slightly better performances than children. They more often produced the correct inferences MP and MT and less often the fallacies AC and DA (see Fig. 1.1).

Nonbinary conditionals presented in restricted contexts led to a more complex pattern of results. As we predicted, this condition elicited a higher production rate of denial inferences in the younger participants and also resulted in lower production rates of the affirmative inferences MP and AC. This could be

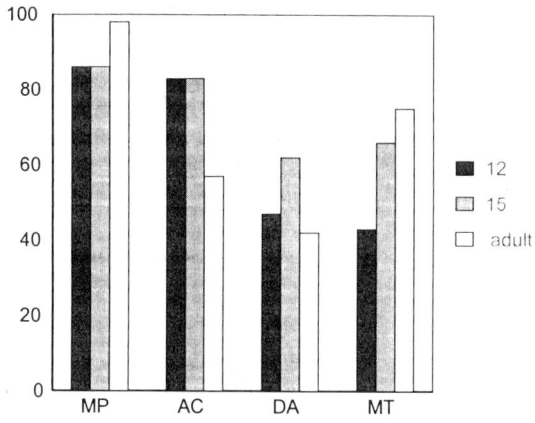

FIG. 1.1.a Production rates of the four inferences (MP: modus ponens; AC: affirmation of the consequent; DA: denial of the antecedent; MT: modus tollens) in the NN condition (conditionals with nonbinary terms) as a function of the age of the participants.

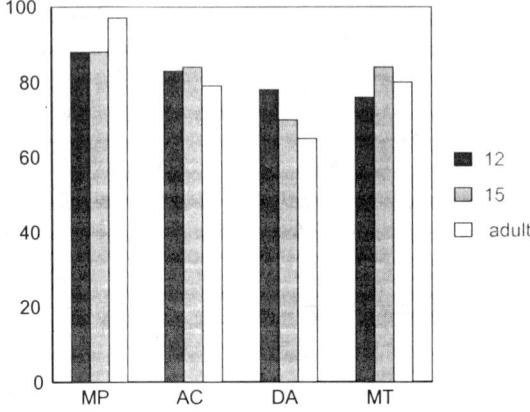

FIG. 1.1.b Production rates of the four inferences (MP: modus ponens; AC: affirmation of the consequent; DA: denial of the antecedent; MT: modus tollens) in the BB condition (conditionals with binary terms) as a function of the age of the participants.

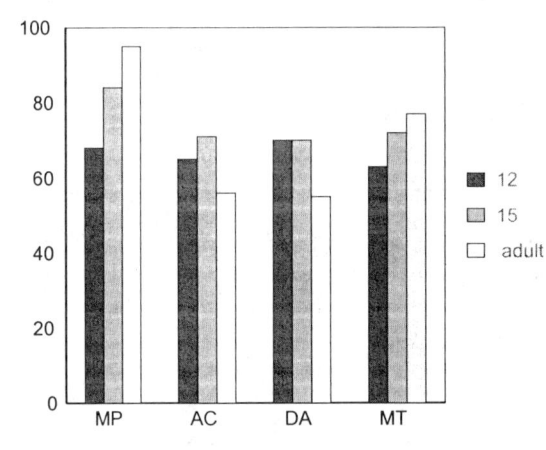

FIG. 1.1.c Production rates of the four inferences (MP: modus ponens; AC: affirmation of the consequent; DA: denial of the antecedent; MT: modus tollens) in the NNR condition (conditionals with nonbinary terms presented in a restricted context) as a function of the age of the participants.

because the restricted context was introduced by means of a scenario that explicitly presented the possible alternative values for both the antecedent and the consequent. Thus, these conditionals could have elicited initial representations that contained not one but two explicit models right from the start. Of course, these representations not only facilitate the production of denial inferences but also impede the production of affirmative inferences because the initial two-model representation from which these inferences are drawn brings about a higher working memory load. Thus, all of the four inferences were produced at roughly similar rates by 12-year-old children (between 63% and 70%). As we anticipated, the biconditional pattern of results was also predominant in 15-year-old children. However, adults did not exhibit the predicted biconditional pattern. In fact, the restricted contexts had only a small effect on adults. Many of them continued to exhibit a main conditional interpretation and produced more logically correct than fallacious inferences (86% vs. 55%). In summary, conditionals involving binary terms had the same effect in adults as in young children, and participants in both groups mainly interpreted these sentences in a biconditional way. In young children, this tendency resulted in an increased production of the denial inferences MT and DA, whereas in adults it led to an increased production of the fallacies AC and DA. However, and contrary to our hypothesis, restricting the context in which nonbinary conditionals appeared did not have the same effect, and the adults' interpretation remained practically unchanged.

Despite this latter fact, our results lend strong support to the mental models approach of conditional reasoning. The mental models theory assumes that the main constraint on human reasoning is the number of models to be constructed and processed because mental models are held in a limited-capacity working memory (Johnson-Laird & Byrne, 1991). Because children have lower working memory capacity than adults, and because this capacity increases with age, they should be limited in the number of the models they can construct and manipulate, and this number of models should progressively increase (Barrouillet & Lecas, 1999). Thus, the interpretation of conditional sentences evolves from a conjunctive to a biconditional and then to a conditional interpretation. The content effect produced by binary terms reinforces the hypothesis that reasoning is a matter of constructing mental models that link together tokens retrieved from long-term memory (Markovits & Barrouillet, 2002). When the retrieval process directly provides individuals with specific and clearly determined alternative values, mental models are easy to construct and young individuals reach a higher interpretational level (i.e., biconditional). However, the retrieval of only one alternative tends to block the fleshing-out process prematurely, and adults tend to regress to a biconditional interpretation. Note that this effect is akin to Cummins' (1995) observations that causal conditional relations that permit few, if any, alternative causes of the effect presented in the consequent mainly result in biconditional patterns of responses.

That restricted contexts did not have the same effect as binary terms in adults suggests that the effects related to the structure of semantic memory supersede the impact of contextual information. It is possible that the fleshing-out process is mainly directed by semantics and that contextual information only modifies the initial model, as suggested by the performance of the 12-year-old children on affirmative inferences. For example, the automatic retrieval process could elicit, in adults, a fleshed-out representation of NNR conditionals as shown in Diagram 5 in which the initial model already contains two explicit models. Such a process would result in the following set of models

$$
\begin{array}{lcl}
(6) \quad p & \to & q \\
p' & \to & q' \\
\text{ind } P & \to & \text{ind } Q
\end{array}
$$

in which p' and q' correspond to the alternative values given by the restricted context. Some results have confirmed this hypothesis. For example, adults produced more denial inferences, DA and MT, with NNR conditionals (57% and 82%, respectively) than with NN conditionals (37% and 72%) when these inferences were cued by minor premises that contained implicit negations (e.g., with the problem of the color of the cars, the DA minor premise was "the car is red" rather than "the car is not blue," and the minor premise of MT was "the car is a Citroën" rather than "the car is not a Peugeot"). Indeed, in the set of models presented in Diagram 6, there is an explicit model that directly matches the implicitly negated minor premise to be considered (i.e., either p' or q').

Thus, context effects and, to a lesser extent, content effects were more pronounced in children than in adults. These developmental differences could be due to the fact that children have less cognitive resources than adults for the retrieval of knowledge from memory and the processing of complex representations. As a consequence, any semantic or contextual factor that facilitates the retrieval of specific values from long-term memory and the construction of models has a stronger impact in young than in older individuals. The same phenomenon is also observed in reasoning from familiar conditional relations.

CONTENT EFFECTS IN REASONING WITH FAMILIAR CAUSAL RELATIONS

As we have stressed earlier, the "if p then q" relation defines a semantic space that is determined by the reasoner's understanding of both the nature of the terms used in the conditional and the relationship between them. We have seen that when unfamiliar relations are used, the nature of the terms and the structure of the semantic space in which they are embedded determines the way individuals understand conditional sentences. When familiar relations are considered, the process of retrieval from memory does not provide the reasoner with alternative values for the antecedent, on the one hand, and the consequent on the other, but with knowledge about cases that link possible values of these two variables. This knowledge underpins the construction of models to be added to the initial representation.

Thus, three classes of cases could be activated that can lead to the construction of three types of models. The first class concerns cases in which both the relationship and the actual objects or events concerned are complementary to those specified in the original conditional, that is, cases where objects or events that are different from p are related to not q (we refer to this as the complementary class). For example, a reasoner who is given a premise such as "if it rains, then the street will be wet" would activate related events such as "if it is sunny, then the street will not be wet" or "if it is only cloudy, then the street will not be wet." The retrieval of one case from this class leads to the construction of a not p . not q model that supports the production of the denial inferences DA and MT. The second class concerns possible objects/events that share the same relation to q as p does, that is, cases in which not-p implies q (we refer to this as the alternatives class). For example, in "if the street cleaner passes, then the street will be wet," note that the retrieval of such an alternative case results in a not p . q model that would block the production of the fallacies AC and DA. Indeed, "it rains" no longer follows from the minor premise "the street is wet" for AC, while "the street is dry" cannot be concluded with certainty from the DA premise "it is not raining." Finally, the third class concerns what Cummins (1995) called disabling conditions, that is, conditions which allow the relationship between p and q to be violated (we refer to this as the disabling class). An example is "if it rains, but the street is covered, then the street will not be wet." The retrieval of disabling conditions should impede the logically correct inferences MP and MT through the construction of a p . not q model. Markovits and Barrouillet (2002) suggested that, at least in children, these three classes should differ in their accessibility: cases from the complementary class should be more accessible than those from either the alternatives class or disabling conditions.

As we stressed earlier, the nature of the conditional relation, either familiar or unfamiliar, has a direct impact on reasoning processes, and models are easier to construct and maintain with familiar relations. Indeed, even young children seem able to construct two-model representations (i.e., p . q, and not p . not q) that lead to a biconditional interpretation, as many studies have demonstrated. However, the content of the conditional sentence still has a major impact on reasoning because it directs the retrieval process.

For example, Markovits, Fleury, Quinn, and Venet (1998) demonstrated that inference production from familiar-class based relations depends on the strength of the association the conditional sentence involves. More precisely, they predicted that correct responses of uncertainty to AC and DA should be more frequent from conditional sentences that involve a weak (e.g., "if something is a butterfly, then it has legs"), rather than a strong relation between the antecedent and the consequent (e.g., "if something is a dog, then it has legs"). The authors reasoned that, within the class of animals that have legs, some cases should have a higher base-level activation than others because they are more typical regarding the legs feature and should thus be easier to retrieve (Anderson, 1993; Anderson & Lebière, 1998). It should be recalled that the retrieval of alternative cases of the form not p . q leads to a correct uncertainty response on the two fallacies AC and DA. Thus, when the conditional premise involves a weak relation such as "if something is a butterfly, then it has legs," those items that are strongly associated with the relevant feature are highly activated and thus easy to retrieve (e.g., dogs, or cows). Now, these items constitute alternative cases that ensure the correct response of uncertainty to AC and DA. On the other hand, when the conditional involves a strong relation (e.g., "if something is a dog, then it has legs"), alternative cases must be recruited from those items that are less strongly activated and thus more difficult to retrieve. Of course, as far as class-based relations are concerned, this difference should have an effect only on individuals who have low retrieval capacities. Thus, the authors hypothesized that young children should more often endorse the fallacies AC and DA from conditionals involving strong rather than weak relations and that this effect should disappear with development because older children have improved retrieval capacities that allow them to evoke alternative cases whatever the strength of the relation presented. The results confirmed these hypotheses. These facts have been recently extended to causal relations in adults: Strong causal relations lead to more frequent fallacies than weak relations (Quinn & Markovits, 1998).

We recently ran a developmental version of this latter experiment in our lab (Barrouillet, Markovits, & Quinn, 2001). We asked 12- and 15-year-old children and adults to perform a conditional syllogism evaluation task on the basis of either strong or weak causal conditional relations. In the former, an event presented as a consequence was linked to its more frequent and probable cause (e.g., "if a dog has fleas, then it will scratch constantly") whereas in the latter the same consequence was associated with a less frequent cause (e.g., "if a dog has a skin disease, then it will scratch constantly"). Following Quinn and Markovits (1998), we hypothesized that alternative causes of the consequent (scratching) should be easier to evoke when the conditional premise involves a weak rather than a strong relation. Indeed, strong relations have a higher base-level activation than weak relations. Thus, the former are easier to retrieve and constitute alternative cases when weak relations are involved in the conditional premise. Thus, those participants who studied weak relations should be less likely to endorse the AC and DA fallacies than those who studied strong relations. Moreover, we hypothesized that this effect should be stronger the younger the participants are because young participants have lower retrieval capacities.

In this study, the participants were presented with four conditional premises that contained either strong or weak relations between antecedent and consequent (e.g., "suppose that if a dog gets fleas, then he will scratch continuously"), along with minor premises corresponding to the four canonical forms MP, AC, DA, and MT (e.g., "a dog does not have fleas" for DA). For each form, the participants were asked to choose between two conclusions, either of certainty or uncertainty (e.g., "it is certain that it will not scratch constantly" or "one cannot be certain whether it will scratch constantly or not" for DA). Fig. 1.2 displays the endorsement rates (i.e., responses of certainty) of the four canonical forms MP, MT, AC and DA.

As we predicted, the strength of the relation affected the production rates of fallacies. Overall, weak relations significantly elicited lower endorsement rates of both DA and AC than strong relations (38% for weak, 54% for strong relations; Fig. 1.2.a-c). Note that this effect did not affect the evaluation of logical inferences. Indeed, logical inferences do not depend on the retrieval of alternative causes (not $p \cdot q$ models) but on either the initial model for MP or the complementary model not $p \cdot$ not q for MT. As far as 12-year-old children were concerned, the strength effect was only significant for AC but not for DA, whereas this effect was significant for both inferences in 15-year-old children. These effects were no longer significant in adults, contrary to the observations reported by Quinn and Markovits (1998). Though the strength effect did not reach significance for DA in the younger group, this developmental trend was, in fact, in line with our theory.

We assumed that the correct response of uncertainty to both AC and DA results from the retrieval of a case from the alternatives class and the construction of a model of the form not $p \cdot q$. This retrieval would be triggered by the content of both the conditional and the minor premises. The content of the conditional premise, the strength of the association it involves, determines the accessibility of the alternative class. However, the minor premises for AC on the one hand and DA on the other differ in their efficiency in activating this relevant knowledge (i.e., the alternative causes). Indeed, the AC minor premise refers to the consequence of the causal relation (e.g., "a dog scratches constantly "), whereas the DA minor premise refers to the absence of the cause involved in the conditional (i.e., "a dog does not have fleas" and "a dog does not have any skin disease" for the strong and weak relations, respectively). Thus, the AC minor premise directly matches alternative cases by evoking the consequence, whereas the DA minor premise should primarily activate cases from the complementary class because it refers to the absence of the cause involved in the conditional. As a consequence, the activation and retrieval of an alternative cause is more probable from AC than from DA. Thus, those participants who have low capacities should be confronted with two difficulties.

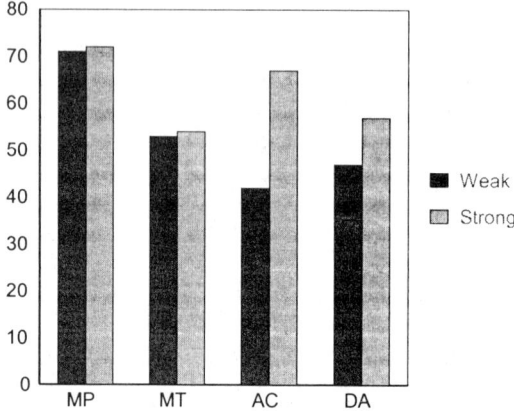

FIG. 1.2.a Production rates of the four inferences (MP: modus ponens; MT: modus tollens; AC: affirmation of the consequent; DA: denial of the antecedent) as a function of the strength of the causal relation involved in the conditional premises used for the 12-year-old children.

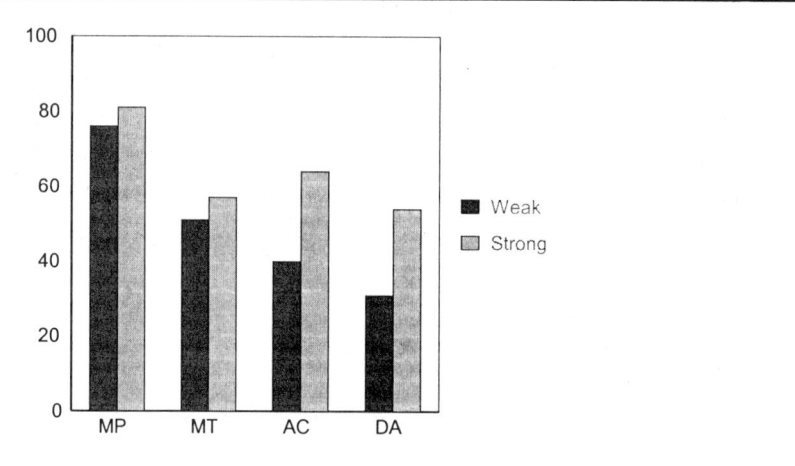

FIG. 1.2.b Production rates of the four inferences (MP: modus ponens; MT: modus tollens; AC: affirmation of the consequent; DA: denial of the antecedent) as a function of the strength of the causal relation involved in the conditional premises used for the 15-year-old children.

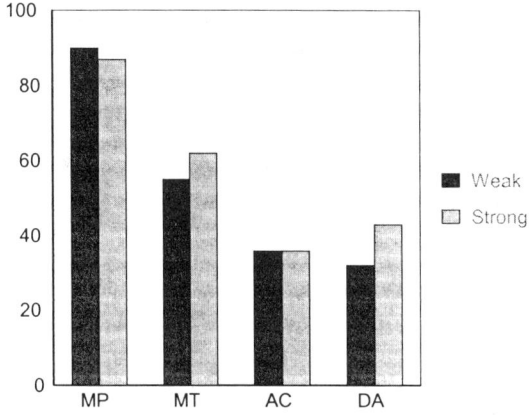

FIG. 1.2.c Production rates of the four inferences (MP: modus ponens; MT: modus tollens; AC: affirmation of the consequent; DA: denial of the antecedent) as a function of the strength of the causal relation involved in the conditional premises used for the adults.

First, they could access the alternatives class only when the conditional involves a weak association, and second, the efficiency of the retrieval process should then depend on the nature of the retrieval cue provided by the minor premise. As a consequence, the strength effect should be more pronounced with AC than with DA, and this is exactly what we observed in our youngest group. Note that the same phenomenon was also observed by Janveau-Brennan and Markovits (1999). The developmental increase in capacities progressively removes these two constraints. Indeed, the strength effect was observed in older children whatever the type of minor premise being investigated, and the performance of adults remained unaffected either by the strength of the relation or the type of minor premise.

Note that this strength effect differs from the phenomena observed by Cummins (1995) and Janveau-Brennan and Markovits (1999), who observed that reasoning from causal conditional relations depends on the number of available alternative causes that can produce the same effect. More precisely, the rate of biconditional responses (i.e., the endorsement of the fallacies AC and DA) is higher from causal conditional relations that allow few rather than many alternatives. Our model easily accounts for this fact because the probability of retrieving a case from the alternatives class that ensures a conditional response to AC and DA is higher when the causal relation under study allows many rather than few alternative causes. In the present experiment, the number of alternative causes was exactly the same for both the strong and the weak causal relations because they referred to the same resulting outcome (e.g., "a dog scratches constantly"). In fact, the effect of the number of alternative causes Cummins (1995) discovered is similar to the effect produced by binary terms. Both rely on the structure of semantic memory. Here, the strength effect results from the relative accessibility of different items of knowledge pertaining to a given semantic structure. Thus, as we stressed earlier, reasoning depends on the semantic structure of the concepts the conditional sentence involves, the nature of the relation between the antecedent and the consequent, the amount of available knowledge in long-term memory concerning both these concepts and this relation, and the relative accessibility of this knowledge

MENTAL MODELS AND THE DEVELOPMENT OF CONDITIONAL REASONING

At the beginning of this chapter, we stressed the need for a mental models theory of reasoning that could account for developmental and content effects. As we suggested, the mental models theory is particularly suitable for accounting for developmental phenomena. Indeed, if reasoning is a matter of constructing and manipulating mental models in a limited-capacity working memory (Johnson-Laird & Byrne, 1991), then the complexity of the representations individuals can construct and process should evolve with development. The first available representation should correspond to the initial model postulated by Johnson-Laird and Byrne (1991), and this representation should increase in complexity as cognitive resources evolve with age.

Accordingly, we observed that the interpretation of conditional sentences and the resulting patterns of inferences evolve with age from a conjunctive to a biconditional and then to a conditional interpretation, which is underpinned by the construction of one, two, and then three models, respectively. This fact lends strong support to the mental models framework. Indeed, it has been claimed that adults outperform children and adolescents in laboratory reasoning tasks because they are more able to set aside the conversational principles that lead to a biconditional interpretation (Braine & O'Brien, 1991). In the same way, O'Brien, Dias, and Roazzi (1998) argued that the mental models theory cannot account for development because it predicts conjunctive responses that would never occur, whereas mental logic predicts an initial biconditional developmental level that has often been observed. The results of the first study presented demonstrated that there is an initial developmental level which is conjunctive in nature. An individual response pattern analysis conducted on the production rates of the four classical inferences with nonbinary conditionals indicated that a majority of 12-year-old children manifested a coherent conjunctive pattern of responses (see Fig. 1.3). This predicted conjunctive level has been systematically observed in many previous studies in children (Barrouillet, 1997; Barrouillet et al., 2000; Barrouillet & Lecas, 1998, 1999;; see also Paris, 1973, and Taplin, Staudenmayer, & Taddonio, 1974, for related observations), and even in adults when the fleshing-out process fails (Barrouillet et al., 2000; Girotto et al., 1997). In line with the mental models theory, the predominant interpretation in 15-year-old children was biconditional in nature, whereas many adults manifested a conditional pattern of responses.

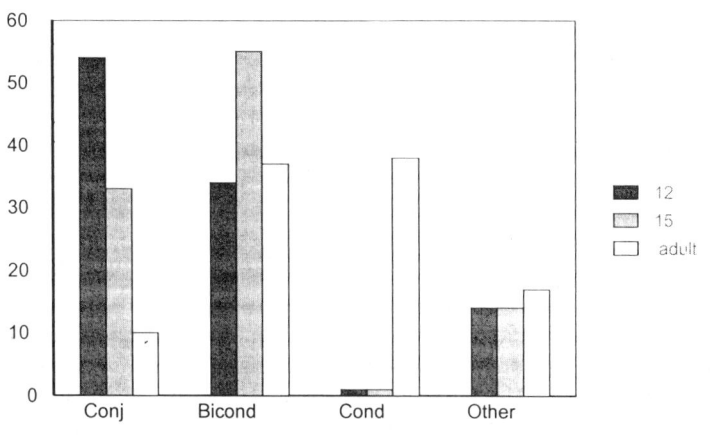

FIG. 1.3 Evolution of the interpretation of conditionals with nonbinary terms (conj: conjunctive; bicond: biconditional; cond: conditional) as a function of age. Percentage of participants who manifested a coherent pattern of responses ($n = 30$).

Moreover, we showed that this developmental trend is modulated by contents in a predictable way. Markovits and Barrouillet (2002) suggested that fleshing out is based on a process of activation and retrieval of available knowledge from long-term memory. Thus, the resulting mental models depend both on the structure of this knowledge and on the available capacities to activate and retrieve it from memory. A first distinction must be made between conditional sentences that involve artificial relations between the antecedent and the consequent and conditionals that refer to familiar relations. The latter facilitate the construction of mental models because the retrieval process provides reasoners with stored relations between possible values of the variable P and their resulting outcomes that constitute ready made models. As a consequence, the cognitive constraints that impede the fleshing-out process in individuals with limited cognitive resources are partly removed, and even young children can construct and process two or even three models. This is probably why O'Brien et al. (1998) proposed that the initial developmental level is biconditional in nature. This is true when familiar relations are studied.

However, whatever the nature of the relation the conditional premise involves, the structure of the available knowledge also has a strong impact on the reasoning process. We have seen that even when participants had to reason from unfamiliar relations, the semantic structure of the concepts involved in the antecedent and the consequent influenced reasoning performances. Even adults regressed to a biconditional interpretation when the conditional premise contained binary terms (73% of them exhibited a coherent biconditional response pattern) and any developmental evolution tended to disappear (the corresponding rates of participants who manifested such a pattern were 70% and 77% in 12- and 15-year-old children, respectively; see Fig. 1.1). Thus, when the structure of semantic knowledge offers clear and readily available alternative values, the fleshing-out process is facilitated, and young participants can go beyond the conjunctive interpretation. However, the resulting representation tends to block any further fleshing out, and most of the adults continue to adhere to a biconditional interpretation.

When the conditional premises contain familiar relations, the structure of the knowledge has more subtle effects that rely on the relative accessibility of different items. Conditionals that involve strong relations between the antecedent and the consequent elicit more fallacies than conditionals that contain weak relations, at least in participants who have limited capacities to activate and retrieve knowledge. When the major premise contains a weak relation, knowledge about strong relations, which is easily retrieved from memory, constitutes alternative not p . q cases that block the classical fallacies. Note that this effect is quite counterintuitive. Indeed, strong relations are probably more familiar than weak relations, and it has been shown that familiarity often improves performance (Markovits, 1984).

Markovits and Barrouillet's (2002) mental models theory accounts for both developmental and content effects. As these authors suggested, there is no need to suppose that reasoning is underpinned by specific cognitive processes or strategies, such as rules or schemas. Development would result from an age-related increase in working memory capacity that allows children to retain and manipulate an increasing number of mental models. Content should modulate this developmental trend through the relative accessibility of the knowledge that provides the building blocks for the construction of models. Thus, both developmental and content effects result from general cognitive constraints that affect the processes by which mental models are constructed and manipulated in working memory. Contrary to what O'Brien et al., (1998) and Bonatti (1994a, 1994b) claimed, the mental models approach has the precise machinery to account for and predict both developmental and content effects.

To decide between competing theories is not the sole object of a developmental approach. Indeed, the developmental evolution we observed sheds light not only on our understanding of children's and adults' reasoning processes but also on the nature of the final state toward which this evolution tends. We suggest that this final state would constitute the norm that human reasoning should conform to.

THE MEANING OF IF THEN AND THE DEVELOPMENTAL PROCESS

The real psychological meaning of the if-then connective has long been a subject of controversy. It has been suggested that the way individuals understand if-then does not correspond to the material implication of the formal logic and that logic-based theories of human reasoning, such as the mental models theory, cannot account for human performances (Oaksford & Chater, 1998). More generally, it has even been suggested that formal logic does not constitute, at least in certain cases, the appropriate normative theory for the assessment of human behavior and reasoning. It has been argued that human reasoning would often conform to an adaptive rationality (a rationality 1) that differs from logical rationality (rationality 2, Evans & Over, 1996). However, it should be noted that many of these assumptions are based on adult studies.

We suggest that focusing exclusively on adult reasoning performances might not be the more appropriate way to investigate these difficult problems. Indeed, adult studies involve two pitfalls that can, and actually do, obscure the debate. First, human performances vary from one task to another and, within a given task, from one content to another (Thompson, 2000). For example, there is no doubt that the poor human performance in Wason's selection task has played a critical role in the debate concerning human rationality by suggesting that human reasoning does not conform to logic. However, though the selection task provides psychologists with striking and puzzling data that need to be accounted for, it must nevertheless be borne in mind that it constitutes only one task among others, and many authors have claimed and provided evidence that it does not require conditional reasoning (Markovits & Savary, 1992). More direct evaluations of the human ability to reason from conditional sentences, such as inference evaluation or production tasks, provide results that conform more closely to the logical norm (see Evans, Newstead, & Byrnes, 1993, for a review). Within this latter kind of task, our results demonstrate that striking differences in performance can result from apparently small content variations (e.g., whether a conditional contains binary terms or not). Such variability makes it difficult to determine the meaning of if-then in adults, even when we consider only indicative or causal conditionals. Second, it seems clear that human reasoning, as well as other high-level cognitive processes, is restricted by limited cognitive capacities. Thus, performance cannot be equated with competence. Young adult studies only provide us with a snapshot from which it is difficult to gain an insight into the real distance between performance and competence.

We claim that a better way to solve the problem of the meaning of if-then would be to adopt the respected approach put forward in Piagetian genetic psychology. As pointed out by Karmiloff-Smith (1992), a developmental perspective is essential to the analysis of human cognition, and the way in which knowledge changes can provide subtle cues to its final state in the adult mind. Developmental studies on conditional reasoning provide a clear delineation of both the age-related evolution of the understanding of conditional statements and the final point toward which this evolution tends. Indeed, though content and context effects modulate this evolution, the different developmental levels observed correspond to an increasing number of mental models that children and adolescents can construct and manipulate. Even if many adults still manifest a biconditional interpretation, it is clear that development tends toward the complete conditional interpretation postulated by Johnson-Laird and Byrne (1991), thus providing evidence that this interpretation actually constitutes the core meaning of both the basic conditionals, as Johnson-Laird and Byrne (2002) have recently assumed. As pointed out by Engel (1989), formal logic constitutes the norm of the truth because it reflects and formalizes the most complete and ideal reasoning processes that human beings can use. Thus, developmental studies provide us with the strongest evidence that, as Johnson-Laird and Byrne (1991) wrote, people are rational in principle but fallible in practice. They are rational in principle because human development tends towards a logical understanding of conditional sentences, and they are fallible in practice because this understanding relies on the construction of representations through cognitive processes that are limited in their efficiency. The strength of the mental models approach stems from the precise account it offers of these processes and their limitations.

REFERENCES

Anderson, J. R. (1993). *Rules of the mind.* Hillsdale, NJ: Lawrence Erlbaum Associates.

Anderson, J. R., & Lebière, C. (1998). *Atomic components of thought.* Hillsdale, NJ: Lawrence Erlbaum Associates.

Barrouillet, P. (1997). Modifying the interpretation of if…then sentences in adolescents by inducing a structure mapping strategy. *Current Psychology of Cognition, 16,* 609–637.

Barrouillet, P., & Camos, V. (2001). Developmental increase in working memory span: Resource sharing or temporal decay. *Journal of Memory and Language, 45,* 1–20.

Barrouillet, P., Grosset, N., & Lecas, J. F. (2000). Conditional reasoning by mental models: Chronometric and developmental evidence. *Cognition, 75,* 237–266.

Barrouillet, P., & Lecas, J. F. (1998). How can mental models account for content effects in conditional reasoning? A developmental perspective. *Cognition, 67,* 209–253.

Barrouillet, P., & Lecas, J. F. (1999). Mental models in conditional reasoning and working memory. *Thinking and Reasoning, 5,* 289–302.

Barrouillet, P., & Lecas, J. F. (2002). Content and context effects in children's and adult's conditional reasoning. *Quarterly Journal of Experimental Psychology, 55*(3), 839–854.

Barrouillet, P., Markovits, H., & Quinn, S. (2001). Developmental and content effects in reasoning with causal conditionals. *Journal of Experimental Child*

Psychology, 81, 235–248.

Bonatti, L. (1994a). Propositional reasoning by model? *Psychological Review, 101*, 725– 733.

Bonatti, L. (1994b). Why should we abandon the mental logic hypothesis? *Cognition, 50*, 17–39.

Braine, M. D. S., & O'Brien, D. P. (1991). A theory of if: A lexical entry, reasoning program, and pragmatic principles. *Psychological Review, 98*, 182–203.

Case, R. (1985). *Intellectual development: Birth to adulthood*. New York: Academic Press.

Cowan, N. (1995). *Attention and memory: An integrated framework*. New York: Oxford University Press.

Cowan, N. (1997). The development of working memory. In N. Cowan & C. Hulme (Eds.), *The development of memory in childhood* (pp. 163–200). Hove, UK: Psychology Press.

Cowan, N. (2001). The magical number 4 in short-term memory: A reconsideration of mental storage capacity. *Behavioral and Brain Sciences, 24*(1), 87–105.

Cummins, D. D. (1995). Naive theories and causal deduction. *Memory and Cognition, 23*, 646–658.

Engle, R. W., Kane, M. J., & Tuholski, S. W. (1999). Individual differences in working memory capacity and what they tell us about controlled attention, general fluid intelligence, and functions of the prefrontal cortex. In A. Miyake & P. Shah (Eds.), *Models of working memory: Mechanisms of active maintenance and executive control* (pp. 102–134). Cambridge, UK: Cambridge University Press.

Engel, P. (1989). *La norme du vrai: Philosophie de la logique*. Paris: Gallimard.

Evans, J. St. B. T. (1993). The mental model theory of conditional reasoning: Critical appraisal and revision. *Cognition, 48*, 1–20.

Evans, J. St. B. T., & Handley, S. J. (1999). The role of negation in conditional inference. *Quarterly Journal of Experimental Psychology, 52A*, 739–769.

Evans, J. St. B. T., Newstead, S. E., & Byrne, R. M. J. (1993). *Human reasoning: The psychology of deduction*. Hillsdale, NJ: Lawrence Erlbaum Associates.

Evans, J. St. B. T., & Over, D. E (1996). *Rationality and reasoning*. Hove, UK: Psychology Press.

Girotto, V., Mazzocco, A., & Tasso, A. (1997). The effect of premise order in conditional reasoning: A test of the mental model theory. *Cognition, 63*, 1–28.

Grosset, N., & Barrouillet, P. (2003). On the nature of mental models of conditional:. The case of If, If then, and Only if. *Thinking and Reasoning, 9*(4), 289–306.

Halford, G. S. (1993). *Children's understanding*. Hillsdale, NJ: Lawrence Erlbaum Associates.

Halford, G. S., Wilson, W. H., & Phillips, S. (1998). Processing capacity defined by relational complexity: Implications for comparative, developmental, and cognitive psychology. *Behavioral and Brain Sciences, 21*, 803–864.

Inhelder, B., & Piaget, J. (1955). *De la logique de l'enfant à la logique de l'adolescent*. Paris: PUF.

Janveau-Brennan, G., & Markovits, H. (1999). The development of reasoning with causal conditional. *Developmental Psychology, 35*, 904–911.

Johnson-Laird, P. N. (1999). Deductive reasoning. *Annual Review of Psychology, 50*, 109–135.

Johnson-Laird, P. N., & Byrne, R. M. J. (1991). *Deduction*. Hillsdale, NJ: Lawrence Erlbaum Associates.

Johnson-Laird, P. N., & Byrne, R. M. J. (2002). Conditionals: A theory of meaning, pragmatics, and inference. *Psychological Review, 109*(4), 646–678.

Johnson-Laird, P. N., Legrenzi, P., Girotto, V., Legrenzi, M. S., & Caverni, J. P. (1999). Naive probability: A mental model theory of extensional reasoning. *Psychological Review, 106*, 62–88.

Johnson-Laird, P. N., & Savary, F. (1999). Illusory inferences: A novel class of erroneous deductions. *Cognition, 71*, 191–229.

Karmiloff-Smith, A. (1992). *Beyond modularity: A developmental perspective on cognitive science*. Cambridge, MA: MIT Press.

Lecas, J. F., & Barrouillet, P. (1999). Understanding of conditional rules in childhood and adolescence: A mental models approach. *Current Psychology of Cognition, 18*, 363–396.

Legrenzi, P. (1970). Relations between language and reasoning about deductive rules. In G. B. Flores D'Arcais & W. J. M. Levelt (Eds.), *Advances in psycholinguistics* (pp. 102–121). Amsterdam: North-Holland.

Markovits, H. (1984). Awareness of the possible as a mediator of formal thinking in conditional reasoning problems. *British Journal of Psychology, 5*, 367–376.

Markovits, H. (1993). The development of conditional reasoning: A Piagetian reformulation of the theory of mental models. *Merrill-Palmer Quarterly, 39*, 133–160.

Markovits, H., & Barrouillet, P. (2002). The development of conditional reasoning: A mental model account. *Developmental Review, 22*(1), 5–36.

Markovits, H., Fleury, M. L., Quinn, S., & Venet, M. (1998). The development of conditional reasoning and the structure of semantic memory. *Child Development, 69*, 742–755.

Markovits, H., & Savary, F. (1992). Pragmatic schemas and the selection task: To reason or not to reason. *Quarterly Journal of Experimental Psychology, 45A*, 133–148.

Markovits, H., & Vachon, R. (1990). Conditional reasoning, representation, and level of abstraction. *Developmental Psychology, 26*, 942–951.

Oaksord, M., & Chater, N. (1998). *Rationality in an uncertain world*. Hove, UK: Psychology Press.

O'Brien, D. P., Dias, M. G., & Roazzi, A. (1998). A case study in the mental models and mental-logic debate: Conditional syllogisms. In M. D. S. Braine & D. P. O'Brien (Eds.), *Mental logic* (pp. 385–420). Mahwah, NJ: Lawrence Erlbaum Associates.

Paris, S. G. (1973). Comprehension of language connectives and propositional logical relationships. *Journal of Experimental Child Psychology, 16,* 278–291.

Piaget, J., & Inhelder, B. (1959). *La genèse des structures logiques élémentaires.* Neuchâtel : Delachaux et Niestlé.

Quinn, S., & Markovits, H. (1998). Conditional reasoning, causality, and the structure of semantic memory: Strength of association as a predictive factor for content effects. *Cognition, 68,* 93–101.

Rosen, V. M., & Engle, W. E. (1997). The role of working memory capacity in retrieval. *Journal of Experimental Psychology: General, 126,* 211–227.

Sperber, D., & Wilson, D. (1986). *Relevance: Communication and cognition.* Oxford, UK: Blackwell.

Swanson, H. L. (1999). What develops in working memory? A life span perspective. *Developmental Psychology, 35,* 968–1000.

Taplin, J. E., Staudenmayer, H., & Taddonio, J. L. (1974). Developmental changes in conditional reasoning: Linguistic or logical? *Journal of Experimental Child Psychology, 17,* 360– 373.

Thompson, V. A. (2000). The task-specific nature of domain-general reasoning. *Cognition, 76,* 209–268.

Thompson, V. A., & Mann, J. M. (1995). Perceived necessity explains the dissociation between logic and meaning: The case of «only if». *Journal of Experimental Psychology: Learning, Memory, and Cognition, 6,* 1554–1567.

2

Representation, Pragmatics and Process in Model-Based Reasoning

Simon Handley
Aidan Feeney

In this chapter we consider the status of the current model theory's assumptions concerning representation and strategies for reasoning in the light of data collected across a range of tasks and paradigms. We argue that this data suggest that the representations on which reasoning is based are richer than is currently thought. Specifically, we show that, as suggested by findings in the literature on situation models (see Zwaan & Radvansky, 1998), people represent information about both the temporal structure and the conversational purpose of the premises about which they are reasoning. We further argue that pragmatic effects in reasoning are not mediated by the inefficient modulation of a model set (see Johnson-Laird & Byrne, 2002) but by the combination of premises in the problem materials and premises from background knowledge. Finally, we discuss the relationship between reasoning by models and the development of strategies for reasoning and suggest that the former often lead to the latter, thus explaining the use of suppositional strategies by adults in conditional reasoning tasks.

INTRODUCTION

We discuss three lines of experimental evidence that focus on the way in which people represent and reason from conditional assertions. Based on this evidence, we argue that the present model based account of conditional reasoning is underspecified in three basic respects. First, in our view, the model based representations of the kind proposed by Johnson-Laird and Byrne (1991; 2002) and Johnson-Laird, Byrne and Schaeken (1992) are too impoverished to capture much of the information that people represent when they are reasoning. Second, the model theory fails to adequately specify the processes by which different conditional forms result in different sets of model based possibilities. We argue that it is crucial to develop an account that clearly specifies the way in which background knowledge, context, and premise based information interact in determining how people understand particular conditional forms. Finally, we argue that the procedures for manipulating models as currently proposed are too deterministic. We suggest that

people are flexible in the strategies and approaches that they employ in reasoning tasks. In particular we show that certain inferences are solved using suppositional strategies that bear a close relationship to the suppositional strategies that have been proposed by rule based theorists.

The chapter begins with a brief description of the current model theoretic account of conditionals. We then describe data from some of our own recent work on the role played by background knowledge about temporal relationships in the suppression effect (Byrne, 1989; Byrne, Espino & Santamaria, 1999; Rumain, Connell and Braine, 1983). We suggest that this data illustrates the need for a consideration of the multiple types of information that people represent during reasoning and a closer integration of model based accounts of text comprehension with those of reasoning. Next, we describe other work examining the way in which people interpret and make inferences from everyday even if conditionals. We use this data to illustrate the importance of specifying clearly how background knowledge is combined with information in an assertion to determine people's understanding of a given proposition and the inferences supported by that proposition. In the penultimate section of the chapter, we describe some developmental data on conditional reasoning, which shows that the means by which participants draw the modus tollens (MT) inference changes over time. Evidence is presented that strongly suggests that older participants employ a flexible strategy in MT reasoning that involves the construction and active manipulation of a single model and the generation, coordination, and manipulation of suppositions. In the final section, the general implications of our work are discussed in the context of the future development of model-based theories of deduction.

THE MODEL THEORY OF REASONING

According to the model theory of conditionals (Johnson-Laird & Byrne, 1991; Johnson-Laird et al., 1992) reasoning proceeds by the construction of models corresponding to the possible states of affairs that the premises describe. In deduction, reasoners normally construct models of the premises of an argument that correspond to a conception of the way the world would be if the premises were true and represent as little information as possible explicitly to reduce demands on working memory. According to this account, a conditional premise such as the following:

(1)   if Jimmy goes fishing, then he will have a fish supper

is represented initially by a single model:

(2) [*F*]   *FS*

...

where *F* corresponds to Jimmy going fishing and *FS* corresponds to Jimmy having a fish supper and each line represents a separate model. The model on the first line corresponds to the situation in which Jimmy goes fishing and has a fish supper. However, two other features of the representation reflect the conditional - rather than conjunctive - nature of the statement. First, the square brackets around F (exhaustivity markers) constitute a mental footnote to the effect that any model in which Jimmy goes fishing is a model in which Jimmy has a fish supper. Second, the presence of the implicit model, represented by the ellipses, signifies that the statement is also consistent with other as yet unspecified states of affairs in which Jimmy does not go fishing. However, initially these alternatives are not fully fleshed out. The full set of models corresponds to the following three states of affairs:

(3)   F   FS
        ¬F   FS
        ¬F   ¬FS

where the initial model is augmented by two additional models in which Jimmy does not go fishing but may or may not have a fish supper.

The study of conditional reasoning ordinarily involves the presentation of a conditional assertion of the kind shown previously together with a second premise that either affirms or denies its antecedent or consequent clause. This results in four conditional argument forms shown in Fig.2.1.

Under a conditional reading, MP and MT are valid inferences, whereas AC and DA are fallacies. The rates at which reasoners endorse the four conditional inferences varies widely. MP is almost universally endosed, whereas MT is drawn at a significantly lower rate. Reasoners also often endorse the fallacies, drawing AC at a generally higher rate than DA. According to the model theory the MP inference can be made by combining a model of the categorical premise with the initial representation of the conditional in Diagram 2. Hence, if people are told that Jimmy went fishing, they readily infer from this initial representation that he had a fish supper. In contrast, if reasoners are told that Jimmy did not have a fish supper, they are unable to combine this information with the initial model of the conditional.

In this case, the full set of models must be fleshed-out (Diagram 3); those models in which Jimmy had a fish supper eliminated leaving a single model in which Jimmy did not go fishing. According to the model theory, the fleshing-out of models is prone to error and hence reasoners are less likely to draw MT, which involves consideration of multiple models, than to draw MP which can be drawn from a single model. In a later section, we will return to the case of MT and discuss evidence that suggests an alternative account of the processes that underly MT reasoning.

MP	MT	AC	DA
if p then q	if p then q	if p then q	if p then q
p	not-q	q	not-p
therefore q	therefore not-p	therefore p	therefore not-q

FIG. 2.1. The four conditional argument forms.

The explanation for the difference in endorsement rates between AC and DA draws on a similar distinction. According to the account, the fallacies are endorsed because reasoners adopt a biconditional representation of the rule, representing only two possible states of affairs in the fully explicit model set:

$$(4) \quad F \quad FS$$
$$\neg F \quad \neg FS$$

AC is endorsed more frequently than DA because the initial representation of the biconditional consists of the first model discussed previously and hence supports the inference, whereas DA requires the initial representation to be fleshed-out.

Recently Johnson-Laird and Byrne (2002) developed their account of conditionals to include five principles that are drawn on in explaining the ways in which people interpret and reason from a range of conditional forms. The major extension to the theory relates to the introduction of an account of the way in which pragmatics and context affect the representation that is consructed. According to Johnson-Laird and Byrne there are two core meanings of conditionals, the conditional interpretation that consists of the three explicit models presented in Diagram 3 and the tautological interpretation. The tautological meaning is associated with conditionals that specify a modal relationship between antecedent and consequent, such as "if A then possibly B". The core tautological meaning is captured in a model set that represents all four truth table cases:

$$(5) \quad A \quad B$$
$$A \quad \neg B$$
$$\neg A \quad B$$
$$\neg A \quad \neg B$$

According to the revised account, the basic conditional and tautological meaning can be moderated by semantics or pragmatics. To illustrate the operation of pragmatic modulation, consider the following assertion (Jonhnson-Laird & Byrne, 2002): "Even if the workers settle for lower wages, the company may still go bankrupt." The core meaning of the assertion can be represented by the tautological model set in Diagram 5. However, context eliminates the possibility in which neither the antecedent nor the consequent is fulfilled; that is, we eliminate the possibility corresponding to the situation in which the workers don't settle and the company does not go bankrupt. This leaves the following three possibilities:

(7)   settle   bankrupt
        settle   ¬bankrupt
        ¬settle   bankrupt

These possibilities capture our intuition that the firm will go bankrupt if the workers do not settle, but settling may disable this outcome. Pragmatic modulation is also invoked to explain why certain conditional forms tend to elicit a biconditional rather than a conditional interpretation. In this case the core conditional meaning is moderated by context that eliminates the model in which the antecedent is false and the consequent true. For example, consider the following assertion: "If Tony Blair wins the next election he will continue to live at no 10 Downing Street." Given our background knowledge, we know that an individual cannot continue to live at 10 Downing street if they are no longer prime minister of Britain, and hence this knowledge eliminates this model from the core conditional meaning. On this modified account, pragmatics and background knowledge determine the way in which we understand assertions through the elimination of a subset of the models associated with the core meanings of conditional assertions.

An aspect of the model theory of conditionals that has received criticism and which in part motivates the first experiment reported here is the way in which knowledge is integrated into a model. As we have seen under the modified account, knowledge is important in determining those models that are retained in a representation. However, many conditionals also appear to convey information that goes beyond a simple description of a series of possible states of affairs in the world. This information may include the plausibility or probability of particular states of affairs (Stevenson & Over, 1995), the utility associated with particular possibilities (Manktelow & Over, 1991), the causal relationship between events (Zwaan & Radansky, 1998), or the temporal order in which events occur (Thompson, 1995; Thompson & Mann, 1995). For example, Thompson and Mann (1995) demonstrated using a semantic rephrasing task that "p only if q" rephrasings are preferred when q is temporally prior to and necessary for p. This evidence was used to argue that the representation of "p only if q", not only encodes necessity relations but also encodes the temporal order of the antecedent and consequent clauses (see also Evans, 1977).

The argument that mental models are informationally rich representations is not unique to the reasoning field. The situation model approach to text comprehension has long emphasized the multidimensional nature of model-based representations. According to this approach, in understanding any piece of discourse, people not only construct a representation of the words in the sentences but also construct a model corresponding to the situation described by those sentences. Hence, they construct a model corresponding to what the text is about rather than a representation of the text itself (see Zwaan & Radvansky, 1998, for a comprehensive review). Situation models constitute a level of representation associated with a deep understanding of a piece of text, and they allow the integration of information in a text with information from background knowledge. This level of representation is multidimensional in nature, encoding a variety of aspects of the situation described in the text. This might include spatial information (Bransford, Barclay, & Franks, 1972; Zwaan & Radvansky, 1998), information about the causal relationships between events (Singer, Halldorsen, Lear, & Andrusiak, 1992), or the goals and intentions of the protagonist (Graesser, 1981; Schank & Abelson, 1977). The situation model account has been successfully applied equally to single sentences (Rinck, Hahnel, & Becker, 2001) and to full story-based texts (Zwaan, Maglioni, & Graesser, 1995). The important point for our purposes is to highlight that there is good evidence that models encode information over and above the possible situations that a premise may describe. Each possibility may also be augmented by additional information based on our knowledge of events in the world. In the next section we illustrate not only that models for reasoning are much richer than has been proposed but also that the information people encode into their representation has a dramatic effect on the inferences they draw.

MODELS, TEMPORAL ORDER AND THE SUPPRESSION OF INFERENCE

In addition to information about causality, intentionality, and space, as discussed in the previous section, situation models encode information about both the relative and absolute times at which the events described in the text or discourse occurred. Despite the ubiquity of temporal information in language (see Miller & Johnson-Laird, 1976), time has received surprisingly little attention in the literature on situation models (for a review see, Zwaan & Radvansky, 1998). The work that does exist (see, e.g., Rinck, Hahnel, & Becker, 2001) suggests that people spontaneously encode temporal information in their mental models and that they have strong expectations about the relationship between the order in which events occur in the world and the order in which they appear in text or discourse.

We believe that temporal information will be encoded into the representations that people use for reasoning and that the temporal aspect of those representations will affect the inferences that are based on them. To test this intuition we decided to use the suppression paradigm (Byrne, 1989; Rumain, Connell & Braine, 1983), in which participants are given two conditional premises each referring to the same consequent and which specify either two alternative or two additional antecedents for that consequent. In the presence of alternative antecedents, the rate at which people draw the fallacious DA and AC inferences is suppressed, whereas in the presence of additional antecedents (i.e. conjoint antecedents for the consequent) people's tendency to draw the valid MP and MT inferences is reduced. So, for example, given a premise pair such as the following:

> If Joe goes fishing, then he will have a fish supper.
> If Joe catches a fish, then he will have a fish supper.

people will endorse the MP inference that Joe will have a fish supper given that he has gone fishing at a low rate relative to a one-rule control.

We agree with Byrne (1989) that to make sense of this text people will integrate the information in the premise pairs. This integration is automatic and online and is supported by the common consequent in each conditional and the common referent in the antecedent clause. According to Byrne, the initial integrated representation consists of a model that encodes the antecedents as conjoint requirements in the following way:

> (7)   [F   C]   FS
>   ...

Although this representation captures the idea that the antecedents are additional requirements, we suggest that people's representations will additionally encode information from background knowledge concerning the temporal order of these antecedents. In the previous example, we know that fishing necessarily precedes catching a fish, and hence the representation not only encodes these events as additional requirements but also encodes their temporal contiguity.

To test this claim we generated eight sets of conditional pairs. Half of the premise pairs specified additional requirements, whereas the other half specified alternative requirements. The additional antecedents were selected on the basis that the first antecedent would ordinarily occur before the second antecedent. We predicted that because people will encode the temporal relationship that normally exists in the world between the additional antecedents, the premise from which they are asked to draw an inference will substantially affect the rates of inference for MP and MT. So, with reference to the previous example if participants are told that Joe went fishing, they will not infer that he had a fish supper because they do not know whether he then caught a fish. In contrast, if they are told that he caught a fish, knowledge about the temporal relationship that holds between the antecedents will enable them to infer that first event had occurred and consequently infer that Jo had a fish supper. However, we would not expect this manipulation to influence the rates at which the fallacies are drawn.

In the remaining four sets of conditional pairings the antecedents specified alternative requirements of the following kind:

> If Joe goes fishing, then he will have a fish supper.
> If Joe goes to the fish-market, then he will have a fish supper.

In these cases, the second antecedent specifies an alternative condition that could lead to the consequent event. As stated previously, the presence of an alternative antecedent leads to a reduction in the rates at which AC and DA are drawn but has little influence on the valid inferences of MP and MT. Due to the lack of a temporal relationship between alternative antecedents, there is no reason to predict that for our materials containing alternative antecedents the premise from which people are asked to draw an inference will influence the inferences that are drawn.

Table 2.1.
Materials From the Experiment on Temporal Order and the Suppression of Conditional Inference

Problem	Consequent	Alternative Antecedents	Additional Antecedents
Fishing	Having a fish supper	Catching a fish Going to the fishmarket	Going fishing Catching a fish
Cashpoint	Withdrawing some money	Remembering PIN Going to a bank	Going to a cashpoint Remembering PIN
University	Going to university	Sitting A levels Going to technical college	Staying at school Sitting A levels
Betting	Winning some money	Placing a bet Buying a lottery ticket	Going to the bookies Placing a bet

Experiment 1

Experiment 1 had a 2 (premise type: alternatives Vs additional) by 2 (reasoning from the first Vs second premise) by 2 (valid Vs invalid inferences) by 2 (affirmative Vs denial inferences) design with repeated measures on the second two factors. Sixty participants were randomly allocated to one of the following four experimental conditions: alternative requirements reasoning from first premise, alternative requirements reasoning from the second premise, additional requirements reasoning from the first premise, and additional requirements reasoning from the second premise. Each participant received a total of 16 problems made up of four contents paired with each of the four inferences (MP, MT, DA, AC). The four contents that we used are displayed in Table 2.1.

The percentage rates of endorsement for the four inferences in each one of the four experimental conditions in this experiment are shown in Table 2.2. The results of a 2 (premise type: alternative Vs additional) by 2 (reasoning from the first Vs the second premise) by 2 (validity) by 2 (negation) ANOVA with repeated measures on the second two factors revealed a significant main effect of condition, $F(1.59) = 13.96, MSE = 2.87, p < .001$. Participants made more inferences from the additional premises (64%) than the alternatives (45%). There was also a highly significant main effect of validity, $F(1,59) = 39.57, MSE = 1.47, p < .001$, with more

Table 2.2.
Percentage of Inference Endorsements in Each of the Experimental Conditions
From Experiment 1

Condition					Inference		
Premise Type	Target Premise	MP	MT	Mean MP/MT	AC	DA	Mean AC/DA
Additionals	One	44	39	41	74	69	71
	Two	81	69	75	72	69	70
Mean Additionals		62	54	58	73	69	70
Alternatives	One	86	74	80	13	13	13
	Two	73	67	70	17	15	16
Mean Alternatives		79	70	75	15	14	14

valid inferences endorsed (67%) than invalid ones (42%). Similarly significantly more affirmative inferences (MP and AC) inferences were made (57%) than denial inferences (52%), $F(1,59) = 6.35, MSE = .52, p < .05$. The analysis also revealed a significant interaction between premise type and the validity of the inference, $F(1,59) = 91.28$, $MSE = 1.48$, $p < .001$. Planned comparisons on this interaction revealed as expected that participants made fewer valid MP and MT inferences than invalid AC and DA inferences from additional premise pairs, $F(1,59) = 5.41$, $MSE = 1.47$, $p < .05$. However, the groups that received premise pairs with alternative antecedents made fewer AC and DA inferences than MP and MT $F(1,59) = 123.51$, $MSE = 1.47$, $p < .001$).

These findings provide evidence that our manipulations served to clearly differentiate between the conditions in terms of additional and alternative requirements. However, our central prediction was that participants would resist drawing inferences from additional premises when these required reasoning from the first antecedent in the temporal sequence but would show no such effect when they reasoned from the second antecedent. As Figure 2.2.a-b illustrates, there was a significant interaction between type of premise pair, the validity of the inference, and the premise that participants reasoned from, $F(1,59) = 9.57$, $MSE = 1.48$, $p <$

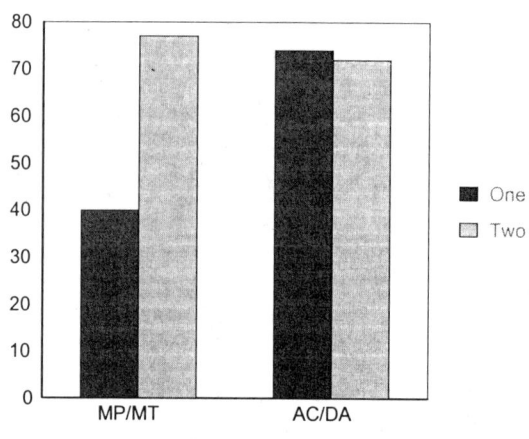

FIG. 2.1.a The interaction between target premise, inference type and type of premise (here additional antecedents) in Experiment 1.

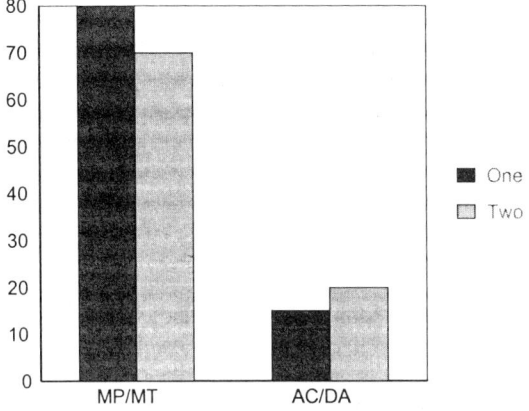

FIG. 2.1.b The interaction between target premise, inference type and type of premise (here alternative antecedents) in Experiment 1.

.005). As predicted, participants presented with alternative premise pairs were not influenced by the premise they were asked to reason from. Planned comparisons showed that there was no effect of premise on valid inferences, $F(1,59) = 1.02$, $MSE = 2.28$, $p < .3$), nor was there any effect of premise on invalid inferences, $F < 1$. In contrast, with additional premise pairs participants endorsed more valid inferences when they reasoned from the second premise than when they reasoned from the first premise, $F(1,59) = 12.68$, $MSE = 2.28$, $p < .005$), but there was no effect of this variable on invalid inferences, $F < 1$.

The findings described in the previous paragraph provide clear evidence that temporal order is spontaneously encoded into the representation of conjoined antecedents in our conditional suppression task. Furthermore, this order information plays a role in determining which inferences people will draw from their representation of the premises. This temporal order effect is predicted by previous work on how information about temporality is encoded in models of text or discourse and is further evidence of the flexibility of mental model level representations of the world. However, it is not clear how Johnson-Laird and Byrne's (1991; 2002) model theory of conditional reasoning would account for this data. We believe that not only does this finding emphasize the common origins and assumptions of model theoretic work on text comprehension and reasoning, but it also challenges workers on mental models for reasoning to specify exactly how background knowledge interacts with the information in the premises to produce representations for reasoning.

REASONING ABOUT EVEN IF

In the previous section, we claimed that the mental model theory, in its current form, does not account for the multidimensionality of people's representations for reasoning. In this section, we argue that the model theory does not adequately specify how participants arrive at representations of conditional forms. The example we wish to use here is that of even-if. In our description of pragmatic modulation in the revised version of the theory (Johnson-Laird & Byrne, 2002), we described how the following assertion:

> Even if the workers settle for lower wages, then the company may go bankrupt.

This is an example of an assertion with a core tautological meaning that is modulated by context so that the situation in which the antecedent and consequent are not satisfied is eliminated from the model set. This model set is presented in Diagram 6. Recently, Rios, Garcia-Madruga, and Byrne (2001) investigated even-if assertions that do not include the modal term *may*:

> Even if the workers settle for lower wages, then the company will go bankrupt.

Byrne and colleagues suggest that assertions such as these are represented by model sets of the following kind:

(8)   settle   bankrupt
       ¬settle   bankrupt

In terms of the revised version of the model theory, such a representation would be arrived at through the pragmatic modulation of the core conditional meaning. In exactly the same manner as in the first example, context eliminates the state of affairs in which the workers don't settle and the company doesn't go bankrupt.

The model sets proposed for even-if assertions of this kind capture the intuition that such statements indicate that the consequent event will happen no matter what. It is this aspect of even if that makes it an intriguing form of conditional assertion and that has made it the focus of debate in the philosophical (e.g., Barker, 1991; Bennett, 1982) and linguistic literatures (e.g., Francescotti, 1995; Lycan, 1991). In many respects, it is a very unusual form of assertion in that the consequent is not conditionalized on the antecedent. On superficial analysis, it provides no more information than does the simple assertion that the consequent event will occur. However, a deeper analysis causes one to more closely evaluate the function performed by an even-if assertion and the inferential process that leads to the representation captured in Johnson-Laird and Byrne's putative model set. In our view, even if has two functions: First, it serves to deny the presupposition that in the communicative context the consequent will not occur in the presence of the antecedent; and second, it serves to activate information in background knowledge that is then combined with the information in the assertion to determine the inferences that are drawn. We believe that simply describing a model set for the assertion, as Johnson-Laird and Byrne did, does not constitute an adequate analysis of the pragmatics of even-if assertions. It simply redescribes our intuitions about the meaning of such statements.

A Modified Account of Even-If

Any analysis of even-if must begin with an understanding of the function that *even* on its own serves in the language. Consider, for example, the following assertion:

> Even Hilary distrusts Bill

In our analysis of *even*, we draw on the work of Jackson (1987) and Sanford (1989) who have suggested that *even* serves to pick out an extreme position: "it is less probable, more surprising, contrary to expectation and so forth – in a contextually determined range of alternatives" (Sanford, 1989, p. 206). The assertion denies a presupposition that the listener might hold that Hilary does not distrust Bill. It also cues the listener to access a range of related statements that are more probable and less surprising (e.g., that George distrusts Bill, that Tony distrusts Bill, that Monica distrusts Bill). In this way it acts to invite the listener to make the inference that Bill is not to be trusted. Consider now, how this account might help us in understanding the pragmatics of even-if. To illustrate imagine that a student makes the following assertion:

> Even if Pete studies hard, he will fail the History exam tomorrow.

The questions, from our point of view, are, first, what presupposition does this assertion serve to deny and, second, what range of alternatives do people access from background knowledge in the course of interpreting this utterance?

As Jackson (1987) argued, the basic analysis of *even* outlined previously can be readily applied to even-if. This account of even if assumes, as does Adams (1975), that the truth of a conditional is its conditional probability. In model theory, the assertion "if p then q" is not incompatible with the assertion "if p then not-q", but of course under conditional probability the truth of one assertion precludes the truth of the other. We will not discuss this point in detail here, but please see Evans et al. (this volume) for a more detailed discussion of conditional probability. The assertion denies a commonly held presupposition that if one studies hard then one will pass an exam. That is, it denies a belief that

> If Pete studies hard, he will pass the history exam.

It also calls to mind a range of conditionals with alternative antecedents that serve to make the consequent more probable. According to Jackson (1987), the range most often consists of the conditional with the antecedent negated. Hence, from background knowledge, people will access information concerning what they commonly understand about the relationship between studying and failing exams:

If Pete doesn't study, then he will fail the history exam.

The combination of the representation of the even-if assertion with this manifest assumption leads directly to the inference that Pete will fail the history exam, whether or not he studies hard. In formal terms this inference is what logicians would term constructive dilemma. Before describing an experiment designed to investigate the pragmatics of even-if, let us first consider again the model-based account of this connective. As we have seen, the initial stage in understanding a connective of this kind involves constructing a fully fleshed-out representation of the core conditional model set. With reference to the even-if assertion, the model set would capture the following possibilities:

(9) S F
      $\neg S$ F
      $\neg S$ $\neg F$

where S represents Pete studying hard, and F represent Pete failing the exam. In the next stage, this representation is modulated through background knowledge. This eliminates the third model in which Pete doesn't study and passes his exam, leaving the following two models:

(10) S F
       $\neg S$ F

We find this account implausible for two reasons. First, it suggests that reasoners initially build a fully fleshed out model set for the assertion. There is ample evidence in the literature that constructing fully explicit models is difficult, and, often, people will reason from just a single model. Indeed, the difficulty of fleshing out models is central to the model theoretic explanation of the difficulties of inferences, such as MT (Johnson-Laird & Byrne, 1991) This objection aside, we are also dissatisfied with the notion that background knowledge influences the interpretation of assertions via the removal of possibilities from the model set.

We favor an alternative account of the processes that lead to the representation of even if assertions specifically and conditional forms in general. There are two key aspects of our proposals that differ substantially from the current mental model account. First we believe that, in line with recent research (Evans & Handley, 1999; Evans, Handley, Harper, & Johnson-Laird, 1999; Evans, Handley, & Over, 2002; Handley & Evans, 2000; Newstead, Handley, & Buck, 1999), people often only consider a single model or one state of affairs when they reason. Hence, people's initial representation of the assertion is likely to consist of just the possible situation in which Pete studies and fails the exam.

Second, we favor an account of pragmatic modulation in which background knowledge causes possibilities to be added to the model set rather than taken away. The knowledge that people access in the context of the assertion includes, as we have argued, the conditional relationship that normally holds between studying and failing exams; that is, we know that, if Pete doesn't study, he will fail the exam. As we argued previously, it is likely that people will initially represent this information in a single model, a model in which Pete doesn't study hard and fails the exam. This single model will then be integrated with the initial model of the assertion, leading to the model set proposed by Johnson-Laird & Byrne. As should be clear from this proposal, background knowledge is serving to add a model to a representation, rather than to eliminate one. Although the final integrated model set under our proposal is the same as that predicted by Johnson-Laird and Byrne, we have specified the principles governing the construction of the model set. These principles may be summarized in the following way:

> In general, people construct only a single model of a possible world in which the antecedent and the consequent are fulfilled.

> The particular connective in the assertion cues the activation of specific information in background knowledge – in the case of even-if this includes the presupposition that the assertion denies as well a range of less surprising and more probable conditional relationships between alternative antecedents and the stated consequent.

> Pragmatic modulation involves adding a single model of background knowledge about more plausible conditional relationships to the initial representation of the assertion.

In addition, concurrent with their representation of the integrated model set, we think it likely that people will represent, in a single model, the conditional relationship that the assertion serves to deny. Because this possibility is inconsistent with the possibilities represented in the integrated model, it is not included in that model. However, as we shall see later, this representation does affect the inferences that people draw from everyday even-if assertions.

Finally, before describing an experiment designed to examine people's even-if reasoning, we wish to point out that the position regarding the multidimensionality of people's representations for reasoning, which we outlined in the previous section, also holds for even-if. In particular, we expect people to represent information about the protagonist's likely intentions to act in a certain way. We return to this point in the discussion of our experimental findings.

Experiment 2

In this section, we report some data collected as part of a larger experiment that was designed to investigate the manner in which people interpret and reason from even-if statements. In the part of the experiment that is most relevant to the current discussion, 48 student participants were presented with the following scenario: Pete and Jimmy are undergraduate students at the University of Plymouth. They are discussing the forthcoming examination. Jimmy says, "Even if I study hard I will fail my history exam." Participants were then asked to complete a task that required them to interpret what Jimmy intended to convey by his assertion, together with a conditional inference task. The order of task presentation was counterbalanced within subjects. In the interpretation task, participants were asked to rate on a nine-point scale the extent to which they agreed that Jimmy intended to convey the following:

> That he will study hard
> That he will not study hard
> That he will fail his history exam
> That he will not fail his history exam

In the conditional inference task, participants were presented with the four conditional argument forms and were asked which of three outcomes was most likely. An example of the MP inference is given below:

> Suppose Jimmy studies hard. According to what he has said, which of the following outcomes is most likely?
>
> Jimmy failed his history exam.
> Jimmy passed his history exam.
> Jimmy may or may not have passed his history exam.

Of course the last disjunctive alternative will always be at least as likely as either of the other two outcomes. The data suggest, however, that participants did not make their selections on this basis.

We present the interpretation data first. We performed a 2 x 2 ANOVA, with conditional clause (antecedent vs. consequent) and polarity (affirmative vs. negative) as the within-participants factors. The main effects in the analysis were subsumed by a significant interaction between these factors, $F(1, 47) = 104.05$, $MSE = 4.90, p < .001$. Planned comparisons carried out on this interaction revealed, as expected, that participants interpreted the speaker's assertion as indicating that he would fail (7.56, $sd = 1.72$) rather than pass the exam (2.38, $sd = 1.54$; $F(1, 47) = 155.14$, $MSE = 4.16$, $p < .001$). This confirms the strong intuition that even-if assertions entail their consequent. Planned comparisons also revealed that participants interpreted the speaker as conveying that he was not going to study (5.13, $sd = 2.05$) rather than that the speaker was going to study (3.79, sd 1.47; $F(1, 47) = 11.12$, $MSE = 3.84, p < .002$).

Before presenting the conditional inference data, we consider the results reported previously in the context of the model set presented in the preceding section. Recall that this model set consisted of the following two models: one in which the speaker studies and fails the exam and another in which he does not study and fails. The immediate inference data, which show that people infer that the speaker will fail the exam, are entirely consistent with this proposed representation, as this holds in both models. However, the second finding, that people infer that the speaker will not study, is not captured by a simple model-based representation of this kind. In our view, this finding again reflects the multidimensional nature of models. In this case, participants have represented in some form the speaker's intention to act. Given that there are two courses of action, both of which lead to the same outcome, it appears that participants have inferred that the speaker is intending to choose the course of action that involves the least effort (i.e., not studying). This suggests, at the very least, that some form of information concerning the relative cost of action and the impact that this may have on the speaker's intentions is encoded into the representation.

Fig. 2a presents the data for the antecedent inferences MP and DA. Recall that the model set we are proposing for even-if represents two possible states of affairs. In both of these models, Pete failed the exam, but in one he studies hard and in the other he does not. Hence, if participants are reasoning only from this model set, we might expect them to infer that Pete failed the exam, whether they are told that he studied (MP) or did not study (DA). Considering DA first, as Fig. 2a clearly shows, the majority of participants inferred that Pete failed the exam on being told that he didn't study (69%). Most of the remaining participants inferred that it was impossible to tell whether Jim passed or failed the exam (29%). Presumably, these participants recognize that it is possible to pass exams without studying, whether through luck or through the setting of a generous assessment. As the reader will recognize, the majority of inferences here are converse inferences; that is, participants are inferring q when they are told not$p$. This provides very good evidence that the model in which Pete doesn't study but passes the exam (not$p$, not$q$ model) is not encoded into the representation of the assertion, whether this be through a process of pragmatic modulation or as we suggest from the fact that people have never represented this possibility in their models in the first place. Turning now to the rates of inference for MP, participants inferred that Pete would fail the exam less (33%) than they did for DA (69%). Here the majority of responses

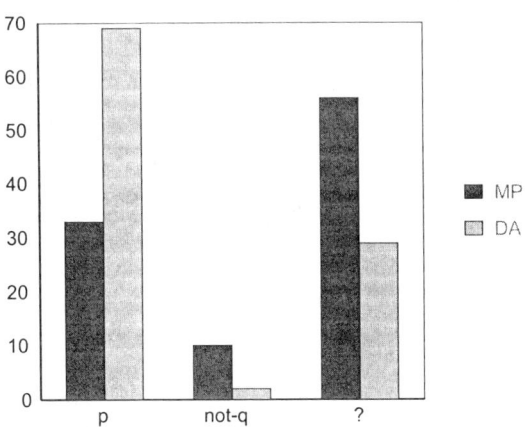

FIG. 2.2.a The pattern of responses to the antecedent inferences on the conditional arguments task in Experiment 2.

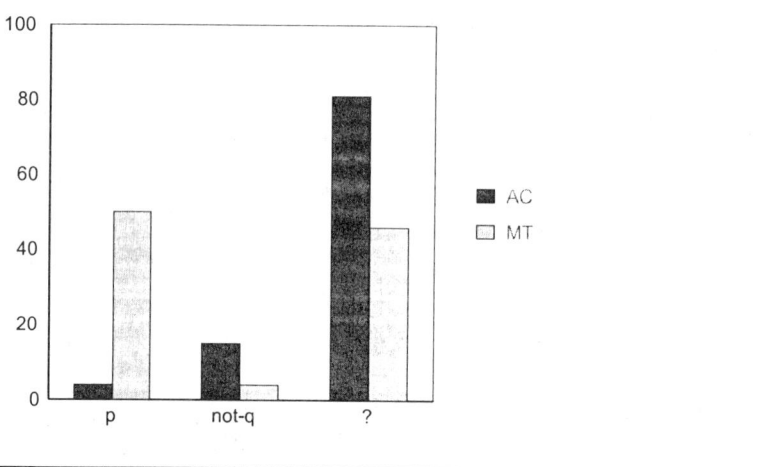

FIG. 2.2.b The pattern of responses to the consequent inferences on the conditional arguments task in Experiment 2.

indicated that it was impossible to tell whether or not he passed (56%). This interaction provides support for our conjecture that people concurrently represent the assertion that even-if serves to deny; that is, they represent from background knowledge that, if you study, then you pass exams. Of course, this is not integrated into the model set of the meaning of the assertion as our immediate inference data show clearly (people infer very strongly that the speaker intended to convey that he would fail). Nevertheless, it affects the inferences drawn. In a sense, being told that Pete studies provides a condition that may disable the outcome that has been inferred. Hence, participants are less likely to reason with certainty that Pete will fail the exam.

We now turn to the consequent inferences MT and AC. As Fig. 2.2.b shows, on the AC inference, the majority of participants inferred that it was not possible to tell whether Pete studied or not (81%). Again, this pattern is entirely consistent with the model set that we propose people construct of the assertion. The pattern of responses for MT was more complex. In many ways, the MT from an even-if assertion is a very peculiar inference to ask people to make. As we showed, even-if serves to cue the immediate inference that Pete believes he will fail the exam. The MT categorical premise "Pete passed the exam" serves to countermand this inference. The question is what should people then infer? Given that this possibility is not present in the model set, this may cause participants to doubt the truth of the assertion. It is not possible to draw any determinate inference from a false premise, and indeed a large proportion of our participants responded that it was not possible to tell whether Pete studies or not (46%). Most of the remaining participants made the converse inference; that is, they inferred that Pete studies hard (50%). Given that the truth of the assertion has been called into question, we suggest that people will fall back on their background knowledge and infer that Pete must have studied hard. As with MP, this finding provides support for our proposal that the possibility that the assertion serves to deny is represented concurrently with a representation of the assertion.

Although we refer to just one example of even-if in this study, the patterns of findings are generally consistent both when alternative thematic content is used and when arbitrary content is included in the assertion (Handley & Feeney, 2004). The immediate inference findings confirm that the representation people construct of the assertion consists only of situations in which the consequent is fulfilled. The pattern of AC and DA inferences suggest that this representation consists of a model in which p and a model in which not$p$ occurs. However, the immediate inferences indicate that participants also encode information concerning such things as the cost of acting and resultant intentions to act. Finally, the inference data for MP and MT indicate that in addition to the representation of the speaker's assertion, a model of the state of affairs that is denied is also represented and determines some of the inferences that are made.

At the very least this experiment demonstrates the richness of the representation constructed and the inferences that people make from everyday conditional assertions. We attempted to clearly specify the manner in which such statements cue the activation of particular kinds of background knowledge and the way in which this knowledge is combined with a representation of the assertion in determining the models constructed and the inferences made. This account is based on the assumption that people generally only construct and represent a single model, one in which the antecedent and hence the consequent hold. Pragmatics serve to add alternatives to this representation rather than eliminating alternatives, as present model-based proposals suggest. In the penultimate section of this chapter we argue that complex inferences, such as MT, can be readily made from a single model based representation.

SUPPOSITIONS IN REASONING: THE CASE OF MODUS TOLLENS

The ability to make temporary suppositions and follow up the consequences of these is a core component of human thinking. Suppositional reasoning underpins our ability to think hypothetically and consider the consequences of possible courses of action. It enables us to identify faults in complex systems, develop acceptable plans for the future, and evaluate and learn from events in the past.

Indeed the extent to which we engage in such thinking in the context of past events may well determine the degree to which we think counterfactually and the associated emotions that we may feel.

Recently, research has begun to investigate the role that suppositions play in human reasoning under the framework of model theoretic accounts of reasoning. For example, Handley and Evans (2000) have argued that people solve complex multipremise propositional reasoning problems through the generation of suppositions based on holistic mental models. Reasoners then check whether these possibilities are consistent with subsequent premises, abandoning them if they contradict and accepting them if they satisfice. Similarly, Byrne and Handley (1997) identified a range of suppositional strategies that people develop and employ spontaneously in solving problems that involve making inferences about the truth and falsity of assertions and the veracity of the assertor. To illustrate, consider the following conversation between two individuals:

> *Sam* :   I am telling the truth, and Sophie is telling a lie.
> *Sophie*: Sam is telling the truth.

The task requires one to determine whether each individual is telling the truth or telling a lie. According to Byrne and Handley (1997), reasoners spontaneously develop higher level strategies in solving these problems that depend on the coordination of suppositions. The hypothesize and match strategy works in the following way: Participants first assume that Sam is telling the truth. It follows from this supposition that Sophie is telling a lie, and from Sophie's assertion it follows that Sam is telling a lie. This contradicts the original supposition, and people hence conclude that Sam is lying. This conclusion is then matched to the content of Sophie's assertion to determine that Sophie is also telling a lie. The identification of suppositional strategies in complex propositional reasoning tasks and in metadeductive reasoning problems suggests that reasoners have the requisite skills that would enable the application of suppositional strategies across a wide range of reasoning tasks.

In conditional reasoning, the role, if any, that suppositions play is unclear. This is somewhat surprising given that conditionals describe hypothetical possibilities and arguably invite one to imagine or suppose a situation in which the antecedent condition is fulfilled. According to rule-based accounts of reasoning, however, people can and do employ suppositional strategies in drawing the MT inference (e.g., Braine & O'Brien, 1991; Rips, 1994). According to this account MT inferences of the following kind are solved by sophisticated reasoners through an inference chain that starts with supposition that *A* holds true:

> If the letter *A* is on the top of the card, then the number 3 is on
> the bottom of the card.
> There is not a 3 on the bottom of the card
> Therefore, there is not an *A* on the top of the card.

This supposition leads to the inference that there is a 3 on the bottom of the card. This contradicts the categorical premise, and reductio reasoning leads to the conclusion that there is not an *A* on the top of the card. In this volume, Evans, Over and Handley argue that the mental model account of MT, in terms of the fleshing out of possibilities, can be viewed as an application of a strategy of this kind. Although we do not intend to repeat this argument in detail here, we also agree that in certain circumstances reasoners will invoke a suppositional strategy in solving MT inferences. Consider, for example, the following argument:

> If *A*, then 3.
> Not3.
> Therefore, not*A*.

The initial model of the conditional together with the models of the categorical premise and conclusion are as follows:

(12)   [*A*]   3
            ...

not3

not*A*

As we know the initial model of the conditional supports the MP inference. All that is needed to draw MT is an ability to generate a temporary supposition that *A* holds, combine this supposition with the initial model, and make the inference that 3 also holds. This contradicts the categorical premise and hence reasoners can conclude that the supposition is false, and not*A* follows. This process does not involve fleshing out the initial representation of the conditional premise to represent the FF case; instead, it only entails generating a single model of the conditional assertion. In these terms, this proposal is consistent with the suggestion that in general people only consider and represent a single possible state of affairs.

The evidence that people employ suppositional strategies of exactly this kind in metadeductive reasoning suggests that people recognize that this strategy is a useful one and that they understand that a supposition that leads to a contradiction is false. There is no reason, in our view, why sophisticated reasoners in conditional reasoning tasks would not develop strategies of this kind. In the experiment that follows, we present evidence from a study on the development of conditional reasoning, which we believe provides support for our conjecture that people engage in suppositional reasoning on MT. Participants were presented with standard MT problems of the kind shown in (12), together with problems of the following kind, in which the conclusion presented was the opposite of the correct conclusion:

(13)   If *A*, then 3.

Not3.
Therefore, *A*.

The task was to decide whether the conclusion is definitely true or definitely false or whether it is impossible to determine its status. In argument (12), the conclusion is of the standard kind, so correctly drawing MT would be indicated by responding "true." In the second example, the conclusion is the opposite of the correct conclusion, so drawing MT requires the "false" response. How might we expect this manipulation to affect the rates at which MT is drawn? Consider first the standard model theoretic account. As we have seen, MT requires the full set of models to be fleshed out:

$$(14) \quad A \qquad 3$$
$$\neg A \quad 3$$
$$\neg A \quad \neg 3$$

The first two models can be eliminated leaving only the third model. In the case of the standard conclusion in (12), there is a match between the contents of the model and the model of the conclusion which will elicit a true response. In contrast, in the case of the opposite conclusion in (13), there is a mismatch with the contents of the model, eliciting a "false" conclusion. In model theory, detecting inconsistency adds to difficulty (Johnson-Laird & Byrne, 1991), and indeed in studies of simple tasks such as sentence verification judging that a case is false with respect to a linguistic description is more difficult than judging it true (Evans, 1982). Hence, on this account, the prediction must be that the opposite conclusion problems will be more difficult and result in lower rates of MT. In contrast, on a suppositional account of reasoning, the opposite conclusion provides the supposition that then can be combined with a representation of the conditional in detecting a contradiction. That is, if people are given the conclusion *A*, their reasoning can proceed as follows: "Given this conclusion is true it follows, from the initial model of the conditional, that there is a 3, but I am told there is not a 3, so the conclusion is false." In the standard problem, the suppositional strategy is not cued by the presence of the conclusion. Indeed, engaging in this strategy entails supposing the opposite of the conclusion, which is likely to be much more difficult.

In summary, in a mental models account, the opposite conclusions should be more difficult to judge as false than the standard conclusions as true, whereas on a suppositional account, the obverse holds. In addition to examining the pattern of inferences in an adult sample, we also examined the inferences developmentally. There is good evidence in the developmental literature that conditional reasoning in younger children is determined by the pragmatic inferences that conditionals cue; that is, MT is supported by pragmatic inferences rather than being solved by the application of an explicit reasoning strategy (Rumain et al., 1983). Hence, we predicted that the effect of the conclusion will interact with the age of the sample.

Experiment 3

A total of 197 participants took part in the experiment. Of these, 26 were in Year 2 ($M = 7.37$ years, $SD = .28$), 27 were in Year 4 ($M = 9.35$ years, $SD = .22$), 28 were in Year 6 ($M = 11. 36$ years, $SD = .30$), 26 were in Year 8 ($M = 13.41$ years, $SD = .28$), 32 were in Year 10 ($M = 15.45$ years, $SD = .36$), 30 were in Year 12 ($M = 17.42$ years, $SD = .28$), and 28 were students at the University of Plymouth ($M = 26.21$ years, $SD = 5.75$). Participants of each age group were presented with a total of 32 experimental problems. Half of the problems had standard conclusions, and half had opposite conclusions. Each set of 16 problems consisted of the four inferences: MP, AC, MT, and DA. For each inference, there were four examples generated through rotating negation within conditional premise (e.g., Evans, Handley, & Buck, 1998). Each of the problems was based on content of the following kind:

If the bottom of the card has a number 7, then the top of the card has the letter V.
The top of the card does not have the letter V.

Is it true that:

The bottom has a 7.

Circle either:

A: Yes, it must be true.
B: No, it can't be true.
C: You can't really tell for definite (there might or might not be a 7).

The problems were presented in a random order, and there was no time limit for the completion of the task.

For the purposes of this chapter we present only the data relevant to the MT inference.

Table 2.3
Percentage of MT Inferences Drawn for Each Age Group in Experiment 3

Problem type	Age Group						
	7	9	11	13	15	17	adults
Standard conclusion	45	45	50	51	34	48	44

Opposite conclusion	45	47	62	56	52	69	66

Table 2.3 shows the percentage inference rates for standard and opposite conclusions for each of the age groups. An ANOVA with age as the between-participants factor and conclusion type within did not show any overall effect of age, $F(6,190) = 1.57$, $MSE = 1403$, $p > .1$. However, there was a significant effect of conclusion type, $F(1,190) = 24.71$, $MSE = 545$, $p < .01$, and an interaction between age and conclusion type, $F(6,190) = 2.21$, $MSE = 545$, $p < .05$). Planned comparisons on this interaction showed that opposite conclusions were correctly rejected more frequently than standard conclusions were accepted in the adult group, $F(1,190) = 13.18$, $MSE = 545$, $p < .001$, the 17-year-old group, $F(1,190) = 11.92$, $MSE = 545$, $p < .001$, and the 15-year-old group, $F(1,190) = 9.46$, $MSE = 545$, $p < .01$. None of the comparisons for the younger age groups was significant.

The data from this experiment confirm the prediction that it will be easier to infer that an opposite conclusion is false than to infer the standard conclusion is true. In our view, outlined previously, this provides good evidence that reasoners can and do apply suppositional reasoning strategies in MT reasoning. Opposite conclusions provide a ready-made supposition that can be integrated with a representation of the conditional assertion to infer the contradiction. Standard conclusions do not provide a cue to generate an appropriate supposition and hence are more difficult. Also, as predicted, this finding interacts with age. The advantage that an opposite conclusion confers is only apparent in the 15-year-old group and older. This might suggest that suppositional strategies are higher level explicit strategies developed during mid- to late adolescence. Prior to this, we would suggest that MT is supported by automatic pragmatic processes. Other evidence present in our data supported this account. In particular, the finding that is also present in other developmental data (e.g., Barouillet, Grosset, & Lecas, 2000) that the rates of the valid inferences MP and MT are no different from the rates of the invalid inferences DA and AC among younger children. This supports the proposal that younger children adopt a pragmatically cued biconditional representation of conditional rules.

CONCLUSIONS

In this chapter we argued that the model theory of deductive reasoning is underspecified in at least three respects. First, we suggested that the models that people construct of conditional assertions are multidimensional in nature; that is, they encode such things as the temporal order of events in the world, the cost associated with alternative actions, and the likely intentions of the protagonist or the speaker. In this respect, the sorts of models that we are suggesting for reasoning bear a close resemblance to the sorts of models that people construct when they understand and represent a piece of text. Indeed, the situation model account of text comprehension was the framework that motivated the first experiment reported here. Given that models of text processing and the mental model account of reasoning have their origins within a common theoretical framework (Johnson-Laird, 1983; van Dijk & Kintsch, 1983), it would be unparsimonious to suggest that the representational structures that underlie reasoning should be any less pragmatically rich than those that underlie other forms of language processing.

The research questions that motivate situation model research concern the conditions under which certain sorts of information, whether this be spatial, causal, or temporal, are encoded into a representation. Given that this information is encoded, the question then arises as to how this may influence the integration of subsequent information into the representation and determine the way in which we understand and process a piece of text. We would argue that these sorts of questions are equally important for reasoning researchers. In the context of the research reported here, it is important to develop the mental model account in such a way as to specify clearly how temporal information is encoded into a model and the manner in which this will influence how models are manipulated and the inferences that are then drawn from them.

The second aspect of the present model theory that we focused on is the role of pragmatics or background knowledge in determining the representation constructed and the inferences drawn. Although Johnson-Laird and Byrne (2002) recently provided an account of the way in which pragmatics modulates a core conditional representation, we are dissatisfied with this account in a number of respects. First, the principle of pragmatic modulation assumes that knowledge eliminates models from a core meaning, which in the case of conditionals consists of the three models corresponding to the fully fleshed-out possibilities. There is increasing evidence in the literature that people generally consider only a single model, and mental model theorists themselves have argued that fleshing-out models is a difficult process and prone to error. Hence, it seems very strange to argue that the representations people construct for everyday conditionals are arrived at by the elimination of models that most people will have difficulty representing in the first place.

Second, the account does not clearly specify how a particular conditional form, content, or context cues the representation of information in background knowledge that then serves to modulate the core representation. In the work presented here on the connective even-if, we developed a modified account that attempts to more clearly specify the way in which the connective cues the activation of specific relationships from background knowledge. We argued that this information is then integrated into a representation of the assertion and that this process determines the inferences drawn. Our account differs in that we assume that people only consider a single model of the assertion and the role of pragmatics is to add a representation to this model rather than to eliminate existing ones. In our view, the development of the model theory depends crucially on more clearly specifying the processes by which background knowledge is activated and integrated with a representation of any given conditional assertion.

In the penultimate section of this chapter, we considered whether the process of fleshing-out an initial representation is a necessary component in explaining people's ability to draw the MT inference. The ability to make suppositions is a core component of human thinking and underlies a whole range of cognitive activities, and we argued that among sophisticated reasoners MT reasoning can be accomplished by employing a strategy based on suppositions. The evidence from Experiment 3 suggests that certain task manipulations facilitate the application of this strategy among more experienced reasoners. As we showed, a suppositional account of MT was proposed by rule-based theorists many years ago (Braine, Reiser, & Rumain, 1984; Rips, 1983). However, we do not feel that proposing an account of this kind commits us to a rule-based account of reasoning. The assumptions that people generally only consider a single model and that reasoning proceeds by the flexible manipulation of this model do not in any way abandon the basic premise that reasoning involves the manipulation of analogical representations of situations in the world. However, we do feel that the idea of fleshing out representations as the only means by which to draw MT is an overly deterministic explanation of such reasoning. People employ a range of strategies in reasoning tasks (see, e.g., Schaeken, DeVooght, Vandierendonck & d'Ydewalle, 2000), and the use of suppositions to guide the inferential process is simply an example of one such strategy.

In conclusion, we are in broad agreement with the notion that reasoning is best viewed as a process that involves the construction and manipulation of mental models corresponding to situations in the world. However, the research reported here highlights the need to modify the account in a way that more adequately captures the self-evident richness of representations and the flexible manner in which such representations are manipulated in human reasoning.

REFERENCES

Adams, E. W. (1975). *The logic of conditionals: An application of probability to deductive logic.* Dordrecht, The Netherlands: Reidel.

Barker, S. (1991). Even, still, and counterfactuals. *Linguistics and Philosophy, 14,* 1-38.

Barrouillet P., Grosset N., & Lecas J. F. (2000). Conditional reasoning by mental models: chronometric and developmental evidence. *Cognition, 75,* 237-266.

Bennett, J. (1982). Even if. *Linguistics and Philosophy, 5,* 403–418.

Braine, M. D. S., & O'Brien, D. P. (1991). A theory of if: A lexical entry, reasoning program, and pragmatic principles. *Psychological Review, 98,* 182–203.

Braine, M. D. S., Reiser, B. J., & Rumain, B. (1984). Some empirical justification for a theory of natural propositional logic. In G. H. Bower (Ed.), *The psychology of learning and motivation* (Vol. 18, pp. 313–371). New York:

Academic Press.

Bransford, J. D., Barclay, J. R., & Franks, J. J. (1972). Sentence memory: A constructive versus interpretative approach. *Cognitive Psychology, 3,* 193–209.

Byrne, R. M. J. (1989). Suppressing valid inferences with conditionals. *Cognition, 31,* 61–83.

Byrne, R. M. J., Espino, O., & Santamaria, C. (1999). Counterexamples and the suppression of inferences. *Journal of Memory and Language, 40,* 347–373.

Byrne, R. M. J., & Handley, S. J. (1997). Reasoning strategies for suppositional deductions. *Cognition, 62,* 1–49.

Evans, J. St. B. T. (1977). Linguistic factors in reasoning. *Quarterly Journal of Experimental Psychology, 29,* 297–306.

Evans, J. St. B. T. (1982). *The psychology of deductive reasoning.* London: Routledge and Kegan Paul.

Evans, J. St. B. T., & Handley, S. J. (1999). The role of negation in conditional inference. *Quarterly Journal of Experimental Psychology, 52A,* 739–769.

Evans, J. St. B. T., Handley, S. J., & Buck, E. (1998). Ordering of information in conditional reasoning. *British Journal of Psychology, 89,* 383–403.

Evans, J. St. B. T., Handley, S. J., & Over, D. E. (2002). Conditionals and conditional probability. *Journal of Experimental Psychology: Learning, Memory and Cognition, 29,* 321–335.

Evans, J. St. B. T., Handley, S. J., Harper, C., & Johnson-Laird, P. N. (1999). Reasoning about necessity and possibility: A test of the mental model theory of deduction. *Journal of Experimental Psychology: Learning, Memory and Cognition, 25,* 1495–1513.

Francescotti, R. M. (1995). Even: The conventional implicature approach reconsidered. *Linguistics and Philosophy, 18,* 153–173.

Graesser, A. C. (1981). *Prose comprehension beyond the word.* New York: Springer-Verlag.

Handley, S. J., & Evans, J. St. B. T. (2000). Supposition and representation in human reasoning. *Thinking and Reasoning, 6,* 273–312.

Handley, S. J., & Feeney, A. (2004). Reasoning and pragmatics: The case of even-if. In I. Noveck & D. Sperber (Eds.), *Towards an experimental pragmatics* (pp. 228–253). Basingstoke, UK: Palgrave MacMillan.

Jackson, F. (1987). *Conditionals.* Oxford, UK: Blackwell.

Johnson-Laird, P. N. (1983). *Mental models.* Cambridge, UK: Cambridge University Press.

Johnson-Laird, P. N., & Byrne, R. M. J. (1991). *Deduction.* Hillsdale, NJ: Lawrence Erlbaum Associates.

Johnson-Laird, P. N., & Byrne, R. M. J. (2002). Conditionals: A theory of their meaning, mental representation, and role in inference. *Psychological Review, 109,* 646–678.

Johnson-Laird, P. N., Byrne, R., & Schaeken, W. (1992). Propositional reasoning by model. *Psychological Review, 99,* 418–439.

Lycan, W. G. (1991). Even and even if. *Linguistics and Philosophy, 14,* 115–150.

Manktelow, K. I., & Over, D. E. (1991). Social roles and utilities in reasoning with deontic conditionals. *Cognition, 39,* 85–105.

Miller, G. A., & Johnson-Laird, P. N. (1976). *Language and perception.* Cambridge, UK: Cambridge University Press.

Newstead, S. N., Handley, S. J., & Buck, E. (1999). Falsifying mental models: Testing the predictions of theories of mental models. *Memory and Cognition, 27* (2), 344–354.

Rinck, M., Hahnel, A., & Becker, G. (2001). Using temporal information to construct, update, and retrieve situation models of narratives. *Journal of Experimental Psychology: Learning, Memory and Cognition, 27,* 67–80.

Rios, S. M., Garcia-Madruga, J. A., & Byrne, R. M. J. (2001). Semi-factual and counterfactual conditionals. *Unpublished manuscript.*

Rips, L. J. (1983). Cognitive processes in propositional reasoning. *Psychological Review, 90,* 38–71.

Rips, L. J. (1994). *The psychology of proof.* New York: MIT press.

Rumain, B., Connell, J., & Braine, M. D. S. (1983). Conversational comprehension processes are responsible for reasoning fallacies in children as well as adults: If is not the biconditional. *Developmental Psychology, 19,* 471–481.

Sanford, D. H. (1989). *If p then q: Conditionals and the foundations of reasoning.* London: Routledge.

Schaeken, W., DeVooght, G., Vandierendonck, A., & d'Ydewalle, G. (2000). *Deductive reasoning and strategies.* Mahwah, NJ: Lawrence Erlbaum Associates.

Schank, R. C., & Abelson, R. P. (1977). *Scripts, plans, goals and understanding: An inquiry into human understanding.* Hillsdale, NJ: Lawrence Erlbaum Associates.

Singer, M., Halldorson, M., Lear, J. C., & Andrusiak, P. (1992). Validation of causal bridging inferences. *Journal of Memory and Language, 31,* 507–524.

Stevenson, R. J., & Over, D. E. (1995). Deduction from uncertain premises. *Quarterly Journal of Experimental Psychology, 48A,* 613–643.

Thompson, V. A. (1995). Conditional reasoning: The necessary and sufficient conditions. *Canadian Journal of Experimental Psychology, 49,* 1–60.

Thompson, V. A., & Mann, J. M. (1995). Perceived necessity explains the dissociation between logic and meaning: The case of "only if." *Journal of Experimental Psychology: Learning, Memory and Cognition, 21,* 1–14.

van Dijk, T. A., & Kintsch, W. (1983). *Strategies of discourse comprehension.* New York: Academic Press.

Zwaan, R. A., Maglioni, J. P., & Graesser, A. C. (1995). Dimensions of situation model construction in narrative comprehension. *Journal of Experimental Psychology: Learning, Memory and Cognition, 21,* 386–397.

Zwaan, R. A., & Radvansky, G. A. (1998). Situation models in language comprehension and memory. *Psychological Bulletin, 123,* 162–185.

3

Whether, Although,
and Other Conditionals

Ruth M. J. Byrne

When we wish to describe a conditional relation in everyday conversation, we can select different connectives to invite our listeners to make different inferences. We may choose to describe a conditional relation using a very wide range of conditional connectives, such as *if*, *unless*, *even if*, *only if*, *whether*, *although*, *suppose*, *whenever*, and so on. These connectives may convey different nuances of meaning, which ensure that listeners represent the events described in subtly different ways. Different interpretations of the conditional relation may in turn lead listeners to make different conditional inferences. We report two experiments that show that different conditional connectives support different inferences. *Whenever* and *supposing* seem similar to *if*, and the initial set of models for *whenever* and *supposing* may be similar to the initial set of models for *if*. The initial set of models for *whether* and *although* are more explicit.

INTRODUCTION

Suppose you wish to explain to a student driver the requirements of a stop sign and a yield sign. To explain the yield sign, you might say, "you must come to a stop if there are any other cars coming." To explain the stop sign, you might say, "you must come to a stop whether there are any other cars coming or not." Approaching a stop sign, you might remind students, "you must stop, although there are no cars." What do these different sorts of connectives - *if*, *whether*, *although* - mean, and why do we use them? The language we use to describe the world is capable of conveying subtle nuances of meaning. Our descriptions of conditional relations can convey a rich variety of interpretations. It is possible that when we wish to describe a conditional relation in everyday conversation, we select different connectives to invite our listeners to make different inferences. We may choose to describe a conditional relation using a very wide range of conditional connectives, such as *if*, *unless*, *even if*, *only if*, *whether*, *although*, *suppose*, *whenever*, and so on. These connectives may convey different nuances of meaning, which ensure that listeners represent the events described in subtly different ways. Different interpretations of the conditional relation may in turn lead listeners to make different conditional inferences. Most of our knowledge about conditional inferences comes from studies of *if*. My aim is to examine other everyday conditional connectives and to compare the frequency with which people make conditional inferences from *if* and these other connectives. I will discuss results from some recent experiments which compare the frequency of inferences from *if* to other connectives such as *whether*, *although*, *suppose*, and *whenever* (Byrne, 2002).

CONDITIONAL INFERENCES FROM *IF*

Most of what we know about conditional inferences is based on experiments with the connective 'if' (see Evans, Newstead and Byrne, 1993 for a review). People readily make the modus ponens inference, from a conditional such as "if the chef used courgettes, he used basil" and the categorical "the chef used courgettes" to the conclusion, "he used basil." They find it more difficult to make the modus tollens inference, from "the chef did not use basil" to the conclusion "he did not use courgettes." The frequency with which they make the affirmation of the consequent inference, from "the chef used basil", to the conclusion "he used courgettes" fluctuates somewhat, but generally, people tend to make it more than the frequency with which they make the denial of the antecedent inference (i.e., from "the chef did not use courgettes" to the conclusion "he did not use basil"; see Johnson-Laird & Byrne, 2002).

One suggestion is that this pattern of inferences reflects the nature and processing of mental models that people have constructed of the conditional (e.g., Johnson-Laird & Byrne, 1991). People may understand a conditional by representing the possibilities that would be true if the assertion were true. Their mental models may be constrained by the limits of working memory, so they may represent some information explicitly and leave some information implicit. For example, the initial set of models for the conditional "if the chef used courgettes, he used basil" may be as follows:

    courgettes   basil
    ...

where "courgettes" represents "the chef used courgettes" and "basil' represents "the chef used basil", and different models are represented on different lines in the diagram. The three dots represent an implicit model, which can be fleshed out to be more explicit if need be and indicates that there are alternatives to the explicit model.

The modus ponens inference may be made readily because it can be made directly from this initial set of models. The information that "the chef used courgettes" can be combined readily with the first model, eliminating the implicit model and allowing the conclusion "the chef used basil" (for details on the combination of information in models, see Johnson-Laird, Byrne, & Schaeken, 1992). The affirmation of the consequent inference may be made in a similar manner, but some reasoners may refrain from making the inference if they flesh out their models to be more explicit and appreciate that the following possibilities can be true when the assertion is true:

courgettes	basil
no courgettes	basil
...	

The modus tollens information "the chef did not use basil" and the denial of the antecedent information "the chef did not use courgettes" may be hard to assimilate into the initial, affirmative, explicit model. The models must be fleshed out to be more explicit. For the modus tollens inference, the models need to be fleshed out to include the following possibility:

courgettes	basil
no courgettes	no basil
...	

The conclusion "the chef did not use courgettes" can thus be made. The denial of the antecedent inference may be made in a similar manner, but again some reasoners may refrain from making the inference if they flesh their models out to be more explicit and appreciate the following possibilities:

courgettes	basil
no courgettes	no basil
no courgettes	basil

CONDITIONAL INFERENCES FROM OTHER CONNECTIVES

People make different inferences from conditionals containing *if* when they contain different contents or contexts (see, e.g., Evans et al., 1993). In fact, there may be many interpretations of conditionals, modulated by semantic and pragmatic factors (Johnson-Laird & Byrne, in press). For example, a conditional such as "if the butter was heated then it melted" may be interpreted by reasoners as consistent with two possibilities:

heated	melted
not heated	not melted

In this biconditional interpretation, the antecedent "the butter was heated" is sufficient and necessary for the consequent "the butter melted." The conditional "if the patient has malaria, then she has a fever" may be interpreted by reasoners as consistent with three possibilities:

malaria   fever
no malaria   no fever
no malaria   fever

and in this conditional interpretation, the antecedent is sufficient for the consequent but not necessary. However, a conditional such as "if oxygen is present, then there may be a fire" may be given an enabling or reversed conditional interpretation consistent with the following three possibilities:

oxygen   fire
oxygen   no fire
no oxygen   no fire

Here, the antecedent is necessary but not sufficient, and the conditional "If the workers settle for lower wages, then the company may still go bankrupt" may be given a disabling interpretation consistent with the following three possibilities:

lower wages   bankrupt
lower wages   not bankrupt
not lower wages   bankrupt

(For these and other examples, see Johnson-Laird & Byrne, 2002; see also Byrne, Espino, & Santamaria, 1999.) Different content and context lead to different interpretations of the meaning of conditionals, and the mental models that reasoners construct differ in the possibilities that they keep in mind.

A second major influence on the inferences that people make from conditionals is the type of linguistic expression used to describe the conditional relation. Different connectives can affect the inferences people make from conditionals. For example, people make different frequencies of inferences from *only-if* conditionals, such as "the chef used courgettes only if he used basil" compared to *if* (e.g., Evans, 1977), and from *unless* conditionals, such as "unless the chef used courgettes, he used basil" compared to *if* (e.g., García-Madruga, Carriedo, Moreno-Rios, & Schaeken, 2000). Different linguistic expressions may make different information explicitly available. Consider the subjunctive mood. People make different frequencies of inferences from conditionals phrased in the subjunctive mood, both counterfactual conditionals such as "if the chef had used courgettes, he would have used basil" (e.g., Byrne & Tasso, 1999; Thompson & Byrne, 2002), and semifactual conditionals, such as "even if the chef had used courgettes, he would have used basil" (e.g., Moreno-Rios, García-Madruga, & Byrne, 2002). These conditionals appear to make available in the initial set of models more information than just the affirmative case (the chef using courgettes and basil). The counterfactual conditional seems to make available in the initial set of models the presupposed factual situation (the chef didn't use courgettes, and he didn't use basil) and accordingly people make many more modus tollens and denial of the antecedent inferences from counterfactual than from factual conditionals (Byrne & Tasso, 1999). Likewise, the semifactual conditional seems to make available in the initial set of models the presupposed factual situation (the chef didn't use courgettes, but he did use basil) and accordingly people make fewer of the affirmation of the consequent and denial of the antecedent inferences from semifactual than from factual conditionals (Moreno-Rios et al., 2002). Different linguistic expressions lead to different interpretations of conditionals, and the mental models that reasoners construct differ in the possibilities that they keep in mind.

These two strands of evidence (the influence of content and context and of linguistic expression) lend some support to the suggestion I make in this chapter: In everyday reasoning, people use different conditional connectives to invite different conditional inferences. In daily life, people use many different conditional connectives, such as *whether, suppose, although, whenever* (e.g., Byrne & Johnson-Laird, 1992). The purpose may be to ensure that reasoners reach subtly different interpretations of a conditional relation, and hence make different inferences from it. I will sketch some recent experimental results that corroborate this suggestion.

THE REPRESENTATION OF *WHETHER, ALTHOUGH, SUPPOSING,* AND *WHENEVER*

It is possible that different connectives make different information available in their initial representation (e.g., Johnson-Laird & Byrne, 1991). Our interest in conditional connectives such as *whether* and *although* is that they appear to convey subtle nuances of meaning, and their initial representation may be more explicit than the initial representation of *if*.

The connective *whether* in "whether there are any cars or not, you must stop" can be used by itself, as in "whether there are any cars ..." or with an explicit negation, as in "whether there are any cars or not ...", or with a specified alternative, as in "whether there are any cars or the road is clear ...". *Whether* can express doubt or a choice between alternatives. My suggestion is that *whether* emphasizes the nonnecessity of the antecedent and may be represented in a rich initial set of models, such as the following:

cars	stop
no cars	stop

The connective *although* in "although there are no cars, you must stop" has a meaning similar to "notwithstanding the fact that..," "but nevertheless ...," or "even on the supposition that..." *Although* emphasizes the facts of the situation, there are no cars and you must stop:

Facts:	no cars	stop

But it also seems to cancel presuppositions, for example, the expectation that when there are no cars you do not need to stop or that it is only when there are cars that you need to stop:

      Cancelled presuppositions: no cars   no stop
                                  cars   stop

In contrast, other connectives seem to function similarly to *if*. The connective *supposing* as in "Supposing there were cars, you must stop," invites a listener to assume the antecedent is the case, and may be very similar to *if* in its meaning and representation:

      cars   stop
      ...

Likewise, the connective *whenever* as in "whenever there are cars you must stop" seems to have the meaning "every time that..," which again seems similar in meaning and representation to *if*, and to *supposing*.

My sketch of the possible representation of these connectives has consequences for the sorts of inferences that people will make readily from them. Given that *supposing* and *whenever* are conjectured to have a very similar representation to *if*, we expect that people will make the same frequency of inferences from these connectives as from *if*. In contrast, given that *whether* and *although* are conjectured to be represented in a more explicit set of initial models, people may make different frequencies of inferences from them than from *if*.

INFERENCES FROM WHETHER, ALTHOUGH, WHENEVER, AND SUPPOSING

I examined the inferences people make from these connectives in several experiments (see Byrne, 2002 for details). Participants in the experiments made the four sorts of inferences (modus ponens, modus tollens, denial of the antecedent and affirmation of the consequent), instantiated in people-in-places content (e.g., "if Laura was in Galway, then Linda was in Dublin") and ingredients content (e.g., "if the chef used lettuce, then she used ginger"). In one experiment, they made these inferences from each of three connectives, *if*, *whether*, and *supposing*. In another, they made them for one of three connectives, *if*, *although* and *whenever*. Their task in both experiments was to select a conclusion from a set of options:

      If the chef used courgettes, he used basil.
      The chef used courgettes.
      What, if anything, follows:
      (1) He used basil.
      (2) He did not use basil.
      (3) He may or may not have used basil.

In the first experiment the participants were 32 members of Trinity's participant panel who were paid for their participation. In the second experiment, 58 undergraduate volunteers participated (see Byrne, 2002, for details). The results showed that conditionals containing *whenever* and *supposing* elicit very similar inferences to *if*, whereas conditionals containing *whether* and *although* do not.

Table 3.1.
The Frequencies of Different Inferences From the Connectives *Whenever* and *Supposing* Compared to *If* in Two Experiments

		MP	*AC*	*MT*	*DA*
Experiment 1	If	89	62	63	52
	Supposing	80	60	39	34
Experiment 2	If	97	53	63	34
	Whenever	95	38	55	33

Note: MP = Modus ponens, AC = Affirmation of the consequent, MT = Modus tollens, DA = Denial of the antecedent.

Supposing and Whenever

Consider *supposing* first. Participants made the same frequency of inferences from *supposing* as from *if* for the affirmative modus ponens inference and affirmation of the consequent inference, as Table 3.1 shows. However, they made reliably fewer of the negative modus tollens inferences (39% and 63%) and denial of the antecedent inferences (34% and 52%) from *supposing* than from *if*. This result suggests that *supposing* focuses attention on the affirmative case represented in the initial set of models, even more than *if* does. Consider *whenever*' next. Participants made the same frequency of inferences from *whenever*' as from *if* for the affirmative modus ponens inference, and there were no reliable differences for the affirmation of the consequent inference either, as Table 3.1 shows. They also made the same frequency of inferences from *whenever*' as from *if* for the negative modus tollens inference and the denial of the antecedent inference.

Whether and Although

Whether elicits a very different pattern of inferences from *if*, in line with our expectations. Participants made the same frequency of inferences from *whether* as from *if* for the affirmative modus ponens inference only, as Table 3.2 shows. They made fewer of the affirmation of the consequent (31% and 62%) and denial of the antecedent inferences (18% and 52%) from *whether* than from *if*. This result corroborates our suggestion that they have access to the case in which the antecedent doesn't occur but the consequent occurs anyway. For example., "whether the chef used courgettes, he used basil" is represented as follows:

> courgettes   basil
> no courgettes   basil

For the denial of the antecedent inference, participants were told "the chef did not use courgettes," and they readily resisted the inference that "he did not use basil." In fact, 64% of their responses were "he used basil". This inference, from notA to *B* provides strong support for our suggestion that reasoners represent the possibility "the chef did not use courgettes and he used basil" as well as the possibility "the chef used courgettes and he used basil." For the affirmation of the consequent, participants were told "the chef used basil," and they readily resisted the inference that "he used courgettes." In fact, 61% of participants responded that "he may or may not have used basil," which provides support for our suggestion that they keep both possibilities in mind. Finally, participants made fewer of the modus tollens inferences from *whether* than from *if* (25% and 63%). This result may reflect the emphasis on the necessity of the consequent, that the chef did in fact use basil.

Last, consider *although. Although* elicits a very different pattern of inferences from *if*, as Table 3.2 shows. Participants made fewer modus ponens inferences from *although* than from *if* (68% and 97%). They made fewer modus tollens inferences (13% and 63%). They also made fewer denial of the antecedent inferences (13% and 34%) but not fewer affirmation of the consequent inferences (71% and 53%). I suggested that the representation of "although the chef used courgettes, he used basil" may be as follows:

> Facts: courgettes   basil
> Cancelled presuppositions: no courgettes   basil
>   courgettes   no basil

Table 3.2.
The Frequencies of Different Inferences From the Connectives *Whether* and *Although*
Compared to *If* in Two Experiments

		MP	*AC*	*MT*	*DA*
Experiment 1	If	89	62	63	52
	Whether	89	31	25	18

| *Experiment 2* | If | 97 | 53 | 63 | 34 |
| | Although | 68 | 71 | 13 | 13 |

Note: MP = Modus ponens, AC = Affirmation of the consequent, MT = Modus tollens, DA = Denial of the antecedent.

The most typical response to the denial of the antecedent information that "the chef did not use courgettes" was to conclude "therefore, he used basil" (45%) and also a frequent response to the modus tollens information that "he did not use basil" was that "he used courgettes" (34%). The high rate of the affirmation of the consequent inference is unexpected given this representation, and further research into the possibilities that people judge to be consistent with assertions containing *whether* and *although* may help clarify their interpretations.

CONCLUSIONS

Different conditional connectives may support different inferences. *Whenever* and *supposing* seem similar to *if*, and the initial set of models for *whenever* and *supposing* may be similar to the initial set of models for *if*. The initial set of models for *whether* and *although* are more explicit, I suggest. The representation of "whether *A*, *B*" may include both the possibility *A* and *B*, and the possibility not*A* and *B*, and hence reasoners make fewer denial of the antecedent and affirmation of the consequent inferences from *whether* than from *if*. The emphasis on *B* also leads them to make fewer modus tollens from *whether*. The representation of "although *A*, *B*" may make explicit not only the suggested facts *A* and *B*, but also the cancelled presuppositions, not*A* and *B*, and *A* and not*B*. Consistent with this suggestion, *although* led to fewer denial of the antecedent and modus tollens inferences. However, the high frequency of affirmation of the consequent inferences requires further exploration.

Overall, our suggestion is that reasoners may select different conditional connectives such as *whether* and *although* to assist their listeners in making certain inferences or resisting certain inferences. The subtle nuances of meaning of different conditional connectives may lead to different information being explicitly represented in the initial set of models, which in turn leads reasoners to make different inferences. The picture that emerges from studies of conditional reasoning based on *if* alone (people are poor at making certain conditional inferences) may be somewhat distorted. In everyday reasoning, people may be adept at relying on the information provided by a speaker, particularly the information available from the connective chosen to describe the conditional relation.

ACKNOWLEDGMENTS

I am grateful to Alice McEleney, Emma Riggs, Michelle Cowley, Rachel McCloy, Clare Walsh, and Regina Cooney for their help and Phil Johnson-Laird and Simon Handley for discussions on the meaning of different connectives. This research was funded by the Arts and Social Sciences Benefactions Fund and the Provost's Academic Development fund of Trinity College, University of Dublin.

REFERENCES

Byrne, R. M. J. (2002). *Conditional reasoning with "whether", "although", "whenever" and "supposing"*. Unpublished manuscript.

Byrne, R. M. J., Espino, O., & Santamaria, C. (1999). Counterexamples and the suppression of inferences. *Journal of Memory and Language, 40,* 347–373.

Byrne, R. M. J., & Johnson-Laird, P. N. (1992). On the spontaneous use of propositional connectives. *Quarterly Journal of Experimental Psychology, 45A,* 89–110.

Byrne, R. M. J., & Tasso, A. (1999). Deductions from factual, possible and counterfactual conditionals. *Memory and Cognition, 27,* 726–740.

Evans, J. St. B. T., Newstead, S., & Byrne, R. M. J. (1993). Human reasoning: The psychology of deduction. Hillsdale, NJ: Lawrence Erlbaum Associates.

García-Madruga, J. A., Carriedo, N., Moreno-Rios, S., & Schaeken, W. (2000). *Comparing conditional reasoning from different formulations: "If then," "if not then," "only if" and "unless."*. Unpublished manuscript.

Johnson-Laird, P. N., & Byrne, R. (1991). *Deduction.* Hillsdale, NJ: Lawrence Erlbaum Associates.

Johnson-Laird, P. N., & Byrne, R. (2002). Conditionals: A theory of meaning, pragmatics, and inference. *Psychological Review, 109,* 646–678.

Johnson-Laird, P. N., Byrne, R., & Schaeken, W. (1992). Propositional reasoning by model. *Psychological Review, 99,* 418–439.

Moreno-Rios, S., García-Madruga, J. A., & Byrne, R. M. J. (2002). *The effects of linguistic mood on if: semifactual and counterfactual conditionals.* Unpublished manuscript.

Thompson, V., & Byrne, R. M. J. (2002). Reasoning about things that didn't happen. *Journal of Experimental Psychology: Learning, Memory, and Cognition, 28,* 1154–1170.

4

Rethinking the Model Theory of Conditionals

Jonathan St. B. T. Evans
David E. Over
Simon J. Handley

In this chapter we discuss some fundamental problems for the mental model theory of conditional reasoning proposed by Johnson-Laird and Byrne (1991, 2002) with reference to the extensive philosophical and psychological literatures on conditionals. First, we show that the theory is fundamentally committed to the notion that people treat the ordinary conditional as a material implication, despite strong philosophical argument and psychological evidence to the contrary. Second, we question the proposal that mental models are no more than truth table cases and demonstrate the inadequacy of attempts to capture a wide range of syntactic and pragmatic factors in terms of the extension of truth table cases that people hold to be true (or consistent) — a mechanism that we term the four-bit semantic device. Finally, we examine closely the notion of fleshing-out and demonstrate that this process conceals inferential processes that occur before models can be derived. This means that people are reasoning to models, not by models, which undermines the semantic principle of deduction that distinguishes mental model theory from the rival rule-based systems. In conclusion, we propose that a fundamental rethink is required, which we suggest should focus on people reasoning about single mental models that are more richly defined than truth table cases.

INTRODUCTION

If the value of a theory is to be judged by the amount of research it stimulates, then the mental model theory of deduction (Johnson-Laird, 1983; Johnson-Laird & Byrne, 1991) must be considered very successful indeed. The theory has a general form as well as specific implementations in application to work in particular paradigms, especially syllogistic reasoning, relational reasoning, and proposition reasoning. The basic idea is that ordinary people do not reason by constructing mental proofs in the manner that a tradition in mental logic would have us believe (Braine & O'Brien, 1998; Rips, 1994). Rather, they consider mental models of the premises of arguments that reflect possible states of the world. Deductions are drawn according to the following fundamental semantic principle: If no models can be discovered in which the premises are true and the conclusion is false, then the argument is valid.

Suppose we are told that Jane is taller than Mary and that Jane is taller than Sally. This information is compatible with two mental models (each model depicted in a different column):

Jane	Jane
Mary	Sally
Sally	Mary

If offered the conclusion "Jane is tallest" people considering these models could safely respond that this is a valid conclusion: It must be true given the information presented. However, they should reject the conclusion "Sally is shortest". There is a state of affairs consistent with the premises in which this conclusion does not hold, so it cannot be a necessary or valid conclusion.

If instructed to draw a valid conclusion from some premises, the theory as presented by Johnson-Laird (1983; Johnson-Laird & Byrne, 1991) proposes that people go through three stages:

1. *Model formation*: A mental model is constructed, which is compatible with the premises.
2. *Conclusion formation*: A conclusion is formed, which is true in this model and semantically informative (e.g., not a repetition of a premise).
3. *Conclusion validation*: A search takes place for counterexamples (i.e. models in which the premises hold and the conclusion does not). If no such counterexample is found, then the conclusion is stated as valid.

This original version of the theory was implemented in detail as a theory of reasoning with classical syllogisms by Johnson-Laird and Bara (1984). They showed, for example, that participants made more errors with syllogisms whose conclusions could be represented by several alternative mental models than by those with a single model. The theory was supplemented in this application by psychological proposals about the mental processing involved. For example, the difficulty of processing multiple models was predicted due to limitations in working memory capacity.

Despite the popularity of this theory, more recent work led researchers to doubt whether people actually validate their conclusions by searching for counterexamples, although direct attempts to measure this have produced conflicting results (Bucciarelli & Johnson-Laird, 1999; Newstead, Handley, & Buck, 1999). In one of the most extensive and complete studies of the syllogistic evaluation task, Evans, Handley, Harper, and Johnson-Laird (1999) found strong evidence that people generally think about only one model of the premises when engaged in syllogistic reasoning. In this study, participants were presented with every possible premise pair together with every possible conclusion and asked to evaluate whether the conclusion followed from the premises. This method led to discovery of a new finding.

A fallacy is an argument whose conclusion could be false given the premises. For example, it would be fallacious to conclude that Sally is shortest, given the information that Jane is taller than both Mary and Sally. What Evans, Handley, et al. (1999) found was that some syllogistic fallacies are consistently endorsed as frequently as valid arguments whereas others are endorsed as infrequently as determinately false arguments (ones whose conclusions must be false if the premises are true). This result clearly suggests that people consider only one model of the premises. With fallacies, if the model that first comes to mind supports the conclusion, then it is endorsed as valid. If the first model considered refutes the conclusion, then the argument is rejected as invalid.

Handley and Evans (2000) recently reported a study of suppositional reasoning in which people were asked to draw conclusions from premises such as the following:

If there is a *p*, then there is a *q*.
Either there is a *p*, or there is a *q*, but not both.

Conclusions can be drawn logically, by the principle of *reductio ad absurdum* (RAA). According to this principle, if a premise is supposed and then a contradiction inferred, the negation of the supposition is a valid conclusion. In the previous case, if we suppose *p* is the case, then we deduce that *q* must be the case by the first premise but that *q* cannot be the case from the second. Hence, logically we can infer not*p*. (Intuitively, we can infer that *p* is not the case because, if it were, we would have a contradiction.. It follows further (from Premise 2) that *q* must be the case.

This kind of indirect suppositional reasoning is supposed to be a basic component of human reasoning ability, according to theorists in the mental logic tradition (Braine & O'Brien, 1998; Rips, 1994). However, error rates were extremely high on problems of the previous kind in this study. Moreover, many participants concluded that *p* and *q* must be the case, a conclusion that is actually impossible given the premises. Handley and Evans(2000) argue that participants imagine some state of affairs suggested by the premises and fail to carry out the logical checks that would refute it (both the finding and the explanation have similarities with Johnson-Laird & Savary, 1999, reports of illusory inferences in propositional reasoning). Handley and Evans presented other experiments that gave strong support to their interpretation.

Both the findings of Evans, Handley, et al. (1999) and Handley and Evans (2000) are compatible with our general theory of hypothetical thinking (Evans, Over, & Handley, 2003). This is a general framework for reasoning and decision making that in common with the mental model theory is based on the idea that people reason by considering possible states of the world. However, it differs from the Johnson-Laird and Byrne (1991) framework in some important respects. First, the mental models which people construct to represent states of affairs are considered to be pragmatically rich. They may for example include representation of their own plausibility and utility for the individual's goals and are related to a relevance principle. Second, the theory is based on the idea that people consider only one model at a time (the singularity principle) and accept it after explicit evaluation if it is good enough (satisficing principle). That is, they accept a model until or unless good evidence is encountered that causes them to give it up. Reasoning is therefore by default both probabilistic and defeasible. Hence, for example, in deductive reasoning tasks, plausible fallacies will normally be accepted without a search for counterexamples, as the data indicate. Erroneous acceptance of an initial model due to shallow reasoning underlies the errors demonstrated by Handley and Evans (2000) and by Johnson-Laird and Savary (1999).

To this point, we have presented our theoretical proposals as broadly sympathetic with the mental models approach while extended and modifying it in significant ways. However, our view of the model theory of conditional reasoning, which is the focus of the remainder of this chapter, is much more critical. A number of significant problems were identified in an earlier critique by Evans (1993) and have not been satisfactorily resolved in our view. Moreover, the development of our theory of hypothetical thinking, together with our own recent research on conditionals, has led us to a fresh and close scrutiny of this particular implementation of model theory. We formed the view that the model theory of conditionals proposed by Johnson-Laird and Byrne (1991; see also Johnson-Laird, Byrne, & Schaeken, 1992) needs fundamental rethinking. We start with a brief summary of the theory and its recent revision and extension by Johnson-Laird and Byrne (2002).

THE MODEL THEORY OF CONDITIONALS

The Johnson-Laird and Byrne (hereafter JLB) theory of propositional reasoning, of which conditional reasoning is a central focus, deviates quite substantially from the general model theory of reasoning discussed previously. First, instead of limiting initial representations to a single mental model, it is proposed that reasoners may sometimes hold two or more models simultaneous to represent a proposition (an idea clearly inconsistent with our own proposals about hypothetical thinking). Second, the theory does not include the notion of a search for counterexamples as such. Rather, it refers to a process of fleshing-out possibilities (models) that were left implicit in people's representations. In addition, the models in the propositional theory are not concrete representations that could correspond to a mental image or some other plausible representation of possible states of affairs (see also Barrouillet, Grosset, & Lecas, 2000). Instead, they contain markers for negation and exhaustivity that make them logical entities. They are, in fact, little more than truth table cases. We show in this chapter why constructing the propositional version of the theory in this way undermines the mental models framework from which it was derived and leads to difficulties that cannot be easily resolved without a complete rethink.

In the JLB theory, a distinction is drawn between initial representations, which are incomplete but may contain more than one mental model, and fully explicit representations, which may (or may not) be fleshed-out. Although Johnson-Laird and Byrne (2002) now talk about propositions allowing possibilities, rather than defining cases as true, we believe this makes no substantive difference to what they term basic conditionals. In a two-value logic (they explicitly reject a three-value system with indeterminate cases allowed) that which is not false is true (as well as possible). Unlike Johnson-Laird and Byrne (1991), Johnson-Laird and Byrne (2002) identify a core meaning for conditionals and distinguish between basic and nonbasic conditionals. Basic conditionals are defined as ones that do not call on background knowledge for their evaluation. Such a basic conditional, with its core meaning, is truth functional. That is to say the statement "if p then p" taken as the basic conditional has the three mental models:

$$
\begin{array}{ll}
p & q \\
\neg p & q \\
\neg p & \neg q
\end{array}
$$

This makes the basic conditional the material conditional of standard two-valued proposition logic. It is equivalent in meaning to "not p or q", which has exactly the same mental models. Moreover, it is clear from the experiments and examples that this basic, material conditional is assumed to represent the conditional of abstract reasoning experiments. But JLB now accept that more realistic and everyday conditionals, to which background knowledge is relevant, are subject to mechanisms that they describe as semantic and pragmatic modulation. As a result, these nonbasic conditionals are nontruth functional.

Basic conditionals are truth functional, but there is more to the JLB theory of them than their truth functionality. First, there is a principle of truth, which "implies that mental models represent only what is true and not what is false" (Johnson-Laird & Byrne, 2002, p. 653). Second, modeling is supposed to be incomplete, so that the full set of models for the basic conditional is not initially represented.

In JLB theory, people typically represent the conditional initially with only one explicit model:

$$
\begin{array}{ll}
p & q \\
\dots &
\end{array}
$$

The three dots indicate that there are other models possible, but they have not been fleshed-out at this point. These dots are required to distinguish this representation as that of a conditional rather than a conjunction. The latter would be represented as just the model p and q. When negatives appear in the rule, then negativity markers are also required in this system. For example, the statement "if p then not q" might (of which, later) be represented as follows:

$$p \qquad \neg q$$
$$\ldots$$

As indicated previously, models so notated are logical entities, not concrete mental models in the normal sense. The theory also proposes that people may or may not flesh-out such initial representations into a fully explicit set of models (those for the basic conditional, shown previously).

Any theory of conditional reasoning must explain a basic finding in the literature (see Evans, Newstead, & Byrne, 1993). There are two valid inferences that may logically be deduced from conditionals called modus ponens (MP) and modus tollens (MT). Given p, q must be true (MP) and given not q, not p must be true (MT). Under standard conditions of presentation, people endorse MP nearly 100% of the time but endorse MT only about 75% of the time. The model theory explains these trends as follows: MP may be read directly from the initial representation, because p is exhausted with respect to q. MT, however, may only be made by those who recover the full core meaning of the conditional by fleshing out the fully explicit model set:

(1) p q, (2) $\neg p$ q, (3) $\neg p$ $\neg q$.

The minor premise— not-q— eliminates models (1) and (2) so that only (3) remains. Hence, the conclusion not p can be derived. Unlike MP, MT will not be made universally because some participants will fail to flesh-out the explicit models. However, it should be noted that this attempt by JLB to explain the difference between MP and MT applies only to basic conditionals. They have no explanation of why MP and MT should differ for nonbasic conditionals.

The rival mental logic theories also have an account of MP and MT that is supposedly distinct from the mental model explanation. These systems (e.g., Braine & O'Brien, 1991) propose that MP is a direct rule of inference that people hold in their mental logic. Hence, the MP inference can be made directly, accounting for its universal endorsement. However, MT requires indirect, suppositional reasoning that is error-prone. This is done by reductio reasoning, referred to earlier. We argue that if there were a p then there would be a q. However, because there is not a q there cannot be a p.

Johnson-Laird and Byrne (2002) develop an interesting principle of pragmatic modulation. The idea is that the core meaning of conditionals may be modified in a given context due to the presence of real-world beliefs and knowledge. This may lead us, for example, to eliminate a logical possibility or to facilitate the fleshing-out process. Such conditionals are clearly not basic and not truthfunctional. We return to this idea in the following section.

THE PROBLEM OF THE MATERIAL CONDITIONAL

As stated earlier, the basic conditional in JLB is the material conditional, which is a truth- functional proposition logically equivalent to "not p or q". The theory hinges upon this, as their explanation of the MT inference shows. People must flesh-out not p and not q as the only true possibility in order to make the inference. Hence, JLB cannot explain why people judge cases in which not p holds to be irrelevant to the evaluation of even basic conditionals, despite much psychological evidence (of which more later) that people do make this judgment. This is a major problem for JLB and in our view a fatal flaw in its own right. Most ordinary indicative conditionals, whether basic in some intuitive sense or not, cannot be material conditionals. Our view on this is supported by the vast weight of opinion among contemporary philosophical logicians who given this matter extensive thought and analysis (see Edgington, 1995 for a review). The problem can be illustrated quite simply. Consider the following two conditional statements:

> (1) If we go to London today, then we will be in France.
> (2) If we go to Paris today, then we will be in France.

Any ordinary person will say at once that the first statement is false and the second is true. However, if we utter these statements today in Brussels, and the conditionals are material, then they are both true. Statement (1) is equivalent to "Either we will not go to London today or we will be in France". Because e will stay in Brussels today, this statement must be true. As Edgington (1995) puts it, anyone who is unable to distinguish true from false conditionals when the antecedent does not hold would be intellectually disabled. Johnson-Laird and Byrne (2002) would not classify statements (1) and (2) as basic conditionals in their sense; all they can say about these examples is that background knowledge will cause us to reject (1) and accept (2). This observation, though true, cannot be called a mental model theory of these conditionals.

The most common way to account for conditionals of this kind in philosophical logic is to use a possible worlds analysis (Edgington, 1995). The Stalnaker conditional (Stalnaker, 1968) is the best example of the result of this kind of semantics. In this semantics, (1) is true if its consequent is true in the nearest possible world in which its antecedent is true; otherwise (1) is false. We prefer to express this by saying that (1) is true if its consequent is true in the most relevant possibility in which its antecedent is true, and otherwise it is false. In either case, we can easily see, on this basis, that (1) is false. Even though we will stay in Brussels today, we can easily imagine a world in which we go to London. There would be no reason to change that world so that London moves across the English channel, so the conditional is clearly false. By similar reasoning, (2) is clearly true. However, there are problems with the Stalnaker semantics that we cannot go into here, so we prefer to base our own thinking on the Ramsey test (see Evans, Handley, & Over, 2002, and Over & Evans, 2003, for detailed discussion of this point.) The Ramsey Test, although proposed and mainly discussed by philosophers (Ramsey, 1931; Stalnaker, 1968), is essentially psychological in nature. We assess the truth of a conditional by a process of hypothetical thinking in which we imagine that p is true. The Ramsey Test implies that the believability of a conditional "if p then q" is related to the conditional probability $P(q/p)$. It follows that (1) is acceptable and (2) is not because it is extremely improbable that we will be in France given that we go to London today, but it is extremely probable that we will be in France given that we go to Paris today. There are technical reasons why the probability of a conditional, treated as a proposition with determinate truth value, cannot be simply identified with the corresponding conditional probability (Edgington, 1995; Lewis, 1976). We cannot go into this technical matter here, but recent experimental evidence shows clearly that most people will assign the conditional probability $P(q/p)$ when asked to judge the probability of a conditionals (Evans et al., in press; Over & Evans, 2003; Oberauer & Wilhelm, 2003). These experiments also provide strong evidence that people do not treat even quite abstract conditionals as material conditionals (see also Over, in press, on problems with the JLB account of the probability of an ordinary conditional).

The principle of pragmatic modulation, introduced by Johnson-Laird and Byrne (2002), modifies the basic conditional in such a way that it is no longer truth-functional. That is to say, its truth depends on wider knowledge of the world. Could the ordinary conditional of everyday language be the basic conditional with pragmatic modulation? The answer is no. Consider the following example given by Edgington (1995):

If the Queen is at home, then she is thinking about me.

Uttered by a normal individual (of whom the queen has never heard), this conditional is clearly false. According to Johnson-Laird and Byrne (2002), the core meaning of this conditional allows the following three possibilities:

(a) Queen is at home, thinking about us.
(b) Queen is away, thinking about us.
(c) Queen is away, not thinking about us.

Now a paradoxical effect of this material reading of the conditional is that on learning that the queen is in Australia, one must consider that the statement is true and this is not avoided by pragmatic modulation. According to this theory, the news that the queen is in Australia eliminates model (a), but leaves the last two. However, pragmatic modulation enables us also to eliminate model (b). Our real-world knowledge tells us that the queen has never heard of us and thus cannot be thinking about us. However, we are still left with model (c) as a true possibility, so the statement cannot be rejected as false, despite the compelling intuition that it is. The Ramsey test, of course, accords with intuition. Once we imagine the queen at home and bring our real-world knowledge to bear, we can easily decide that whatever else she may be doing, it is most improbable that she is not thinking about us.

THE DEFECTIVE TRUTH TABLE

The problem of the material conditional arises in a two-valued propositional logic, which assigns the value true to three of the cases: TT, FT, FF and false to just the case TF (true antecedent and false consequent). As noted earlier, this makes "if *p* then *q*" equivalent to "not *p* or *q*". Because of the difficulties of treating the ordinary conditional as material, some philosophers have suggested that the truth table for the conditional is defective. According to this hypothesis, the false antecedent cases should be assigned a third truth value: I (indeterminate). This third value can be interpreted in one of two ways. It could mean that such cases are intrinsically indeterminate; that is, one will never be able to tell if a conditional is true or false if the antecedent does not hold. Our preferred interpretation under the Ramsey test is that people are telling us that the false antecedent states are irrelevant because only by reference to a hypothetical world in which the antecedent holds can the truth of the conditional be determined (see Evans et al., 2002).

Either way, there is strong psychological evidence that ordinary people do in fact regard FT and FF in at least abstract cases as irrelevant. This has been shown by a set of published studies using truth table tasks (reviewed by Evans et al., 1993, chap. 2). The most recently published study using this task is that of Evans, Legrenzi, and Girotto (1999). In the evaluation truth table task, people are given a conditional such as "if there is a *D* on the left, then there is a 6 on the right" and asked to evaluate the following examples as true, false or irrelevant:

D 6 (TT)
D 6 (FT)
H 4 (FF)

The findings are somewhat complicated by the presence of a matching bias (Evans, 1998) due to the use of implicit negations in the cases. However, the underlying pattern of evaluation is that of the defective truth table: TT as T, TF as F, FT and FF as I. In the construction version of the task (Evans, 1972; Oaksford & Stenning, 1992), people are asked to give all possible verifying and all possible falsifying cases. This produces exactly the same results. People omit to construct, as either true or false, exactly the same cases that they describe as irrelevant in the evaluation task (Evans, 1975).

Research on the truth table task presents two problems for the model. First, if the conditional is material, then participants should be treating the FT and FF cases as making the true, rather than the irrelevant. Second, we need some model theory account of how these evaluations are actually produced. Both points are addressed briefly by Johnson-Laird and Byrne (2002). First, they argue against the defective truth table. They do this in the case of the biconditional "if and only if *p* then *q*" that they rightly say must be treated as the conjunction of two conditionals:

"if p then q, and if q then p."

The argument they give is that the (material) biconditional is true in two cases: TT and FF, which cannot be derived by conjoining two defective truth tables for material conditionals. This assumes a material biconditional truth table: TT (T), TF (F), FT (F), FF (T), or TFFT for short. However, they overlook a truth table for the defective biconditional: TFFI. This pattern occurs commonly in truth table experiments and is the conjunction of two defective truth tables, as Table 4.1 shows.

Table 4.1.
Patterns than Occur Commonly in Truth Table Experiments

Case	If p then q	If q then p	Iff p then q
TT	T	T	T
TF	F	I	F
FT	I	F	F
FF	I	I	I

This analysis assumes that a case will be treated as false if either rule has a case for false. So, in our example "if there is a D on the left, then there is a 6 the right" is a conjunction of (1) "if D, then 6" and (2) "if 6, then D." In either case, $D6$ is true, $D3$ is false by rule (1) and $X6$ is false by rule (2). $H4$ (FF) is indeterminate by either rule, so it remains indeterminate. Data on truth table tasks are compatible with a mixture of defective conditional and defective biconditional patterns.

Whether or not there is really a defective truth table, people still behave as if there were on the truth table task, a behavior that the model theory must explain. Johnson-Laird and Byrne (2002) appeal to the distinction between initial and fully explicit representations and propose that people describe as irrelevant cases that are not initially represented. This argument has two serious problems, however: The TF case is also not explicitly represented in the initial models, but this is evaluated as false and not as irrelevant, and if the FF case is considered irrelevant, how is it that reasoners often succeed in fleshing it out as a true case to support the MT inference?

Johnson-Laird and Savary (1999) emphasized the principle of truth in offering their mental models account of illusory inferences. That is, people strongly tend to represent only true possibilities. This makes one wonder why people so easily identify TF as the falsifying case on the truth table task. In our own theory (Evans et al., 2001), we propose instead a principle of relevance in the construction of mental models. By default, this leads us to construct the most plausible, probable, or believable cases, but this default is easily changed according to the goals of the reasoner (e.g., an instruction to find false cases). The answer to the first problem identified previously surely has to be that people construct the TF falsifying case from the initial representation:

p q

...

Because p is exhausted with respect to q, p cannot occur in the absence of q. Understanding that TF falsifies the rule is equivalent to understanding what this exhaustivity marker means. Note, however, that this involves reasoning about a model, not reasoning by model. It does not accord with the fundamental semantic principle that distinguishes model theory from rule-based reasoning (the idea that conclusions are inferred when they are allowed by models of the premises). We return to this point a little later. For the moment, we conclude that we are not at all satisfied by the account given by Johnson-Laird and Byrne (2002) of the defective truth table and the experimental findings using the truth table task.

Evans, Ellis, and Newstead (1996) reported some research on a novel task related to but distinct from the truth table task. In their first experiment, people were asked to evaluate conditionals as true or false with regard to distribution of the cases in which examples of TT, TF, FT, and FF cases were given multiple representations. In subsequent experiments, they were asked to fill in a grid with examples of the four cases to produce their own distributions. A couple of their findings are particularly relevant to the current arguments:

1. In roughly equal frequency, people constructed a number of FT and FF cases, both when representing situations where the conditional was true and also where it was false. This is entirely consistent with the defective truth table. Including such irrelevant cases may be a way of indicating the conditionality of the connective (it only sometimes applies).
2. Distributions for true conditionals included some TF cases but a high ratio of TT to TF. Distributions for false cases had a high ratio of TF to FF. This suggests that people were representing two ends of a continuum with the probability of q given p being equated with the truth value of the conditional. Logically, you only need one TF case to make the rule false and cannot have any in the true condition.

Note that these findings are consistent with other evidence, cited earlier, that people treat the conditional as though its probability were the conditional probability of q given p. We comment further on this study later in the chapter.

MULTIPLE MENTAL MODELS AND THE FOUR BIT SEMANTIC DEVICE

We already noted that in the JLB account of conditional reasoning (and more generally propositional reasoning) models are essentially truth table cases representing logical possibilities. Moreover, a great deal of explanatory work is required of the notion that a mental representation consists of a set of such models that are held to be possible. Leaving aside the representation of counterfactual conditionals, which we discuss in a later section, there are just four such cases in which a connective, such as a conditional, can hold or not hold, making just $2^4 = 16$ possible truth functional connectives. Hence, we refer to this idea as the four-bit semantic device.

The device is manifest in both initial and fully explicit representations. The core theory of conditionals presented by Johnson-Laird and Byrne (2002) employs the device with regard to full representations and uses the majority of the 16 possibilities to try to account for a variety of conditionals.

The four-bit device, as applied to initial representations, has been in use for some time to account for a wide range of effects. It has been used to distinguish if-then from only-if conditionals, to account for matching bias effects with negated conditionals, and to explain a range of pragmatic factors influencing representation of conditionals. A priori it seems to us that a four-bit device simply cannot do so much work. However, we consider a couple of these cases in detail here. The conditional "p only if q" has the same truth table as "if p then q" in truth functional logic. Both conditionals are false only when we have p without q. However, it is known that there are differences in the pattern of reasoning shown in psychological experiments with these two forms. For example, there are more MP inferences on if-then conditionals and more MT inferences on only-if conditionals (see Evans et al., 1993, p. 46). Johnson-Laird and Byrne (1991) tried to account for this difference by proposing that "p only if q" has an initial representation that makes explicit two models as follows:

$$
\begin{array}{ll}
p & q \\
\neg p & \neg q \\
\ldots &
\end{array}
$$

Evans (1993) criticized this proposal on the grounds that there were other differences between the two forms of conditionals in the experimental literature that this difference in representation could not explain. However, our more fundamental objection is that people are proposed to consider two models at once, in contradiction of the singularity principle of the hypothetical reasoning model (Evans et al., 2001). In fact, Johnson-Laird and Byrne's (1991) hypothesis can be rejected on the basis of three main experimental findings. First, research on truth table tasks employed only-if as well as if-then conditionals (e.g., Evans & Newstead, 1977). The findings fail to confirm the obvious prediction that the FF case will be rated as true (rather than as irrelevant) on only-if conditionals or even that this will occur with greater frequency than on if-then conditionals

Second, the truth functional account of only-if was explicitly examined by Evans et al. (1996) with their novel task. In Experiment 2, people constructed distributions for only-if as well as if-then conditionals. Participants actually included slightly fewer FF cases when modeling only-if than true if-then conditionals as true, and substantially more when modelling false conditionals, contrary to the predictions of the JLB hypothesis. Finally, (Evans, Legrenzi, & Girotto, 1999, Experiment 3) tested the hypothesis by comparing if-then and only-if conditionals on the Wason selection task. The model theory of the selection task proposes that people choose cards explicitly modeled provided an inferential justification can be found for them (Johnson-Laird, 1995). Because all four cards are available in the initial models of the only-if statement, the correct cards should be identified by reasoning. In particular, the not q card— notoriously omitted in most standard selection tasks experiments— should be found. In fact, people made somewhat fewer correct choices on only-if rules contrary to predictions. Evans et al. also tested an alternative hypothesis put forward by Evans (1993), which was that there is a directionality difference between the representation of the two rules (which cannot be captured by the four-bit device). This led to the prediction that people would choose relatively more antecedent than consequent cards on if-then rules, as indexed by adding p and not-p selection and subtracting q and not q selections. This prediction was significantly supported in their experiment.

Hence, research on only-if conditionals clearly shows that there are differences between them and if-then conditionals that cannot be captured by the four-bit device. The answer again lies in enriching the nature of the mental models so that they are more than just truth table cases. As Evans (1993) suggested, the preferred direction of reasoning that distinguishes if-then from only-if conditionals must reflect the nature of the mental models used to represent them. Moreover, there is no reason to violate the singularity principle and propose that people consider multiple mental models when representing only-if conditionals.

CONDITIONALS IN CONTEXT

Pragmatic effects in conditional reasoning are many and varied, and we seriously doubt that the four-bit semantic device will be able to cope with them all. For example, valid—as well as fallacious—conditional inferences may be suppressed when real-world knowledge comes into play (see Evans et al., 1993, pp. 55–61, for a review of relevant studies). Consider the following from (Byrne, 1989):

> If she meets her friend, she will go the play.
> (If she has enough money, she will go to the play).
> She meets her friend.
> Therefore, what follows?

If the second conditional is omitted, most people make the MP inference and draw the conclusion that she goes to the play. Considerable suppression of this inference is observed, however, if the second (logically irrelevant) inference is included. The mental models account has to be that pragmatic modulation causes people to represent the TF case (she meets her friend and does not go to the play) as a possibility, thus suppressing the MP inference. An alternative account is that the believability of the conditional premises is reduced and that people are reluctant to draw conclusions from false or uncertain premises (Politzer & Bourmaud, 2002; Politzer & Braine, 1991; Stevenson & Over, 1995). Because mental models do not include representation of their own plausibility in the present model theory, the account has to be that some participants represent the TF case and some do not, causing a drop of MP from 100% to around 35% in Byrne's (1989) study. However, research with alternative methodologies is problematic for the model theory. When participants are allowed to indicate the likelihood that the conclusion follows, then they lower this estimate belief because the major premise is undermined (Stevenson & Over, 1995; and see Stevenson & Over, 2001, on undermining the minor premise). Hence, people must represent degrees of belief, or probabilities, not simply unweighted logical possibilities (for related evidence and argument, see George, 1995, 1997; Liu, Lo, & Wu, 1996; Oaksford, Chater, & Larkin, 2000;

Over, in press). This is not achieved by the mechanisms of pragmatic modulation as defined by Johnson-Laird and Byrne (2002).

Conditionals can be classified into different types according to their use, such as contingent and causal conditionals, threats, promises, tips, and warnings, with subtle differences in inference rates being observed (Newstead, Ellis, Evans, & Dennis, 1997). One finding of Newstead et al. was that people tended to draw more inferences of all kinds, both valid and invalid, when conditionals were presented as threats and promises compared with those presented as warnings and tips. Evans and Twyman-Musgrove (1998) later showed that this was due to perceived control of the speaker over the consequent event being higher in the former cases. This is hard finding for model theory to explain. Typically people treat say promises as biconditionals, making all the following inferences with high frequencies:

Sam was told by his father, "if you pass your exams, I will buy you a bike."

Sam passed his exams; therefore, his father bought him a bike (MP).
Sam failed his exams; therefore, his father did not buy him a bike (DA).
Sam's father bought him a bike; therefore, he passed his exams (AC).
Sam's father did not buy him a bike; therefore, he did not pass the exams (MT).

This biconditionality is not surprising: Why make a promise conditional if you intend to deliver it anyway? Nor in itself is this a problem for mental model theory. Pragmatic modulation removes the FT case (Sam does not pass the exam; his father buys him a bike) from the core list of possibilities. What is a problem for the model theory is what happens when we turn this into a tip by substituting the first sentence: Sam's friend says to him, "if you pass your exams, your father will buy you a bike."

In the tip form, substantially fewer inferences of all four kinds will be drawn (but still well above zero). How can the four-bit device (plus pragmatic modulation) explain this? Only it would seem by representing the tip because a tautology in which all four truth table cases are possible. However, this will not do. A tautology by definition conveys no information and should thus never be uttered as it violates the communicative principle of relevance (Sperber & Wilson, 1995). In any case, a tip does convey information. It indicates a raised probability of q given p, but not as high a conditional probability as applies on a promise where the speaker has control of q. Without some means of representing probability, plausibility, or degrees of belief in the mental models themselves, we are simply not going to be able to explain effects of this kind.

COUNTERFACTUAL CONDITIONALS

All the conditionals we discusse have been indicative conditionals, but there are also counterfactuals:

(3 If Peter were a smoker, then his health would get better.
(4)   If Peter were a smoker, then his health would get worse.

Suppose we know that Peter is not a smoker. It would obviously be absurd to conclude on that basis alone that (3) and (4) are true, and thus (3) and (4) cannot be material conditionals. This is so clear that not even JLB treat these as material conditionals. According to JLB, people model (3) in the following way:

Fact:	Peter is not a smoker. Peter's health is not getting better.
Counterfactual possibility:	Peter is a smoker. Peter's health getting better.

In other words, people would understand (3) to be the statement that, although Peter is in fact not a smoker and his health is not getting any better, there is a counterfactual possibility in which he does smoke and his health is getting better. However, this analysis is too weak, because it does not explain why people with knowledge of the harmful effects of smoking would reject (3). Counterfactual possibilities exist as long as they are not logically inconsistent. The significant question is which counterfactual possibility (in which the antecedent holds) is the most relevant, as we would put it, for making a judgment about the counterfactual.

Suppose that (4) is asserted after (3). Then the JLB model theory implies this analysis:

Fact:	Peter is not a smoker. Peter's health not getting worse.
One counterfactual possibility:	Peter is a smoker. Peter's health is getting better.
Another counterfactual possibility:	Peter a smoker Peter's health getting worse

We are assuming that it is a fact that Peter is not a smoker and that his health is neither getting better nor worse. Given that, there is certainly one counterfactual possibility in which he is a smoker and his health gets better, and another counterfactual possibility in which he is a smoker and his health gets worse. Hence, if the JLB analysis is correct, (3) and (4) are compatible propositions. But it is clear that (3) and (4) cannot both be acceptable, and no sensible ordinary person would assert or believe both. In short, the present model theory of counterfactuals cannot show why obviously incompatible counterfactuals are incompatible (see also Over, in press).

Counterfactuals (3) and (4) present no problems for the Ramsey test. The closest, or, as we would prefer to say, the most relevant, possibility in which Peter is a smoker is one in which his heath gets worse and not better. Our default knowledge about health and lifestyle will apply unless we have other special information, such as Peter has some genetic protection from the harmful effects of smoking. The first counterfactual possibility is inconsistent with what we know about smoking and health. Ordinary people would not consider that first counterfactual possibility to be the most relevant possibility for assessing the acceptability of either (3) or (4). The most relevant counterfactual possibility for both (3) and (4) is the second one, in which Peter is a smoker and his health gets worse, with the result that (3) is false and (4) is true. Without any place for greater or less relevance of counterfactual possibilities, the present model theory of counterfactuals is currently inadequate in our view.

REASONING BY, FROM, AND ABOUT MODELS

In our discussion of the truth table task earlier, it was pointed out that if the falsifying case TF is constructed by reasoning about the initial representation of the TT case, then this implies a method of reasoning not captured by the fundamental semantic principle. As a reminder this principle is the following: If no models can be discovered in which the premises are true and the conclusion is false, then the argument is valid. What distinguishes deduction in the model theory from that of rule theories is this idea that inferences are drawn by identifying possibilities allowed by the models of the premises. We return to this issue now in consideration of the models account of MT reasoning.

Our rejection of the material conditional, as an analysis of the ordinary conditional in natural language, implies that we cannot accept the standard JLB account of the MT inference, which requires people to flesh-out the FF case as a true possibility. We know also that this case is typically rejected as irrelevant in truth table tasks. However, we note that Johnson-Laird himself has introduced a different idea about the MT inference, which may be drawn in giving an account of the double negation effect (Evans & Clibbens, 1995; Evans & Handley, 1999). Johnson-Laird's account was cited as a personal communication by Evans and Handley (1999) but has now been confirmed by Johnson-Laird and Byrne (2002). Consider the following arguments:

(5) If there is a C on the left, then there is a 7 on the right.
There is not a 7 on the right.
Therefore, there is not a C on the left.

(6) If there is not a C on the left, then there is a 7 on the right.
There is not a 7 on the right.
Therefore, there is C on the left.

In the psychological literature, these are both referred to as MT inferences, although this is not strictly correct. The second problem leads by MT to the conclusion "there is not not a C on the left", and by a further step of double negation elimination to the conclusion "there is a C on the left." The conclusion is, however, valid in both cases. Ordinary participants, however, endorse the conclusion for problem (6) much less frequently. This result could be explained by the mental logic theory as due to the extra step of double negation elimination (although the current systems included double negation as a direct rule of reasoning, which should be much easier to process than it apparently is). However, how can the model theory explain the effect?

The account of Johnson-Laird and Byrne (2002), in our view, introduces a significant change to the theory of MT. He says that the FF case is fleshed-out by reasoning about the initial representation. For problems (5) and (6) these representations are as follows:

(7) C 7   (8) $\neg C$ 7
    ...   ...

Now when the premise "not 7" is introduced in problem (5), people reason that since C is exhausted with respect to 7, any model in which 7 is not present will exclude C. Hence, they flesh-out the model $\neg C$ $\neg 7$. In problem (6) the same reasoning hits the double negation problem. Since $\neg C$ is exhausted, any model without a 7 must exclude $\neg C$. This does not immediately make it apparent that such models must include C.

Our point is not to dispute this explanation, which we believe is substantially correct. However, we believe this account both undermines the fundamental semantic principle and obviates the need to propose that conditionals are material. On the first point, this account shows that the fleshing-out process is the reasoning process. By the time the FF model has been derived the conclusion is drawn and the problem solved. This is not reasoning by model at all; it is reasoning about one model and to another. The second point is that a suppositional account of MT does not require the unsatisfactory proposal of a material conditional that the standard JLB theory entails. MT can be derived in this way for conditionals with a defective truth table. Suppose we have a conditional that applies only in worlds where the antecedent is true. The statement "if there is a B, then there is a 7" now means that a 7 is always present in B worlds. If we are told that there is not a 7 in the actual world, we can easily infer that the actual world is not a B world and that therefore "not B". MT is valid simply because we cannot have a world with a B and not a 7.

CONCLUSIONS AND ALTERNATIVES

Our purpose in this chapter has been to identify significant weakness in the current mental models account of conditionals, rather than to propose a detailed alternative account. However, we point in this final section to the rough shape of the theory we develop as an alternative. We argued strongly against the material conditional analysis of indicative conditionals in natural language. Current mental model theory relies heavily on this analysis. Inferences that do not conform to the analysis are illusory (Johnson-Laird & Savary, 1999), and the correct probability judgment about an indicative conditional makes it equal to the probability of the material conditional (Johnson-Laird, Legrenzi, Girotto, Legrenzi, & Caverni, 1999). This analysis allows JLB to claim that people can flesh out "not p, not q" as a true possibility for "if p then q." They made this claim to explain MT reasoning in line with their fundamental semantic principle. In the first place, this explanation applies only to basic conditionals. In the second place, as we showed in the preceding section, Johnson-Laird and Byrne (2002) have already given up their fundamental principle to account for the double negation effect in conditional reasoning. If a suppositional account of Modus Tollens reasoning is allowed, then there is no reason at all to propose the unsatisfactory material conditional analysis of the ordinary indicative conditional.

If the Ramsey test is used to evaluate the ordinary conditional, then we can resolve the problems of the material conditional analysis, account for counterfactual and indicative conditionals with the same mechanism, and give a coherent account of the truth table task as well. There must, in addition, be a general relation between people's representation of an ordinary conditional and their conditional probability judgments (see Evans et al., 2002; Over & Evans, 2003). In our view, people represent the assertion of an ordinary conditional, 'if p then q', as the expression of conditional probability judgment. This is the judgment that q is highly probable (in the context of the assertion) given p. In addition, they do not represent this conditional as a statement about any world in which p does not hold. Where the probability of q given p is high, and the minor premise is highly probable, we can have some confidence in the conclusions of MP and MT.

We know from the experimental literature that biconditional inference patterns are common. People often endorse the fallacies of DA and AC (e.g., Evans et al., 1993). We assume that a biconditional reading is a conjunction of two probabilistic conditionals representing "if p then q," and "if q then p." This will, of course, support all four conditional inferences. In the truth table task, it will produce the pattern for defective equivalence, discussed earlier. That is, people will identify "not p, q" as a falsifying case while continuing to describe "not p, not q" as irrelevant.

The proposed representation of conditionals linked to conditional probability is necessary to account for the kinds of pragmatic effects discussed earlier in this chapter. It is impossible to account for pragmatic influences merely in terms of unweighted logical possibilities, using only what we have termed the four-bit device. For example, a promise conveys a high probability of q given p, whereas a tip conveys a raised (relative to base rate) probability but one that is not so high as that for a promise. This account also explains why participants, when permitted to do so by the procedure, will endorse conditional inferences with a range of confidence or probability ratings. It is also supported by some recent research conducted by the authors on probability judgments made about conditional statements. Our experiments to date clearly indicate that the probability of q given p is the major determinant of people's judgments about the probability of an ordinary conditional statement.

In terms of the general mental model theory of deduction, the major step to take, in our view, is to advance beyond logical possibilities that are not weighted in terms of probability. There must be more to a theory of conditional reasoning than what we have called the four-bit device. More generally, current mental model theory is deeply committed a kind of logicism that restricts itself to manipulating simple logically possibilities. Even the mental model account of probabilistic reasoning, in Johnson-Laird et al. (1999), is confined to the notion of probability defined in terms of unweighted logical possibilities, which has the result, as the authors themselves stress, that probabilistic reasoning in this sense is purely deductive. Such a notion of probability does not even allow us to learn from experience. To avoid this problem and others, mental models must be weighted in terms of a nondeductive, nonlogicist concept of probability (Over, in press). We must also acknowledge that people reason using suppositions, taking into account probabilities that are directly represented. Although a suppositional account blurs the distinction between model and rule theory, we most definitely do not wish our analysis to be taken as argument for an extant mental logic based on inference rules. The existing accounts of this kind are most unsatisfactory to us because they propose a core deductive mechanism with separate pragmatic mechanisms added on and require a different account for reasoning than for other kinds of hypothetical thinking such as decision making and forecasting. In common with mental model theory of Johnson-Laird and Byrne (1991, 2002), the hypothetical thinking model of Evans et al. (2001) proposes that people think about mental models representing hypothetical possibilities. What we hope to have shown in this chapter, is that proposals about both the nature of the models and the reasoning processes that are applied need to be fundamentally rethought.

REFERENCES

Barrouillet, P., Grosset, N., & Lecas, J.-F. (2000). Conditional reasoning by mental models: Chronometric and developmental evidence. *Cognition, 75,* 237–266.

Braine, M. D. S., & O'Brien, D. P. (1991). A theory of if: A lexical entry, reasoning program, and pragmatic principles. *Psychological Review, 98,* 182–203.

Braine, M. D. S., & O'Brien, D. P. (Eds.). (1998). *Mental logic.* Mahwah, NJ: Lawrence Erlbaum Associates.

Bucciarelli, M., & Johnson-Laird, P. N. (1999). Strategies in syllogistic reasoning. *Cognitive Science, 23,* 247–303.

Byrne, R. M. J. (1989). Suppressing valid inferences with conditionals. *Cognition, 31,* 61– 83.

Edgington, D. (1995). On conditionals. *Mind, 104,* 235-329.

Evans, J. St. B. T. (1972). Interpretation and matching bias in a reasoning task. *Quarterly Journal of Experimental Psychology, 24,* 193–199.

Evans, J. St. B. T. (1975). On interpreting reasoning data: A reply to Van Duyne. *Cognition, 3,* 387–390.

Evans, J. St. B. T. (1993). The mental model theory of conditional reasoning: Critical appraisal and revision. *Cognition, 48,* 1–20.

Evans, J. St. B. T. (1998). Matching bias in conditional reasoning: Do we understand it after 25 years? *Thinking and Reasoning, 4,* 45–82.

Evans, J. St. B. T., & Clibbens, J. (1995). Perspective shifts in the selection task: Reasoning or relevance? *Thinking and Reasoning, 1,* 315–323.

Evans, J. St. B. T., Ellis, C. E., & Newstead, S. E. (1996). On the mental representation of conditional sentences. *Quarterly Journal of Experimental Psychology, 49A,* 1086–1114.

Evans, J. St. B. T., & Handley, S. J. (1999). The role of negation in conditional inference. *Quarterly Journal of Experimental Psychology, 52A,* 739–769.

Evans, J. St. B. T., Handley, S. J., Harper, C., & Johnson-Laird, P. N. (1999). Reasoning about necessity and possibility: A test of the mental model theory of deduction. *Journal of Experimental Psychology: Learning, Memory and Cognition, 25,* 1495–1513.

Evans, J. St. B. T., Handley, S. H., & Over, D. E. (2002). Conditionals and conditional probability. *Journal of Experimental Psychology: Learning, Memory and Cognition, 29,* 321–335.

Evans, J. St. B. T., Legrenzi, P., & Girotto, V. (1999). The influence of linguistic form on reasoning: The case of matching bias. *Quarterly Journal of Experimental Psychology, 52A,* 185–216.

Evans, J. St. B. T., & Newstead, S. E. (1977). Language and reasoning: A study of temporal factors. *Cognition, 5,* 265–283.

Evans, J. St. B. T., Newstead, S. E., & Byrne, R. M. J. (1993). *Human reasoning: The psychology of deduction.* Hillsdale, NJ: Lawrence Erlbaum Associates.

Evans, J. St. B. T., Over, D. E., & Handley, S. H. (2003). A theory of hypothetical thinking. In D. Hardman & L. Maachi (Eds.), *Decision making and reasoning* (pp. 3–21). Chichester, UK: Wiley.

Evans, J. St. B. T., & Twyman-Musgrove, J. (1998). Conditional reasoning with inducements and advice. *Cognition, 69,* B11–B16.

George, C. (1995). The endorsement of the premises: Assumption based or belief-based reasoning. *British Journal of Psychology, 86,* 93–111.

George, C. (1997). Reasoning from uncertain premises. *Thinking and Reasoning, 3,* 161– 190.

Handley, S. J., & Evans, J. St. B. T. (2000). Supposition and representation in human reasoning. *Thinking and Reasoning, 6,* 273–312.

Johnson-Laird, P. N. (1983). *Mental models.* Cambridge, UK: Cambridge University Press.

Johnson-Laird, P. N. (1995). Inference and mental models. In S. E. Newstead & J. St. B. T. Evans (Eds.), *Perspectives in thinking and reasoning* (pp. 115–146). Hillsdale, NJ: Lawrence Erlbaum Associates.

Johnson-Laird, P. N., & Bara, B. G. (1984). Syllogistic inference. *Cognition, 16,* 1–61.

Johnson-Laird, P. N., & Byrne, R. (1991). *Deduction.* Hillsdale, NJ: Lawrence Erlbaum Associates.

Johnson-Laird, P. N., & Byrne, R. (2002). Conditionals: A theory of meaning, pragmatics and inference. *Psychological Review, 109,* 646–678.

Johnson-Laird, P. N., Byrne, R. M. J., & Schaeken, W. (1992). Propositional reasoning by model. *Psychological Review, 99,* 418–439.

Johnson-Laird, P. N., Legrenzi, P., Girotto, V., Legrenzi, M., & Caverni, J.-P. (1999). Naive probability: A mental model theory of extensional reasoning. *Psychological Review, 106,* 62–88.

Johnson-Laird, P. N., & Savary, F. (1999). Illusory inferences: A novel class of erroneous deductions. *Cognition, 71,* 191–299.

Liu, I.-M., Lo, K.-C., & Wu, J.-T. (1996). A probabilistic interpretation of "if-then." *The Quarterly Journal of Experimental Psychology, 49A,* 828–844.

Newstead, S. E., Ellis, C., Evans, J. St. B. T., & Dennis, I. (1997). Conditional reasoning with realistic material. *Thinking and Reasoning, 3,* 49–76.

Newstead, S. E., Handley, S. H., & Buck, E. (1999). Falsifying mental models: Testing the predictions of theories of syllogistic reasoning. *Journal of Memory and Language, 27,* 344–354.

Oaksford, M., Chater, N., & Larkin, J. (2000). Probabilities and polarity biases in conditional inference. *Journal of Experimental Psychology: Learning, Memory and Cognition, 26,* 883–889.

Oaksford, M., & Stenning, K. (1992). Reasoning with conditional containing negated constituents. *Journal of Experimental Psychology: Learning, Memory and Cognition, 18,* 835–854.

Oberauer, K., & Wilhelm, O. (2003). The meaning(s) of conditionals—Experiments with a probabilistic truth-table evaluation task. *Journal of Experimental Psychology: Learning, Memory and Cognition, 29*, 680–693.

Over, D. E. (in press). Naïve probability and its model theory. In V. Girotto & P. N. Johnson-Laird (Eds.), *The shape of reason. Essays in honour of Paolo Legrenzi*. Hove: Psychology Press.

Over, D. E., & Evans, J. St. B. T. (2003). The probability of conditionals: The psychological evidence. *Mind and Language, 18*, 340–358.

Politzer, G., & Bourmaud, G. (2002). Deductive reasoning from uncertain conditionals. *British Journal of Psychololgy, 93*, 345–381.

Politzer, G., & Braine, M. D. S. (1991). Responses to inconsistent premises cannot count as suppresion of valid inferences. *Cognition, 38*, 103–108.

Ramsey, F. P. (1931). *The Foundations of mathematics and other logical essays*. London: Routledge and Kegan Paul.

Rips, L. J. (1994). *The Psychology of Proof.* Cambridge, MA: MIT Press.

Sperber, D., & Wilson, D. (1995). *Relevance* (2nd ed.). Oxford, UK: Blackwell.

Stalnaker, R. (1968). A theory of conditionals. *American Philosophical Quarterly Monograph Series, 2*, 98–112.

Stevenson, R. J., & Over, D. E. (1995). Deduction from uncertain premises. *The Quarterly Journal of Experimental Psychology, 48A*, 613–643.

Stevenson, R. J., & Over, D. E. (2001). Reasoning from uncertain premises. Effects of expertise and conversational context. *Thinking and Reasoning, 7*, 367–390.

5

Mental Models and Falsification:
It Depends on the Task

Maxwell J. Roberts

This chapter reviews a number of task factors that have previously been shown to increase the likelihood that a falsification strategy will be applied when reasoning by using mental models. These are (1) the presence of unbelievable conclusionsn (2) enhanced instructions to improve the understanding of a task, and (3) reducing the cognitive load of a task. In addition, a new factor is discussed: task construal. It is suggested that people adopt nonlogical quantifier interpretations when solving categorical syllogisms, with the consequence that the prevalence and success of falsification behavior at this task has been underestimated in the past. Overall, it is argued (1) that in appropriate circumstances, falsification will be widespread and robust, (2) that care is required to ensure that methods of identifying falsification behavior do not themselves alter its prevalence, and (3) that care is required not to make widespread generalizations from one or a small number of tasks.

INTRODUCTION

How does a person decide whether a conclusion is definitely true, rather than merely possible? This question is at the heart of the issue of whether humans possess deductive competence. If it is found that people do not naturally possess this skill, and it can only be applied sporadically and with great difficulty, then the implications for everyday reasoning would be somewhat disturbing. For example, untrained jurors are expected only to pass a verdict of guilty if this is beyond reasonable doubt. In other words, a person should only be declared guilty if this is necessarily true, not merely possibly true.

Mental models theory (see Johnson-Laird & Byrne, 1991) incorporates a procedure known as falsification or the search for counterexamples to explain how people determine whether a conclusion necessarily follows from the information given (i.e., that the conclusion is valid). Briefly, the full procedure for making a deduction is as follows:

1. Construct an integrated mental model of the information given (equivalent to a spatial array). Draw a putative conclusion from

85

this.

2. Attempt to construct further models to falsify the conclusion. If no falsifying models can be constructed, announce the conclusion as the answer.
3. Once the conclusion is contradicted, identify a new conclusion compatible with all models. If no conclusion can be identified, announce no valid conclusion.
4. Repeat steps 2 and 3 as necessary.

This procedure is most easily illustrated using the two-dimensional relational inference task (e.g., Roberts, 2000b). For example, consider the following multiple-model problem with no valid conclusion:

A is behind C.
B is behind C.
D is to the right of A.
E is to the right of B.
Where is D in relation to E?

The first step (i.e., constructing an integrated model) might give the following:

A   D
B   E
C

This yields the putative conclusion that D is behind E. However, an attempt to construct further models gives the following:

B   E
A   D
C

The previous conclusion is now falsified, and no other conclusion is possible linking the D and E terms, so "no valid conclusion" is announced.

Having illustrated the falsification procedure, how do we know whether people reason in this way? One starting point is that people are able to respond "no valid conclusion" when this is the correct answer. If only one single model were ever considered, then an erroneous answer would always be given instead. However, as Table 5.1 shows, error rates for problems with no valid conclusion can be somewhat on the high side, and this might suggest that the consideration of all possible models is somewhat rare. This is where one of the key predictions of mental models theory becomes important: The more mental models required to make a correct inference, the more demands on working memory and hence the more likely that errors will occur. Compared with one-model problems (where the information specifies just one model, and there must always be a valid conclusion), multiple-model problems with no valid conclusion are therefore predicted to be more difficult to solve. Hence, multiple-model problems will lead to errors either (1) because increased demands on working memory lead to incorrectly constructed models—or incorrect inferences from models—or (2) construction of further models is terminated when working memory reaches capacity. Of course, (2) is simply another way of stating that falsification is unlikely to occur except where working memory capacity is high, and hence we are faced with two possibilities. When people reason by using mental models, are multiple-model problems difficult because people do attempt to falsify, but not very well or people do not attempt to falsify?

The overall stance taken in this chapter is that reasoning by the use of mental models is an important general strategy that people often apply when reasoning. No assumptions are made concerning whether these inference processes form the basis of some sort of hardwired fundamental reasoning mechanism. Indeed, I have argued elsewhere that this is very unlikely to be the case, and instead it is more fruitful to investigate reasoning from the point of view of identifying and attempting to understand individual differences in strategy usage (Roberts, 1993, 1997, 2000a). However, given that people do often use mental models to make deductions, it is interesting for the strategy researcher to consider the circumstances in which the additional strategy of falsification is applied over and above making an inference from the construction of one single model. Hence, the focus of this chapter is intrastrategic differences: How are the fine details of inference procedures varied within a general class of strategy (e.g., the mental models strategy)? The alternative, interstrategic differences—how people differ in the classes of strategies that they use (e.g., mental models, deduction rules, or various task-specific shortcuts)— has been discussed by Roberts (2000a).

To simplify my arguments, I take a weaker than usual definition of falsification. In theory, falsification entails a strict serial sequence of procedures: An initial model is constructed, a tentative conclusion drawn, a second model is constructed to falsify the conclusion, and so on. This is therefore a special case of reasoning by the use of multiple models. For example, an alternative use of multiple models could involve first constructing all possible models and then seeing which conclusion is common to all. Hence, for the this chapter, falsification denotes the general class of strategies in which a person attempts to make deductions by constructing more than one model whenever possible, as opposed to strategies where only one possibility is ever considered. In other words, I simply consider whether reasoning is likely to involve the consideration of multiple mental models.

WHAT ARE THE ACCURACY DATA?

Table 5.1 shows a selection of studies in which accuracy has been calculated as a function of the number of models necessary to make an inference. These days, it is usual for mental models researchers to refer one-model problems versus multiple-model problems, the only distinction for multiple-model problems being whether or not they support a valid conclusion. From this, we can see that the major prediction of mental models theory is borne out. Multiple-model problems are always harder than one-model problems. However, comparisons between tasks are difficult because of differences in the nature of the mental models and in the task properties.

Table 5.1.
Accuracy Levels for Various Inference Tasks as a Function of Problem Type.

Deduction Task	N	One Model	Multiple Model (Valid Conclusion)	Multiple Model (No Valid Conclusion)
Categorical Syllogisms[1]	40	83%	22%	50%
Categorical Syllogisms[2]	56	80%	20%	33%
Conditional Syllogisms[3]	40	97%	56%	---
2D Relational Inference[4]	33	66%	48%	16%
2DRelational Inference[5]	72	67%	54%	31%
2D Relational Inference[6]	72	79%	55%	52%
Multiple Quantifiers[7]	14	72%	23%	23%

[1] Data aggregated from Johnson Laird & Steedman (1978), Experiment 2, and Johnson-Laird & Bara (1984), Experiment 3.
[2] Calculated from data reported by Roberts, Newstead, & Griggs (2001).
[3] Data aggregated from Johnson Laird, Byrne, & Schaeken (1992), Experiments 2 and 3.
[4] Data aggregated from Byrne & Johnson Laird (1989), Experiments 1 and 2.
[5] Data aggregated from Roberts (2000a), Experiments 1 to 3, serial presentation only.
[6] Data aggregated from Roberts (2000a), Experiments 1 to 3, parallel presentation only.
[7] Data from Johnson Laird, Byrne, & Tabossi (1989), Experiment 3.

For example, for the two-dimensional relational inference task, failure to construct all models for multiple-model valid problems will still yield the correct answer, but failure may not do so for categorical syllogisms. In addition, multiple-model problems for the two-dimensional relational inference task are always two-model, but for categorical syllogisms these headings include both two- and three-model problems. Nonetheless, Table 5.1 indicates two important pointers as to when to expect falsification to be prevalent, and as to why.

The first clue is that the decline in accuracy from one-model to multiple-model valid problems is particularly spectacular for categorical syllogisms. Hence, for this task, perhaps falsification is simply not being applied, and people are making inferences from one single model. Not surprisingly, critics of falsification focus on this task. However, this decline is far less marked for conditional syllogisms. If people were generally failing to falsify, the decline should be equally marked for this task. Instead, rather than concluding from just one type of reasoning task that people rarely falsify, it may be better to consider the unique qualities of categorical syllogisms to see whether any of these may particularly inhibit falsification.

The second clue on Table 5.1 is the waywardness of accuracy for multiple-model problems where there is no valid conclusion. For categorical syllogisms, unlike the other tasks, accuracy is markedly higher when compared with multiple-model valid problems. Again, this suggests something unique about this task in terms of sources of inaccuracy for multiple-model problems. Also, for the two-dimensional relational inference task, compare the differences in accuracy for multiple-model valid versus invalid problems. The sizes of these differences range widely and are linked to presentation format. Premises presented one at a time (verbally or in writing) are associated with large differences, but premises presented simultaneously (in writing) are associated with far smaller differences. Considering why task presentation can influence patterns of data is also relevant to the issue of the prevalence of falsification.

CHALLENGES TO FALSIFICATION

Many people have queried whether falsification is prevalent, although virtually all research leading to such doubts is based on various investigations of categorical syllogisms. The first challenges arose from studies concerned with belief bias (i.e., where people's beliefs influence the conclusions they endorse or produce). The most frequent demonstrations of belief bias use conclusion evaluation tasks (e.g., Evans, Barston, & Pollard , 1983; the results for conclusion production tasks are generally compatible, e.g., Oakhill & Johnson-Laird, 1985; Oakhill, Johnson-Laird, & Garnham, 1989). For example, consider the following categorical syllogism:

> No addictive things are inexpensive.
> Some cigarettes are inexpensive.
> Therefore, some addictive things are not cigarettes.

Although believable, the conclusion is not valid. In this example, it is compatible with some but not all states of affairs implied by the premises, so it is possible but does not necessarily follow. In the laboratory, this type of conclusion is usually accepted almost as frequently as believable valid conclusions. Overall, when looking at the proportions of conclusions accepted, there are usually main effects of conclusion believability and logic, but these factors also interact. Believable conclusions tend to be accepted irrespective of validity; likewise, unbelievable valid conclusions are accepted. However, unbelievable invalid conclusions tend to be rejected. Hence, the belief bias effect is primarily due to the acceptance of too many believable invalid conclusions.

A mental models account of the interaction is shown in Fig. 5.1 (see also Oakhill & Johnson-Laird, 1985). Evidence in support of this comes from Newstead, Pollard, Evans, and Allen (1992), Experiments 1 and 2, in which it was shown that the interaction disappears when conclusions to be evaluated are determinately invalid, i.e. are impossible given the premises (e.g., "all cigarettes are addictive things" is believable but impossible given the earlier premises). In addition, the believability by validity interaction has also been shown in similar circumstances for conditional inference (Thompson, 1996) and for relational inference (Roberts & Sykes, 2003), so, presumably, believable conclusions curtail falsification in a similar way for these tasks.

Thus far, it appears that falsification is not an obligatory strategy when reasoning: A particularly believable conclusion will halt the search for further models that may refute it. Unfortunately, for categorical syllogisms, Newstead et al.

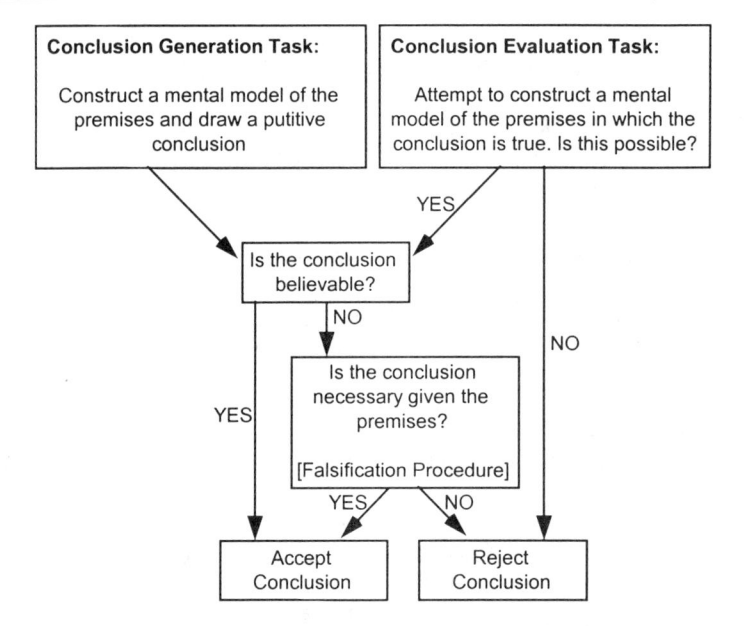

FIG. 5.1 Summary of the mental models explanation of belief bias.

(1992), Experiment 4, additionally found that the acceptance patterns of neutral conclusions matched those for believable conclusions. In other words, falsification appears not to be routinely attempted when evaluating conclusions in general; one single compatible model will suffice for most people. Only where conclusions are unbelievable do people search for models that may falsify them. Similar data are not yet available for the other deduction tasks where belief bias has also been shown, but, overall, this finding leads to the first of the generally accepted task-related factors that determines whether falsification is likely to occur:

1. *Belief conflicts*: Where problems have everyday content, unbelievable conclusions will particularly trigger attempts to falsify them by constructing further models. Neutral and believable conclusions are more likely to be accepted without further processing.

A further task-related factor can also be derived from Newstead et al. (1992). For Experiment 5, subjects were given augmented instructions that stressed that conclusions should only be accepted if definitely true, not merely possible. The interaction between believability and logic was now reduced. Believable invalid conclusions were now rejected, possibly showing that falsification was now being applied more generally, hence the following:

2. *Instructions*: Where instructions are phrased so as to encourage falsification, these have been shown to be reasonably successful at improving performance.

However, this effect can be difficult to replicate (Evans, Newstead, Allen, & Pollard, 1994), and quite complex instructions, concerning syllogistic logic in general, may be necessary.

Thus far, if we accept from the evidence that falsification is a rare strategy during reasoning, we need a mechanism to explain how people are able to respond "no valid conclusion" at all. Considering the categorical syllogism data sets compiled by Roberts, Newstead, and Griggs (2001), "no valid conclusion" responses ranged from more than 20% to just less than 40%, and in fact this was the modal answer. One possibility is that people use some sort of cutoff heuristic so that the search for a conclusion is abandoned when certain criteria are met or fail to be met. A formal theory to this effect, and intended to account for all deduction tasks (but mainly based on an analysis of categorical syllogisms), was put forward by Polk and Newell (1995). For this, problems are solved by repeated attempts to formulate an adequate single representation, and a conclusion is drawn from this. If a legal conclusion cannot be identified, then further encodings of the premises are attempted until a conclusion can be drawn, or else "no valid conclusion" is announced. Adding a procedure for falsification over and above this yielded virtually no additional predictive power to their model. Hence, Polk and Newell assert that people identify "no valid conclusion" as an answer when they are unable to draw any conclusion to a problem and that untrained individuals rarely consider multiple models when reasoning.

It is worth pausing here to consider the psychological plausibility of Polk and Newell's (1995) model. One reason for its apparent success is undoubtedly because of the inclusion of more than 20 parameters, with even their reduced parameter space permitting more than 35 million different permutations. Parameters were fit to individuals without any apparent attempt to do so in a principled way, for example, by considering coherent strategies. Despite this, the model was only able to account for 60% of responses in their data as a whole. Also, it is worth questioning whether it is plausible to assert that people announce "no valid conclusion" having failed to identify any possible conclusion at all. This would imply a failure to comprehend tasks to an extent that is simply not observed in the laboratory. The problem for subjects is surely that sometimes there are too many possible conclusions for them to consider, rather than too few (for discussions of why Polk & Newell's model has difficulty accounting for relational inference task data, see Roberts, 2000b).

Despite problems with Polk and Newell's (1995) model, recently there has been considerable interest in whether there really is evidence for falsification in deduction tasks, in which conclusions are neutral in terms of believability. For example, Newstead, Handley, and Buck (1999) found that for multiple-model syllogisms, subjects were neither more likely to report more intermediate conclusions nor draw additional diagrams while solving them, compared with one-model syllogisms. In addition, Newstead and Griggs (1999) found that by disambiguating premise meanings, syllogistic accuracy was improved, and they suggested that this is compatible with people only constructing single models to solve syllogisms and that the task modifications increased the likelihood that the initial model for a problem would support the appropriate conclusion. Furthermore, Evans, Handley, Harper, and Johnson-Laird (1999) found that when subjects evaluated whether presented conclusions necessarily followed, different syllogisms varied in the extent to which people erroneously endorsed conclusions that were merely possible. Incorrect conclusion endorsements for any particular syllogism tended to be compatible with its predicted initial mental model as suggested by mental models theory. Hence, Evans et al. (1999) suggested that the difficulty of any particular syllogism was related to the likelihood that the initial mental model would support the correct conclusion. Thus, they concur that multiple model construction is a rare strategy, at least for categorical syllogisms, concluding that "people *can* search for alternative models, but do not necessarily do so spontaneously" (p. 1507; see also Evans, 2000b). However, they do not discuss a mechanism for obtaining "no valid conclusion" responses.

A further blow to falsification comes from Evans, Handley, and Harper (2001) and Evans (2000a). The selective processing model for explaining belief bias in the conclusion evaluation task posits that the believability by validity interaction need not be a falsification phenomenon. Instead, the exact reasoning procedure depends on the believability of the conclusion. A confirmatory mental model will be sought for believable and neutral conclusions. If this is possible, then the conclusions will be accepted. A disconfirmatory model will be sought for unbelievable conclusions. If this is possible, then the conclusions will be rejected. This explains the large belief bias effect for conclusions that are possible but not necessary. For these, there are potentially both confirmatory and disconfirmatory models, and either can be found depending on what is sought. A similar model has also been proposed by Klauer, Musch, and Naumer (2000). However, these are task-specific models, and it is not clear whether anything similar can be applied to conclusion-generation tasks.

SUPPORT FOR FALSIFICATION

All of the evidence against the widespread use of falsification is derived from studies of categorical syllogisms, but this task has also yielded some support for the use of this strategy. Bucciarelli and Johnson-Laird (1999; see also Johnson-Laird, Savary, & Bucciarelli, 2000) gave subjects physical tokens to manipulate by hand. The use of multiple models was observed in all subjects at least some of the time, albeit with a wide range of adoption. This was the case whether subjects generated their own or evaluated presented conclusions. Sequences of models were frequently constructed for solving multiple-model problems. Hence, there was suggestive evidence for falsification, at least in the general sense, although the opportunity to externalize did not improve accuracy. However, caution is required in interpreting any study where there is an opportunity for externalization. Roberts, Gilmore, and Wood (1997) and Newton and Roberts (2000) showed that the opportunity to externalize for a compass-point directions task markedly inhibits normal strategy development: People were far less likely to discover simplification strategies that would improve performance at the task. For people who would normally make such discoveries, the opportunity to externalize therefore actually reduced their performance markedly. Hence, for categorical syllogisms with externalization, one possibility is that the use of physical tokens (but not pencil and paper, as shown by Newstead et al., 1999) reduces the task demands to the extent that subjects no longer economize by considering a minimal number of models. This leads to the unfortunate possibility that the manipulations intended to reveal falsification are instead responsible for inducing this strategy.

Turning to other tasks, Bell and Johnson-Laird (1998) investigated judgments of necessity and possibility with conditionals and disjunctions. The important point here is that if multiple models are being constructed, then it should be easier to determine whether a conclusion is possible than whether it is impossible. For the former, just one compatible model is required, whereas for the latter all models must be considered. Conversely, it should be easier to determine whether a conclusion does not necessarily follow than whether it necessarily follows. For the former, just one incompatible model is required, whereas for the latter, all models must be considered. Data were in line with this, and levels of accuracy were high compared with categorical syllogisms. This suggests that falsification was a commonly applied strategy for this particular task.

FALSIFICATION AND DEPENDENCE ON COGNITIVE LOAD

Thus far, evidence against widespread falsification has largely been based on categorical syllogism tasks. Evidence to the contrary comes either from a categorical syllogism task where the cognitive load was markedly reduced or from a study of conditionals and disjunctions. For the latter task, Bell and Johnson-Laird's (1998) participants clearly found it rather easy: 63% correct was the lowest score obtained for any one item (p. 42). Table 5.1 likewise shows that reasoning with conditionals appears to be a relatively easy task. Hence, given that it is agreed that falsification is not an obligatory procedure, and given that falsification requires more processing than not falsifying, this then leads us to the next task factor that is likely to influence whether this strategy is likely to occur, as suggested by Roberts (2000b):

> 3. *Cognitive load*: Falsification is more likely for a deduction task that is less cognitively demanding than for a task that is more demanding.

This factor is most straightforward when used for making predictions within different formats of the same task. If we consider the two-dimensional relational inference task, traditionally this has been presented verbally (i.e., serial presentation). With four premises linking five different objects, this clearly makes the task of constructing an integrated model quite demanding, and indeed the low accuracy rate for multiple-model problems without a valid conclusion (Byrne & Johnson-Laird, 1989; see also Table 5.1) does imply that people rarely construct all necessary models. One important question, therefore, is, if the cognitive load for the relational inference task were reduced, would the patterns of performance indicate more use of falsification? Roberts (2000b) tested this by presenting subjects with either written serial or parallel presentation, and the aggregate findings across experiments are shown in Fig. 5.2.

Once ideal patterns of behavior are considered, the data in Fig. 5.2 clearly support falsification: A person who never falsifies should have similar accuracy for one-model and multiple-model valid problems, where all models support the same answer. However, accuracy should be zero for multiple-model invalid problems, where a possible answer (that does not necessarily follow) will always be reported. If falsification is always to be applied, predictions are less straightforward but are still possible. For a multiple-model valid problem, a correct response will depend on both models being constructed correctly, and the probability of this can be estimated from the error rate for one-model problems. Multiple-model invalid problems are more interesting because if the same error is made for both models, then the correct answer of "no valid conclusion" will still be made. Hence, if falsification is applied, these problems should be easier than multiple-model valid problems.

Why should a person wish to expend more effort considering all possibilities if this will damage his or her accuracy for multiple-model valid problems? The most likely reason is that subjects are unable to identify any simple way of distinguishing between the valid versus invalid multiple-model problems from the premises, and constructing multiple models is therefore the only way of raising accuracy at invalid problems above floor level. Hence, for Roberts (2000b), parallel presentation leads to improved accuracy at one-model problems (cognitive load is reduced compared with serial presentation) and improved accuracy at multiple-model invalid problems (reduced cognitive load means that falsification is applied more widely) but no improvement for multiple-model valid problems (gains from the reduced cognitive load are cancelled out because falsification makes such items harder). Overall, by using error rates of one-model problems to predict the probability of successfully constructing any one model, Roberts (2000b) suggested that, for parallel presentation, falsification was attempted roughly 90% of the time where possible, but this figure fell to 50% for serial presentation.

Taking a wider view of deduction, people are rarely subjected to serial presentation for other tasks, so further data are required on the effects of task presentation before the findings of Roberts (2000b) can be generalized. Exceptions are Gilhooly, Logie, Wetherick, and Wynn (1993) and Gilhooly, Logie, and Wynn (2002), who investigated parallel, serial verbal, and serial written presentation for categorical syllogisms. They found lower levels of accuracy for serial presentation, but did not investigate this in terms of the number of mental models required.

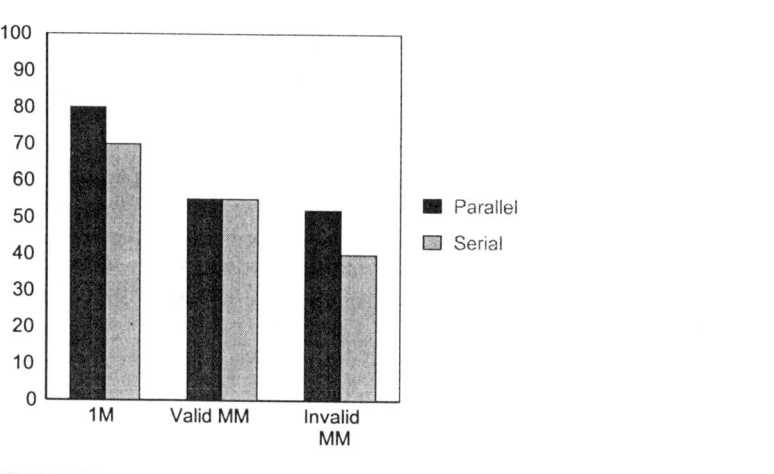

FIG. 5.2.a Aggregate data for the 2D relational inference task from Roberts (2000a).

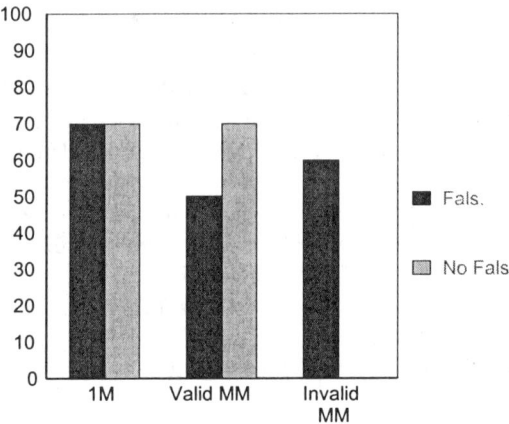

FIG. 5.2.b Predicted levels of accuracy when falsification is always applied (Fals.) and never applied (No Fals..) The probability of constructing a single model correctly is taken to be 70%.

Another means by which cognitive load can be manipulated is by the use of concurrent tasks, which can be used to vary working memory load while reasoning (e.g., Gilhooly, 1998; Gilhooly et al., 1993). If the cognitive load hypothesis is correct, then increasing the working memory load would be expected to reduce falsification. Studies thus far have not provided a direct test of this, although Gilhooly, Logie, and Wynn (1999) present evidence suggesting that for categorical syllogisms, increased memory load can lead to the abandonment of the use of mental models altogether and the substitution of various low-cost coping strategies, such as atmosphere, matching, and guessing. Hence, it appears that categorical syllogisms even without concurrent tasks and with parallel presentation are so demanding to solve that the slightest increase in cognitive load effectively causes reasoning to cease. Conversely, data from Bucciarelli and Johnson-Laird (1999) suggest that reducing the cognitive load for categorical syllogisms may well increase the prevalence of falsification. Hence, one challenge for the future may be to make this task easier to increase falsification as well as to explain why externalization via pencil and paper appears not to do so (Newstead et al., 1999).

Overall, we have highly suggestive evidence that cognitive load manipulations can alter the prevalence of falsification: For any given task, increasing the load reduces this. Two manipulations, presentation and concurrent tasks, are both likely to be of great importance for this purpose in the future, although cognitive load could be manipulated by other means, for example the number of premises and entities that need to be considered. Hence, compare the following multiple-model invalid relational inference problems:

A is behind C.   A is behind X.
B is behind C.   X is behind C.
D is to the right of A.   B is behind Y.
E is to the right of B.   Y is behind C.
Where is D in relation to E?   D is to the right of A.
                                            E is to the right of B.
                                            Where is D in relation to E?

For researchers, the best strategy is probably to focus on tasks where there is currently reasonably clear evidence for falsification. For example, modus tollens (MT) is a fairly widespread multiple-model inference for conditional reasoning, likewise the prevention of erroneous denial of the antecedent (DA) and affirmation of the consequent (AC) inferences. For conditional reasoning, there is therefore almost certainly measurable scope for reducing MT and raising DA and AC inferences by raising cognitive load. However, Toms, Morris, and Ward (1993), Experiment 3, found that although raising working memory load reduced the number of MT inferences without influencing modus ponens (MP), there was no increase in denial of the antecedent and affirmation of the consequent inferences. Other working memory studies have tended not to report changes in accuracy by item type, and this is therefore an important consideration for future reporting and interpretation of data.

Thus far, the cognitive load hypothesis can predict differences in the frequency of falsification between different versions of the same task. Predicting differences in prevalence between deduction tasks is somewhat more challenging. For example, one reason why it is hard to observe the use of multiple models for categorical syllogisms may be that this task is particularly demanding in general. However, with high accuracy for one-model problems—at or near 80% (see Table 5.1)—this is not an obvious starting point for explaining lack of falsification, especially because Bucciarelli and Johnson-Laird (1999) found that the opportunity to externalize did not assist performance in any way. Hence, as suggested earlier, the somewhat peculiar data for categorical syllogisms suggest that we should scrutinize this task carefully.

FALSIFICATION AND DEPENDENCE ON TASK CONSTRUAL

Roberts (2000b) suggested a speculative fourth factor for determining whether falsification is likely to occur—and a recent analysis of categorical syllogisms by Roberts, Newstead, and Griggs (2001) will enable the suggestion to be made more explicit—and supplies some evidence in its support. In its original form, the factor was stated as follows:

> 4. *Task type*: Multiple model construction is more likely for deduction tasks where the demands and underlying logic are better understood or where the components of the task are more easily mapped onto spatial representations, or both.

Some evidence in favor of this suggestion already comes from the instruction effects of the Newstead et al. (1992) and Evans et al. (1994) belief bias studies, hence Factor 2 stated previously may be seen as a special case of this. Obviously, if a person does not understand a task, then all performance will be poor, let alone performance at multiple-model problems. However, performance at one-model categorical syllogisms is generally good, so unless it is to be suggested that high accuracy at certain problems is due to other reasons—for example, premise atmosphere biasing people's guesses in favor of the correct answers—then a more specific explanation needs to be sought. In addition, these effects of instruction were sporadic; and one important finding of Evans, Handley, Harper, and Johnson-Laird (1999) is that participants apparently had little difficulty in understanding the meanings of necessity and possibility for this task. Hence, where observed, instructional effects may be overcoming a reluctance to falsify that is due to the lengthy procedure that this entails, rather than overcoming a misunderstanding of the task, so we should not rely too much on a general claim of a lack of task understanding.

Instead, a more specific claim can be made: People do understand the general meaning of logical validity and the requirements of the categorical syllogism task. However, the way in which people construe the meanings of quantifiers actually means that they are solving different problems than those set by the experimenters and that the apparent lack of falsification behavior can be explained by this.

Table 5.2
Comparison of Logical and Nonlogical Quantifier Interpretations

Quantifier	Relationship
Logical Interpretations	
all A are B	(A=B) (A inside B)
no A are B	(A) (B)
some A are B	(A=B) (A overlap B) (A inside B) (A, B overlapping)
some A are not B	(A) (B) (A overlap B) (A, B overlapping)
Reversible Interpretations (all and some-not modified)	
all A are B	(A=B)
some A are not B	(A) (B) (A, B overlapping)
Gricean Interpretations (some and some-not modified)	
some A are B	(A overlap B) (A, B overlapping)
some A are not B	(A overlap B) (A, B overlapping)
Reversible Gricean Interpretations (all, some and some-not modified)	
all A are B	(A=B)
some A are B	(A, B overlapping)
some A are not B	(A, B overlapping)

The conventional meanings of syllogistic quantifiers are shown in Table 5.2. It should be noted here that certain quantifiers are very ambiguous indeed: up to four different meanings for some. To ensure that a syllogism has been solved correctly, it may be necessary to consider all possible meanings, but failure to do so will undoubtedly simplify the task. Theories of syllogistic error based on quantifier interpretation are not new, although direct evidence in their favor has been hard to come by in the past. Indirect evidence includes immediate inference and Euler circle interpretation tasks, whose data imply that people are particularly inclined to adopt so-called Gricean interpretations, in which *some* versus *all* are taken to be mutually exclusive, likewise *no* versus *some not* (see Table 5.2). Although utilizing Gricean interpretations may superficially appear to simplify the categorical syllogism task, direct evidence that people actually use these is virtually nonexistent (Newstead, 1995). One problem with these interpretations, highlighted by Roberts et al. (2001), is that if *some* and *all* are taken to be mutually exclusive when encoding, this must also be the case when identifying a conclusion from a set of represented possibilities. A very large number of syllogisms result in an ambiguity in which a subset of the possibilities imply *all* as the conclusion, while other possibilities imply *some*. Hence, mutually exclusive conclusions are simultaneously possible. This is also the case for other problems in which the quantifiers *some not* versus *no* are simultaneously possible. Hence, Roberts et al. (2001) suggested that experience of this ambiguity will cause people to abandon Gricean interpretations, either by adopting logical interpretations or other misinterpretations.

Roberts et al. (2001) also discussed reversible interpretations. For these, the quantifiers *all* and *some not* are modified only to include the meanings that permit reversibility so that "all *A* are *B*" implies that "all *B* are *A*", and "some *A* are not *B*" implies that "some *B* are not *A*" (see Table 5.2). This is distinct from conversion, in which premises are reversed so that "all *A* are *B*" is converted to "all *B* are *A*" and *all* is interpreted correctly thereon. Gricean and reversible interpretations can also be combined (see Table 5.2).

Roberts et al. (2001) compared the different interpretation strategies across three data sets by determining the precise expected answer for every one of these strategies for every possible premise pair. Aggregating over the analyzed data sets, the authors found only 46% of responses matched the logically correct answer. The best of the Gricean interpretation strategies was even worse; Only 41% of responses matched the expected answers for this. However, reversible interpretations were a considerable improvement over logic, with 58% of responses corresponding with the expected answer for these, whereas the best reversible Gricean strategy was not far behind at 57%. It should be noted that these figures are not far behind the 60% figure obtained by Polk and Newell (1995) and also that the figures of Roberts et al. (2001) were not obtained by assigning quantifier interpretation strategies on an individual basis. Had this been possible, then the proportion of responses accounted for would undoubtedly have been even higher.

Overall, Roberts et al. (2001) concluded that when solving categorical syllogisms, the majority of people adopt reversible interpretations, although the issue of whether people tend to adopt Gricean interpretations over and above these remains open. The widespread use of reversible interpretations is certainly not suggested by immediate inference and Euler circle interpretation tasks, and this highlights the difficulty in making between-task comparisons. The evaluation of categorical syllogisms requires people to integrate information and perform a lengthy falsification procedure. This may lead them to adopt unusual quantifier interpretations to reduce the number of processing steps.

What has this got to do with the prevalence of falsification? Previously, it has been suggested that the very low accuracy rates for multiple-model problems are caused by one of two possibilities: (1) that people attempt to falsify, but not very well, and (2) that people do not attempt to falsify. However, it is probable that people's quantifier interpretations differ from those used by researchers when they calculate the number of mental models required to solve a problem correctly. This suggests that (2) can be divided into two distinct subcategories, depending on the cause of the failure to falsify.

Johnson-Laird and colleagues frequently acknowledge the importance of quantifier interpretation as an influence on reasoning performance. However, this has never been a major part of their theorizing. For example, Bucciarelli and Johnson-Laird (1999) acknowledge that quantifier interpretation is important but suggest that this is highly variable and unpredictable. Overall, then, although it has been suggested that, for example, interpretations may bias initial models, no extensive provision has been made for these to constrain falsification procedures so that correctly applied reasoning processes will always lead to the logically correct answer. Hence, an important possibility is that people routinely attempt to falsify, but their proficiency at this is underestimated because the predicted mental model counts do not take account of people's quantifier interpretations.

For example, if we take the syllogism "all *A* are *B* and all *C* are *B*," which is a multiple-model syllogism with no valid conclusion, many subjects erroneously report all as the conclusion. Its high error rate might indicate that subjects are poor at falsifying or have neglected to do so. However, if people apply reversible interpretations to the premises, this makes it a one-model syllogism with *all* as its expected answer. In this case, the error rate for this syllogism is not a measure of the difficulty of falsification nor the tendency for people to neglect to apply this procedure. Instead, the interpretation of the premises used by the subjects means that no falsification can ever be attempted because this is impossible. Hence, it is reasonable to suggest that using mental model counts as an estimate of problem difficulty is only effective when the interpretation of the quantifiers is known. This is because the interpretation can send a person to a different answer than the one expected so that even if his or her logic is impeccable from then on and falsification is applied meticulously wherever possible, this cannot be detected. Hence, if we do not take account of quantifier interpretations, we cannot tell the difference between correct encoding but poor deduction and incorrect encoding but proficient deduction (cf. Henle, 1962). This also explains why Bucciarelli and Johnson-Laird (1999) found no influence of externalization on accuracy: Irrespective of the effect of this on the likelihood of falsification, if quantifier interpretations nonetheless remain unchanged, then the prevalence of falsification will continue to be underestimated for the same reasons as before.

We therefore have three possible situations regarding the proficiency/prevalence of falsification and the underlying reasons for the possible lack of this. It is important to make a distinction between these because they make different predictions and have different implications regarding the prevalence of falsification in general.

> 1. People attempt to falsify wherever this is possible, but make many errors when doing so—for example due to working memory capacity restrictions (e.g., Johnson-Laird & Byrne, 1991). *Prediction*: Falsification will be easily detected but will be found to be very inaccurate. *Remediation*: Any intervention that addresses the reasons for inaccuracy should improve performance (e.g., by easing the working memory load).
> 2. People are able to falsify in principle but in practice generally neglect to do so. This might, for example, be caused by a general lack of understanding of the importance of necessity versus possibility or by working memory constraints, meaning that an attempt to apply an arduous lengthy procedure is only made where absolutely necessary (e.g., Evans et al., 1999). *Prediction*: Falsification will be applied sporadically and unsystematically; where detected, it will not be linked to particular items in any way. *Remediation*: General instructions and encouragement may be of assistance, particularly if working memory load is simultaneously reduced.
> 3. People are able to falsify in principle and generally do so wherever possible. However, for particular cases, misinterpretations of quantifiers mean that it is impossible for them to do so. *Prediction*: Falsification will be applied sporadically but highly systematically. It will be detectable only for items in which falsification is still possible despite misinterpreted quantifiers. Remediation: Instructions to use different quantifier interpretations may be successful but only if the reasons for incorrect interpretations are also addressed.

To test the quantifier misinterpretation hypothesis comprehensively, it would be necessary to determine whether falsification is possible for every premise pair in which misinterpretations might manifest themselves. This entails calculating the number of mental models required for more than 100 premise pairs with modified quantifier meanings. Given that there is some disagreement concerning the number of mental models necessary, even with logical quantifier interpretations (e.g., Hardman, 1996; Newstead & Griggs, 1999; Rips, 1994), such an exercise is beyond the scope of this chapter. However, there exists a systematic means of estimating mental model counts, which enables the plausibility of this hypothesis to be tested.

At first sight, categorical syllogisms appear to be very complicated. If we consider the number of qualitatively different permutations linking the A, B, and C terms, these range from 2 (e.g., for "no A are B" and "all C are B") in the simplest case to 80 (e.g., "some B are A" and "some B are C"). The greatest number of permutations for a premise pair with a valid conclusion is 16. Unfortunately, numbers of permutations do not predict problem difficulty because some of the invalid syllogisms with large numbers of permutations are somewhat easier than some of the valid syllogisms with considerably smaller numbers. This by itself might suggest a cognitive overload theory for responding "no valid conclusion", but even for valid syllogisms, A-B-C permutation counts are not related to difficulty.

Syllogisms are somewhat more straightforward when the numbers of permutations linking just the A and C terms is considered (the A and C terms appear only once each in the premises and must appear in the conclusion). From this point of view, there are only seven different syllogisms, and these are shown in Table 5.3.

Table 5.3
Euler Circles Denoting the Seven Possible Outcomes for Categorical Syllogisms
When Using Logical Quantifier Interpretations

Example	N	Outcomes compatible with the premises	C-A Conclusion	A-C Conclusion
All B are A All C are B	1	(C=A)　(©C A)	All (some)	Some
No B are A All C are B	4	(C)(A)	No (some-not)	No (some-not)
All A are B All B are C	1	(C=A)　(C(A))	Some	All (some)
All B are A All B are C	5	(C=A)　(C(A)) (©C A) (C(A))	Some	Some
No A are B All B are C	8	(C)(A) (C(A))　(C((A))	Some-not	NVC
All B are A No C are B	8	(C)(A)　(©C A) (C((A))	NVC	Some-not
All A are B All C are B	37	(C=A) (C)(A) (C(A)) (©C A) (C((A))	NVC	NVC

Note: Parenthesis indicates conclusions that are technically also correct. *C-A* and *A-C* indicate the direction of terms in the conclusions. Hence, for example, *all C are A* versus *all A are C*.

However, even here, permutation counts are not particularly successful at predicting problem difficulty, this time because of the huge variation in accuracy within categories. In addition, problems with *some* as the correct answer (four permutations) tend to be easier than problems with *some not* as the correct answer (three permutations). This is undoubtedly what led Johnson-Laird and colleagues to the square-bracket notation to denote the exhaustive representation of sets. The working of this will not be discussed here, but suffice it to say that an integrated mental model of all three terms from both premises is analogous to a Venn diagram, but the mental model also contains notations to constrain which additional models can be constructed. However, the information in Table 5.3 enables mental model counts to be estimated relatively easily, which will then enable a comparison of logical and reversible quantifier interpretations to take place.

Looking at Table 5.3, all syllogisms with *all* and *no* as the correct answer are clearly one-model problems, likewise multiple-model syllogisms with no valid conclusion are easily identified. Syllogisms with *some* and *some not* as the correct answer are harder to categorize. Taking the former, sometimes the initial model will support the putative conclusion *all*, and hence further models must be constructed for the correct conclusion to be identified (in other words, falsification is required). At other times, the correct answer may be given by the first model. Although Johnson-Laird and Byrne (1991) give precise predictions, there must surely be individual differences in initial model construction. For the following analyses, syllogisms with *some* and *some not* as the correct answer will be categorized together as multiple-model valid. Whereas this will not always be true for particular premise pairs, or individuals, on average it must be true that, as a whole, solving syllogisms successfully in this category will require more mental models than one-model problems and hence will lead to more difficulty. The consequence of this categorization is that the difficulty of multiple-model valid problems will be slightly underestimated.

Table 5.4 shows the expected solutions to premise pairs if people adopt reversible quantifier interpretations and then reason logically from then on. Exactly the same categorization as before may be applied to estimate mental model counts. This leads to a change in status for 14 syllogisms. Six multiple-model syllogisms are reclassified as one-model problems. For these, the "correct" answer using reversible interpretations is very easy to obtain. The remainder of the changes are for multiple-model invalid syllogisms, which are now multiple-model valid. The modified "correct" answer still requires falsification to obtain it. How successfully can subjects achieve this?

Having recategorized certain problems, we can now ask the question, given the system of assigning mental model counts here, how difficult are problems that require falsification when assuming logical quantifier interpretations compared with those that require falsification when assuming reversible quantifier interpretations? The answer to this is shown in Table 5.5.

Table 5.4

Euler Circles Denoting the Seven Possible Outcomes for Categorical Syllogisms When Using Reversible Quantifier Interpretations

Quantifiers	N	Outcomes Compatible With the Premises		C-A Conclusion	A-C Conclusion
All–all	4	(C=A)		All (some)	All (some)
All–no No–all	8	(C)(A)		No (some-not)	No (some-not)
All–some Some–all	8	(C=A) (C(A)) (C A) (C)(A)		Some	Some
All–some-not Some-not–all	8	(C)(A) (C)(A)		Some-not	Some-not
No–some	4	(C)(A) (C(A)) (C)(A)		Some-not	NVC
Some–no	4	(C)(A) (C A) (C)(A)		NVC	Some-not
Remainder	28	(C=A) (C)(A) (C(A)) (C A) (C)(A)		NVC	NVC

Note: Parenthesis indicates conclusions that are technically also correct. C-A and A-C indicate the direction of terms in the conclusions. Hence, for example, *all C are A* versus *all A are C*.

If we first consider logical interpretations, despite the underestimation of the difficulty of multiple-model problems, their decline in accuracy remains spectacular for three of the four data sets considered. The exception, derived from studies by Dickstein (see Roberts et al., 2001) used a five-option multiple-choice task, which assists subjects for several reasons (Hardman & Payne, 1995). For the other data sets, written answers were required, with conclusions in either direction permitted. If we next consider reversible interpretations, there is a decline in accuracies for one-model problems compared with logical interpretations, but error rates remain well within the range expected on the basis of other deduction tasks. In addition, "success" both for valid and invalid multiple-model problems is always greater with reversible interpretations than with their equivalents assuming logical interpretations. Overall, Table 5.5 shows that if we base mental model counts on reversible interpretations, we obtain considerably greater "accuracy" on multiple-

Table 5.5
Accuracy Levels (in %) for Various Categorical Syllogism Data Sets as a Function of Problem Type and Quantifier Interpretation

Deduction Task	One Model	Multiple Model	Multiple Model (NVC)
Johnson-Laird aggregate (see Table 5.1)			
Logical interpretations	80	34	50
Reversible interpretations	70	49	57
Roberts, Newstead, and Griggs (2001)			
Logical interpretations	77	33	33
Reversible interpretations	79	54	39
Dickstein aggregate (see Roberts, Newstead, & Griggs, 2001)			
Logical interpretations	94	60	49
Reversible interpretations	77	71	59
Bucciarelli and Johnson-Laird (199), Experiment 4			
Logical interpretations	90	36	58
Reversible interpretations	74	48	68

model syllogisms than has previously been suspected. Hence, arguments that falsification is rare for this task, based on extremely poor accuracy for problems that were asserted to require falsification, are based on an assumption that people are using logically appropriate quantifier interpretations. Assuming reversible interpretations, and having identified those problems where falsification is likely to be necessary, we can now observe far more respectable levels of "accuracy". This is despite a reclassification of only 14 syllogisms. Overall then, we can assert that task construal is another factor that determines both whether falsification is likely to take place and whether this is likely to be detectable.

BELIEF BIAS REVISITED: SOME SPECULATIONS

Having discussed task factors that may influence the prevalence of falsification, it is worth returning to the topic of belief bias. It was here that doubt was originally cast on whether falsification is a prevalent strategy. Belief bias has primarily been investigated by the administration of categorical syllogisms, and, given the suggestion that these have unique properties that may make falsification hard to detect where it does occur, it is useful to speculate about expected patterns of data if belief bias were investigated by the use of other tasks.

Roberts and Sykes (2003) completed a series of studies concerning belief bias effects for the relational inference task. These require subjects to evaluate the truth of various spatial (e.g., "London is north of Edinburgh") or temporal (e.g., "World War II took place before the Battle of Hastings") conclusions in the light of premises:

> Churchill was prime minister before Thatcher.
> Blair was prime minister before Thatcher.
> Nelson Mandela was released while Blair was prime minister.
> Prince Charles was born while Churchill was prime minister.
> Therefore, Prince Charles was born before Nelson Mandela was released.
> True or false?

Like categorical syllogisms, these conclusions can be necessarily true, merely possible, or impossible, given the premises, and equivalent conclusions have yielded exactly the same patterns of data, including the believability by validity interaction as shown in Fig. 5.3 (where temporal problems were used). The next step is to add neutral conclusions to the items to see how these compare with believable/unbelievable conclusions. Assuming that falsification is rare unless conclusions are unbelievable, then accuracy for neutral conclusions should match accuracy for believable conclusions. However, given Roberts' (2000b) suggestion that with parallel presentation falsification is highly prevalent for the relational inference task, accuracy for neutral conclusions should resemble unbelievable conclusions, whereas for serial presentation, where falsification is less likely to be prevalent, neutral conclusions should more closely resemble believable conclusions. Hence, whereas the prevalence of falsification for categorical syllogisms is an interesting issue, if an answer for the question of the prevalence of falsification in general is required, then other tasks need to be investigated too, especially if the properties of categorical syllogisms mean that research based on these leads to an underestimation of the prevalence of falsification in general.

CONCLUSIONS

When are people most likely to falsify? This almost certainly depends on the properties of a task. In the light of the previous discussion, Factors 1 and 3 can probably remain unchanged. Hence, falsification is most likely to occur when a task involves at least some conclusions that are particularly unbelievable (Factor 1), where the cognitive demands of a task are relatively low (Factor 3), or both. On the other hand, Factor 2 probably could be made more general, taking on some of the components of Factor 4:

> 2. *General task understanding*: Falsification is more likely for deduction tasks where the demands and underlying logic are well understood. If a lack of understanding is the only barrier to falsification, appropriate instructions may be able to increase this behaviour.

This leaves us with a more specific but better defined Factor 4, which may well apply to other tasks where logical terms have multiple meanings and hence are ambiguous or where logical meanings differ from everyday meanings of the same words:

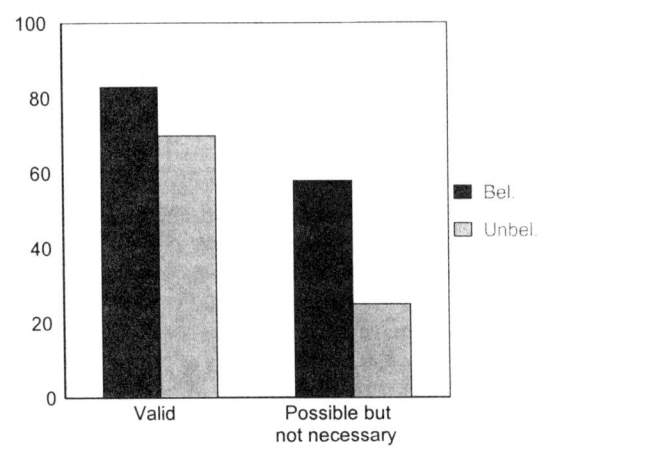

FIG. 5.3.a Believability x validity interaction for a temporal conclusion evaluation task (Roberts & Sykes, 2003, Experiment 3).

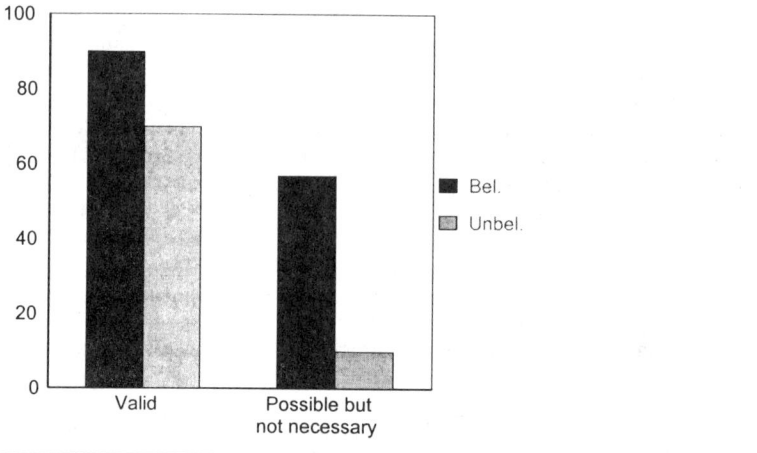

FIG. 5.3.b Believability x validity interaction for an equivalent (with the temporal task in Fig. 5.3.a) categorical syllogism conclusion evaluation task (aggregated data, based on Evans, Barston & Pollard, 1983).

4. *Task construal*: Falsification may be impossible for certain items, or be difficult to detect for others, or both, where a person's interpretation of its logical terms differs from the experimenters'. This may occur because the need to simplify a task rather than because a general lack of understanding.

Hence, falsification may not be prevalent for categorical syllogisms because the task is not necessarily well understood, its cognitive demands are relatively high, and the construal of quantifier meanings results in falsification behavior of subjects that cannot match the expectations of the experimenter. More than one of these may turn out to be important, and until the quantifier interpretation issue is settled, we may have to conclude that falsification is merely hard to detect for this task, rather than unlikely to be applied. Simply instructing people to use correct quantifier meanings is unlikely to be a useful manipulation, given that people are generally aware that *all* and *some not* are not reversible in real life. People may well adopt these interpretations to shorten lengthy solution procedures. In contrast, when we consider two-dimensional relational inference, we see a task whose requirements are easily understandable by subjects, whose interpretations of relational terms are less likely to disagree with the experimenter's in any way that will have implications for performance, and whose cognitive load is relatively light for parallel presentation. Here, falsification appears to be widespread.

Overall, having identified additional task parameters that are likely to be linked to the prevalence of falsification, particularly cognitive load, the next step is to gather more data. This will involve manipulating such variables as task presentation and memory load and extending findings to as wide a range of deduction tasks as possible. However, a note of caution is required here. Care is required to ensure that the means of detecting falsification does not also become a task variable itself, encouraging or suppressing falsification beyond what would normally be expected. This is particularly the case when asking subjects to externalize, because this will have direct consequences for cognitive load. As another example, the relatively undemanding nature of immediate inference and Euler circle evaluation tasks is likely to result in different quantifier interpretations compared with categorical syllogisms, where altered meanings simplify the task and reduce its demands.

One possibility not considered here, and far less likely to be considered by researchers of today than those of 10 years ago, is that there is a simple dichotomy to resolve: Do people apply falsification or don't they? If this were the case, we could focus on one single type of deduction task and answer the question very easily. However, many researchers in this domain appear to assume a virtual dichotomy (witness comments to the effect by certain researchers that falsification is so rare that to all intents and purposes it does not occur for everyday reasoning). Even so, it would be a mistake to answer this question on the basis of just one deduction task, particularly one where falsification may be particularly difficult to detect. Hence, the only viable research strategy is to identify task-related factors, such as those outlined previously, so that we can have a thorough understanding of which task properties promote or suppress falsification and why.

Finally, one issue absent from this chapter is whether there may be stable individual differences in people's falsification behavior: When reasoning by the use of mental models, are some people more likely than others to use a falsification strategy? It is certainly possible that this is the case, although the data discussed here do not address this issue. Given that people differ in their cognitive capacities, such as working memory and general intelligence (e.g., Carpenter, Just, & Shell, 1990; Stanovich & West, 2000), it is likely that these will be related to the tendency to falsify in a similar way to the cognitive load task factors discussed earlier. Hence, psychometric test scores may well be a useful predictor of falsification. Similarly, people will almost certainly differ in their levels of task understanding and their task construals, also potentially leading to strategy differences. Here, large sample sizes or within-subjects manipulations will ensure that individual differences will not obscure the search for task variables that are linked to falsification. However, the eventual goal must be an understanding of all factors that may be linked to reasoning processes, and hence performance, whether task-based or individual based.

POSTSCRIPT

Since writing this chapter, a fifth factor associated with the likelihood that falsification will be applied has been identified by Schroyens, Schaeken, and Handley (2003):

5. *Time*: Falsification is a lengthy procedure and is less likely to be applied where decisions must be taken rapidly.

Research by Schroyens et al. (2003) indicates that this is a plausible factor. Findings by Roberts and Newton (2001), in which subjects were presented with speeded versions of the Wason selection task, are also compatible with this.

REFERENCES

Bell, V. A., & Johnson-Laird, P. N. (1998). A model theory of modal reasoning. *Cognitive Science, 22,* 25–51.

Bucciarelli, M., & Johnson-Laird, P. N. (1999). Strategies in syllogistic reasoning. *Cognitive Science, 23,* 247–303

Byrne, R. M. J., & Johnson-Laird, P. N. (1989). Spatial reasoning. *Journal of Memory and Language, 28,* 564–575.

Carpenter, P. A., Just, M. A., & Shell, P. (1990). What one intelligence test measures: A theoretical account of the processing in the Raven Progressive Matrices Test. *Psychological Review, 97,* 404–431.

Evans, J. St. B. T. (2000a). Thinking and believing. In J. García-Madruga, N. Carriedo, & M. J. González-Labra (Eds.), *Mental models in reasoning* (pp.41–55). Madrid, Spain: UNED.

Evans, J. St. B. T. (2000b). What could and could not be a strategy in reasoning? In W. Schaeken, G. De Vooght, A. Vandierendonck, & G. d'Ydewalle (Eds.), *Deductive reasoning and strategies* (pp. 1–22). Mahwah, NJ: Lawrence Erlbaum Associates.

Evans, J. St. B. T., Barston, J. L., & Pollard, P. (1983). On the conflict between logic and belief in syllogistic reasoning. *Memory and Cognition, 11,* 295–306.

Evans, J. St. B. T., Handley, S. J., & Harper, C. N. J. (2001). Necessity, possibility and belief: A study of syllogistic reasoning. *Quarterly Journal of Experimental Psychology, 54A,* 935–958.

Evans, J. St. B. T., Handley, S. J., Harper, C. N. J., & Johnson-Laird, P. N. (1999). Reasoning about necessity and possibility: A test of the mental model theory of deduction. *Journal of Experimental Psychology: Learning, Memory and Cognition, 25,* 1495–1513.

Evans, J. St. B. T., Newstead, S. E., Allen, J. L., & Pollard, P. (1994). Debiasing by instruction—the case of belief bias. *European Journal of Cognitive Psychology, 6,* 263–285.

Gilhooly, K. J. (1998). Working memory, strategies, and reasoning tasks. In R. H. Logie & K. J. Gilhooly (Eds.), *Working memory and thinking* (pp. 7–22). Hove, UK: Psychology Press.

Gilhooly, K. J., Logie, R. H., Wetherick, N. E., & Wynn, V. (1993). Working memory and strategies in syllogistic-reasoning tasks. *Memory and Cognition, 21,* 115–124.

Gilhooly, K. J., Logie, R. H., & Wynn, V. (1999). Syllogistic reasoning tasks, working memory and skill. *European Journal of Cognitive Psychology, 11,* 473–498.

Gilhooly, K. J., Logie, R. H., & Wynn, V. (2002). Syllogistic reasoning tasks and working memory: Evidence from sequential presentation of premises. *Current Psychology, 21,* 111–120.

Hardman, D. K. (1996). Mental models: The revised theory brings new problems. *Behavioral and Brain Sciences, 19,* 542–543.

Hardman, D. K., & Payne, S. J. (1995). Problem difficulty and response format in syllogistic reasoning. *Quarterly Journal of Experimental Psychology, 48A,* 945–975.

Henle, M. (1962). On the relation between logic and thinking. *Psychological Review, 69,* 366–378.

Johnson-Laird, P. N., & Bara, B. G. (1984). Syllogistic inference. *Cognition, 16,* 1–61.

Johnson-Laird, P. N., & Byrne, R. M. J. (1991). *Deduction.* Hove, UK: Psychology Press.

Johnson-Laird, P. N., Byrne, R. M. J., & Schaeken, W. (1992). Propositional reasoning by model. *Psychological Review, 99,* 418–439.

Johnson-Laird, P. N., Byrne, R. M. J., & Tabossi, P. (1992). Reasoning by model: The case of multiple quantification. *Psychological Review, 96,* 658–673.

Johnson-Laird, P. N., Savary, F., & Bucciarelli, M. (2000). Strategies and tactics in reasoning. In W. Schaeken, G. De Vooght, A. Vandierendonck, & G. d'Ydewalle (Eds.), *Deductive reasoning and strategies* (pp. 209–240). Mahwah, NJ: Lawrence Erlbaum.

Johnson-Laird, P. N., & Steedman, M. (1978). The psychology of syllogisms. *Cognitive Psychology, 10,* 64–99.

Klauer, K. C., Musch, J., & Naumer, B. (2000). On belief bias in syllogistic reasoning. *Psychological Review, 107,* 852–884.

Newstead, S. E. (1995). Gricean implicatures and syllogistic reasoning. *Journal of Memory & Language, 34*(5), 644–664

Newstead, S. E., & Griggs, R. A. (1999). Premise misinterpretation and syllogistic reasoning. *Quarterly Journal of Experimental Psychology, 52A,* 1057–1075.

Newstead, S. E., Handley, S. J., & Buck, E. (1999). Falsifying mental models: Testing the predictions of theories of syllogistic reasoning. *Memory and Cognition, 27,* 344–354.

Newstead, S. E., Pollard, P., Evans, J. St. B. T., & Allen, J. L. (1992). The source of belief bias in syllogistic reasoning. *Cognition, 45,* 257–284.

Newton, E. J., & Roberts, M. J. (2000). An experimental study of strategy development. *Memory and Cognition, 28,* 565–573.

Oakhill, J., & Johnson-Laird, P. N. (1985). The effect of belief on the spontaneous production of syllogistic conclusions. *Quarterly Journal of Experimental Psychology, 37A,* 553–570.

Oakhill, J., Johnson-Laird, P. N., & Garnham, A. (1989). Believability and syllogistic reasoning. *Cognition, 31,* 117–140.

Polk, T. A., & Newell, A. (1995). Deduction as verbal reasoning. *Psychological Review, 102,* 533–566.

Rips, L. J. (1994). *The psychology of proof.* Cambridge, MA: MIT Press.

Roberts, M. J. (1993). Human reasoning: deduction rules or mental models, or both? *Quarterly Journal of Experimental Psychology, 46A,* 569–589.

Roberts, M. J. (1997). On dichotomies and deductive reasoning research. *Current Psychology of Cognition, 16,* 196–204.

Roberts, M. J. (2000a). Individual differences in reasoning strategies: A problem to solve or an opportunity to seize? In W. Schaeken, G. De Vooght, A. Vandierendonck, & G. d'Ydewalle (Eds.), *Deductive reasoning and strategies* (pp. 23–48). Mahwah, NJ: Lawrence Erlbaum Associates.

Roberts, M. J. (2000b). Strategies in relational inference. *Thinking and Reasoning, 6,* 1–26.

Roberts, M. J., Gilmore, D. J., & Wood, D. J. (1997). Individual differences and strategy selection in reasoning. *British Journal of Psychology, 88,* 473–492.

Roberts, M. J., Newstead, S. E., & Griggs, R. A. (2001). Quantifier interpretation and syllogistic reasoning. *Thinking and Reasoning, 7,* 173–204.

Roberts, M. J., & Newton, E. J. (2001). Inspection times, the change task and the rapid-response selection task. *Quarterly Journal of Experimental Psychology, 54A,* 1031–1048.

Roberts, M. J., & Sykes, E. D. A. (2003). Belief bias in relational inference. *Quarterly Journal of Experimental Psychology, 56A,* 131–154.

Schroyens, W., Schaeken, W., & Handley, S. J. (2003). In search of counter examples: Deductive rationality in human reasoning. *Quarterly Journal of Experimental Psychology, 56,* 1129–1145.

Stanovich, K. E., & West, R. F. (2000). Individual differences in reasoning: Implications for the rationality debate? *Behavioral and Brain Sciences, 23,* 645–665.

Thompson, V. A. (1996). Reasoning from false premises: The role of soundness in making logical deductions. *Canadian Journal of Experimental Psychology, 50,* 315–319.

Toms, M., Morris, N., & Ward, D. (1993) Working memory and conditional reasoning. *Quarterly Journal of Experimental Psychology, 46A,* 679–699.

Oakhill, J., Johnson-Laird, P. N., & Garnham, A. (1989). Believability and syllogistic reasoning. *Cognition, 31,* 117–140.

Polk, T. A., & Newell, A. (1995). Deduction as verbal reasoning. *Psychological Review, 102,* 533–566.

Rips, L. J. (1994). *The psychology of proof.* Cambridge, MA: MIT Press.

Roberts, M. J. (1993). Human reasoning: deduction rules or mental models, or both? *Quarterly Journal of Experimental Psychology, 46A,* 569–589.

Roberts, M. J. (1997). On dichotomies and deductive reasoning research.*Current Psychology of Cognition, 16,* 196–204.

Roberts, M. J. (2000a). Individual differences in reasoning strategies: A problem to solve or an opportunity to seize? In W. Schaeken, G. De Vooght, A. Vandierendonck, & G. d'Ydewalle (Eds.), *Deductive reasoning and strategies* (pp. 23–48). Mahwah, NJ: Lawrence Erlbaum Associates.

Roberts, M. J. (2000b). Strategies in relational inference. *Thinking and Reasoning, 6,* 1– 26.

Roberts, M. J., Gilmore, D. J., & Wood, D. J. (1997). Individual differences and strategy selection in reasoning. *British Journal of Psychology, 88,* 473–492.

Roberts, M. J., Newstead, S. E., & Griggs, R. A. (2001). Quantifier interpretation and syllogistic reasoning. *Thinking and Reasoning, 7,* 173–204.

Roberts, M. J., & Newton, E. J. (2001). Inspection times, the change task and the rapid-response selection task. *Quarterly Journal of Experimental Psychology, 54A,* 1031–1048.

Roberts, M. J., & Sykes, E. D. A. (2003). Belief bias in relational inference. *Quarterly Journal of Experimental Psychology, 56A,* 131–154.

Schroyens, W., Schaeken, W., & Handley, S. J. (2003). In search of counter examples: Deductive rationality in human reasoning. *Quarterly Journal of Experimental Psychology, 56,* 1129–1145.

Stanovich, K. E., & West, R. F. (2000). Individual differences in reasoning: Implications for the rationality debate? *Behavioral and Brain Sciences, 23,* 645–665.

Thompson, V. A. (1996). Reasoning from false premises: The role of soundness in making logical deductions. *Canadian Journal of Experimental Psychology, 50,* 315–319.

Toms, M., Morris, N., & Ward, D. (1993) Working memory and conditional reasoning. *Quarterly Journal of Experimental Psychology, 46A,* 679–699.

6

Modeling Something That Is Believed to Be False:
The Competition of Scripts and Models in Linear Reasoning

Vicky Dierckx
André Vandierendonck

This chapter studies the effect of the believability of a temporal ordering described by linear reasoning problems on model construction and on model maintenance. It appears harder to process premises stating an unbelievable ordering than premises stating a believable or an arbitrary ordering. Furthermore, conclusion evaluation on the basis of an unbelievable model is less accurate and slower than on the basis of a believable or neutral model. These disrupting effects prove to be quite robust and hard to control. Taken together, the findings presented in the chapter indicate that the content of the model is an important factor affecting reasoning performance.

INTRODUCTION

Within the field of categorical (e.g., Johnson-Laird & Bara, 1984), conditional (e.g., Johnson-Laird & Byrne, 1991) propositional (e.g., Johnson-Laird, Byrne, & Schaeken, 1992), modal (e.g., Bell & Johnson-Laird, 1998), and relational reasoning (e.g., Vandierendonck & De Vooght, 1996), studies have provided a substantial amount of evidence corroborating the mental models theory (e.g., Johnson-Laird & Byrne, 1991). According to this theory, reasoning is in essence a semantically based operation consisting of the construction and manipulation of mental models. These models represent possible relations between entities as conveyed in the premises. To construct a model or a set of models, reasoners first have to interpret the information in the premises and to model the premises' meaning into an integrated representation in working memory (model construction phase). On the basis of the model(s) constructed, a putative conclusion can be drawn or evaluated (conclusion generation/evaluation phase). To make sure that this conclusion necessarily follows from the premises, reasoners should try to construct alternative models of the premises in which the conclusion does not hold (conclusion validation phase). If such an alternative model can be found, the putative conclusion is falsified and should be rejected. If no falsifying model can be found, the conclusion may considered to be valid. Because working memory only has a limited capacity, the

more models have to be constructed, the harder reasoning becomes and the more mistakes are made (e.g., Johnson-Laird & Byrne, 1991; Johnson-Laird et al., 1992).

The conclusion validation phase is the critical component in the mental models theory and has been the subject of several recent studies (e.g., Bell & Johnson-Laird, 1998; Evans, Handley, Harper, & Johnson-Laird, 1999; Newstead, Handley & Buck, 1999; Polk & Newell, 1995;; Schaeken & Van der Henst, 2004; Vandierendonck, De Vooght, Desimpelaere, & Dierckx, 2000). The principal objective of these studies was to discover whether untrained reasoners, given their working memory limitations, always engage in attempts at falsifying the putative conclusion. In relational reasoning with simple spatial and temporal relations, reasoners seem to construct only one model of multiple-model problems including the indeterminate relation into the problem representation (Schaeken & Van der Henst, 2004; Vandierendonck et al., 2000). This is realized by placing a marker in the model, indicating that from that point on the relation is ambiguous (annotated mental model; Vandierendonck et al., 2000). If a conclusion to be evaluated deals with the indeterminacy, the marker is fleshed out into a fork-like structure, explicitly representing all possible relations in one single representation (see Table 6.1, right panel). If, however, the conclusion queries a determinate relation between the premise terms, the conclusion can be evaluated on the basis of the annotated model, and the model does not have to be fleshed out. The forked model may also be constructed immediately if reasoners are provided with external means, decreasing working memory load (isomeric model; Schaeken & Van der Henst, 2004).

Because untrained reasoners often do not falsify the putative conclusion, reasoning performance becomes almost totally dependent on the initial model constructed. This refocuses the attention from the conclusion validation to the model construction and conclusion generation/evaluation phase, enabling the study of other research questions. One of these questions concerns the nature of the initial model. It is important to know which model is constructed initially of a multiple-model problem and whether it is possible to influence this construction process such that, under certain circumstances, another model is built. This question is among others dealt with in recent research on relational reasoning. The aforementioned work of Vandierendonck et al. (2000) and Schaeken and Van der Henst (2004) explored the nature of the model constructed of simple relational reasoning problems. Furthermore, Rauh and colleagues (e.g., Knauff, Rauh, & Schlieder, 1995; Rauh, 2000) established that reasoners have the tendency to construct the same initial model of multiple-model problems describing more complex relations, like Allen's interval relations (e.g., "X overlaps Y from the left"). They were able to map out all these preferred models for each combination of two Allen relations. Although there is a preference for constructing a specific model first, Kuβ (cited in

Rauh, 2000) reported that it is possible to change this preference by placing the problem within a specific context that can be approached from two different perspectives. If each of these perspectives makes another model of the relation pertinent, and one of the models does not correspond to the preferred model, reasoners base their conclusion on the other model and no longer on the preferred one. Older research on categorical reasoning (e.g., Revlin, Leirer, Yopp, & Yopp, 1980; Wason & Johnson-Laird, 1972) showed that also the content of a reasoning problems determines the nature of the initial model. It was found that the content of a problem directed the interpretation of the logical quantifier and consequently the representation constructed of this interpretation. For instance, the quantifier *some* was given a universal interpretation in "some jerseys are jumpers" whereas it was interpreted as meaning "some but not all" in "some books are novels." Both interpretations are translated into different initial models.

Another research question concerning the first two phases of the mental models theory pertains to the factors influencing the model construction process and the maintenance of the model during conclusion generation or evaluation. This question does not concern what is represented in the model but the ease with which the premise information is translated into a model and the ease with which the model is kept active in working memory. In other words, the question deals with the factors influencing the amount of resources needed to construct and to maintain the mental model in working memory. One of these factors is the use of external means. Allowing reasoners to model the information externally reduces the amount of resources needed to solve the problems and often leads to a better performance (e.g., Schaeken &Van der Henst, 2004, but see Bucciarelli & Johnson-Laird, 1999).

Another relevant factor that may affect the amount of resources needed during model construction and maintenance may be the content of a reasoning problem. The meaning of the relation to be represented may determine not only the interpretation of the premise information, as contended before, but also the ease with which a model can be constructed and kept active in working memory. It may be harder to represent a relation that is believed to be false and to maintain this representation in working memory than to represent and maintain a relation that is believed to be true. This hypothesis is explored in this chapter, working with temporal linear reasoning problems.

REASONING ABOUT SCRIPT RELATIONS

People have a lot of experience with the temporal order in which everyday actions are executed. This knowledge is represented in long-term memory (LTM) as a cognitive schema commonly referred to as a script (Graesser & Nakamura, 1982; Schank & Abelson, 1977). There is compelling evidence that scripts influence information processing in a number of ways. Incomplete texts, describing a situation consistent with a script, may be understood because the activated script knowledge fills in the gaps (e.g., Graesser & Nakamura, 1982). Furthermore, scripts also affect the maintenance of the information processed. If people have to recall a text describing a scriptlike situation, they also recall actions that are typical for the script, but did not appear in the text (e.g., Bower, Black, & Turner, 1979; Vandierendonck & Van Damme, 1988). Moreover, if script actions are presented in an atypical order and people are asked to reproduce the actions in the order in which these were presented to them, they have the tendency to recall the misordered actions closer to their normal position in the script (Bower et al., 1979).

In view of these powerful effects of activated scripts, it may be expected that this knowledge also plays a role when people have to reason about the temporal order of script actions. The activated script may influence the processing of the information in the model construction phase. It may for instance be easier to construct a model representing a relation that is consistent with a script and is thus believable than to construct a model representing a relation that is not consistent with a script and is hence unbelievable. This should be reflected in a difference in processing time of the two types of relations.

In the same vein, the activated script may affect the maintenance of the model in working memory. If the order represented in the model corresponds to a script, probably fewer resources are needed to keep this believable model active in working memory because of the support by the script. Consequently, more resources are left for the evaluation of the conclusion, increasing the probability of a correct and fast evaluation. On the contrary, it seems plausible that more resources are required to keep a model active in working memory that conflicts with a script. At the same time, the script order may also interfere with the order represented in the model, making it hard to keep the correct representation active. The extra amount of resources needed and the interference of the script will result in slower and less accurate evaluations of the conclusions.

These predictions were tested in a series of experiments. To this end, one- and two-model problems were created on the basis of scripts. Four types of problems were devised by combining the believability of the relation(s) described in the problems (script consistent or believable and script inconsistent or unbelievable) with the number of models that can be constructed of the problems (one- and two-model problems). Table 6.1 displays an example of each problem type together with examples of neutral problems.

The one-model believable problems describe an order of four actions, which is consistent with a script. The model that can be constructed of these problems represents a believable order of the premise terms in the sense that the order corresponds to a script. Similarly, the two-model believable problems state two believable orders of the premise terms, both compatible with a script. These relations can be represented in a believable annotated model, which can be fleshed out later in a forked structure representing two possible and believable orders.

To create the unbelievable problems, one script action was put out of order. In the one-model unbelievable problems, the order of the last and the last-but-one action was switched and in the two-model unbelievable problems, the first action of the script was moved to the last premise, locating the action at the last or last-but-one-position in the script. The model constructed of the relation of the one- and the two-model unbelievable problems is unbelievable for both problems because the order represented in this model violates the script order.

We also created one- and two-model neutral problems. These problems described an arbitrary relation between actions selected from different scripts (see bottom of Table 6.1). Because processing these problems will not activate a script, comparison of these problems with the one- and two-model believable and unbelievable problems reveals whether script knowledge either facilitates or inhibits model construction and conclusion evaluation (cf. Evans, 2000).

Table 6.1.
An Example of Each Problem Type.

One-Model Problems	Two-Model Problems
Believable Problems	
Preparing speech before being announced	Putting on beachwear before looking for chair
Being announced before mounting the podium	Looking for a chair before sunbathing
Mounting the podium before giving speech	Looking for a chair before diving into the sea
	S
P B M G	P L
	D
Unbelievable Problems	
Being caught before being arrested	Stretching muscles before running distance
Being arrested before serving one's time	Running distance before taking a shower
Serving one's time before being condemned	Running distance before putting on running clothes
	T
B A S C	S R
	R
Neutral Problems	
Being caught before diving into the sea	Mounting the podium before sunbathing
Diving into the sea before preparing speech	Sunbathing before being condemned
Preparing speech before stretching muscles	Sunbathing before putting on running clothes
	B
B D P S	M S
	P

In a first experiment the premises were presented sequentially and in a self-paced manner, allowing registration of the time needed to process each premise separately. After the last premise had been presented, participants were requested to evaluate a proposed conclusion. This conclusion always expressed a relation between the third and the fourth premise term. For the one-model problems, this was a determinate relation, and for the two-model problems, an indeterminate one. Filler problems were added with a conclusion querying another relation. Reasoners had to indicate whether the conclusion was correct, incorrect or equivocal because of insufficient information. After the experiment, the reasoners' script knowledge was tested by a questionnaire, and the problems, for which they were unable to put the actions in the correct script order, were removed from the analyses. The rationale behind this selection is that script knowledge is a precondition for script activation.

The one- and two-model problems were analyzed separately with respect to premise processing time, solution accuracy, and solution time. Because only the last premise differed between the believable and unbelievable problems, only the processing time of this premise is considered here. The analyses revealed an effect of the believability of the order described in the problems on model construction and on conclusion evaluation. For the one-model problems, participants required more time to process the last premise of an unbelievable problem (5.6 s) than the corresponding premise of a believable problem (3.3 s) and a neutral problem (3.2 s). A similar difference was observed for the two-model problems (6.7 s, 5.3 s and 4.5 s, respectively). However, there was no difference in the processing time of the last premise between the believable and neutral problems. Script knowledge thus seems not to be explicitly relied on to model the premises. However, this knowledge may have influenced premise processing more indirectly. Indeed, due to the active script, reasoners might have been aware of the problems describing a typical order of the actions, and this awareness may have resulted in a more stable representation of the information, compared with the model constructed of the arbitrary relation of the neutral problems. If, on the contrary, the information in the last premise conflicts with the script, this premise will draw the attention of the reasoners and will probably bring about an explicit comparison between what has to be represented and what is true following the script. This process will require extra time and will possibly result in a less stable representation of the information.

These expectations about the differences in the stability of the model were confirmed by the accuracy data. As can be seen in the Table 6.2, the believable problems were solved more accurately than the unbelievable and the neutral problems. Furthermore, the neutral one-model problems were solved more accurately than the unbelievable one-model problems. Conclusion evaluation is thus facilitated if the model represents a believable ordering of the premise terms and is inhibited—at least for the one-model problems—if the model represents an unbelievable order. The time needed to evaluate the conclusions only reflected a slowing due to belief: Both the one- and the two-model unbelievable problems were solved more slowly than the neutral problems, which were solved equally fast as the believable problems (see Table 6.2).

Table 6.2
The Accuracy (ACC) and Conclusion EvaluationTimes (ET) as a Function of the
Believability of the Model and the Number of Models That Can Be Constructed
of the Problems

	One-Model Problems ACC (%) ET (s)		Two-Model Problems ACC (%) ET (s)	
Believable model	98	4.4	64	4.3
Unbelievable model	67	6.2	36	7.0
Neutral model	91	4.4	42	5.0

These findings show that the believability of the order of the terms is an important factor affecting the ease with which a model can be constructed and be maintained in working memory during conclusion evaluation. A possible critique, however, concerns a covariation between the believability of the order to be represented in a model and the believability of the last premise. Every unbelievable problem consists of one unbelievable premise, whereas every believable problem consists only of believable premises. Because previous research (e.g., Thompson, 1996) showed that the believability of the premises affects reasoning performance, the poorer and slower conclusion evaluation of the unbelievable problems may be due to the unbelievable premise and not to the unbelievable model. Furthermore, the believability of the model, the believability of the conclusion, and the validity of the conclusion did not vary systematically between the different types of problems. The believable conclusions of the one-model believable problems were always valid, whereas for the one-model unbelievable problems the believable conclusions were always invalid. Likewise, the indeterminate conclusions of the two-model believable problems were always believable, whereas the indeterminate conclusions of the two-model unbelievable problems could be believable or unbelievable depending on the order of the terms in the conclusion. To unravel these entanglements a new experiment was run in which all problems consisted of believable premises and the conclusions to be evaluated were believable valid as well as invalid ones.

UNFOLDING SOURCES OF BELIEVABILITY

To create believable and unbelievable problems consisting of only believable premises, an extra premise term was added to the previously used problems. In each problem, this term belonged to the same script as the other four actions but did not have a fixed position in the script. This extra premise term was inserted as the first term of the last premise such that this premise was also believable for the unbelievable problems (see Table 6.3). Yet the overall order of the premise terms of the unbelievable problems remained unbelievable.

Table 6.3
An Illustration of the Adaptation of the Unbelievable Problems.

One-Model Unbelievable Problem	Two-Model Unbelievable Problem
Being caught before being arrested	Stretching muscles before running distance
Being arrested before serving one's time	Running distance before sneezing
Serving one's time before swearing frequently	Sneezing before taking a shower
Swearing frequently before being condemned	Sneezing before putting on running clothes
	T
B A S SW C	S R SN
	P

All conclusions, presented for evaluation, were believable. The valid conclusions always queried a determinate relation between two premise terms, whereas the invalid conclusions were determinate for the one-model problems and indeterminate for the two-model problems. To create invalid believable conclusions for the one-model problems, the relation between the extra premise term and the second premise term was queried.

We hypothesized before that a script only interferes with model construction if there is an explicit clash between the information to be modeled and the script. In the new problem set, all premises provided information consistent with a script, and, in line with the hypothesis, no differences in processing time of the last premise were expected or detected. Script knowledge, however, did influence the maintenance of the model as reflected in the accuracy and the conclusion evaluation time. Table 6.4 displays the accuracy of the evaluation of the valid and invalid conclusions of the different types of problems. As could be expected, solutions of valid problems were more accurate than solutions of invalid problems, both in one- and two-model problems. More important for our present concerns, however, is that believable and unbelievable problems with a valid conclusion were solved more accurately than neutral problems, both in the one-model and two-model conditions. This performance difference may be due to a facilitating influence of the script because all valid conclusions query a relation belonging to a believable part of a model, except for the one-model unbelievable problems. Indeed, the first part of the model, representing the first three premises, is for both types of problems consistent with a script. The activated script may thus support the activation of this part of the model, making it easier to keep the correct representation active in working memory. This facilitating influence, however, was not reflected in the evaluation time. The valid conclusions of the unbelievable problems were still evaluated more slowly than the valid conclusions of the believable and neutral problems.

The invalid conclusion problems reflected only impairment due to the believability of the model. The unbelievable problems were solved less accurately and more slowly than the believable and the neutral problems (see Table 6.4). Hence, in contrast to the first experiment, the believable problems were solved equally accurately as the neutral problems. This difference may be due to sample variations. To observe a facilitating influence of script knowledge on the two-model believable problems, reasoners should correctly represent the indeterminate relation of these problems. Possibly, the reasoners of the second study might have experienced more difficulties to correctly represent the problems through which no facilitation could be observed. For the one-model believable problems, however, the absence of facilitation may be due to the status of the unfixed term of which the relation is queried in the invalid conclusions. Because the term may occur anywhere in the sequence, script knowledge does not necessarily bring about a stable representation of this term relative to the other terms. Consequently, during conclusion evaluation, doubts might have been risen about the exact position of the term in the sequence.

Table 6.4

The Accuraccy (ACC) and the EvaluationTime (ET) of the Valid and Invalid Conclusions of the One-Model and Two-Model Problems as a Function of the Believability of the Model

	Valid conclusions ACC (%) ET (s)		Invalid conclusions ACC (%) ET (s)	
One-model problems				
Believable model	94	4.5	82	5.5
Unbelievable model	93	6.0	77	6.9
Neutral model	83	4.9	83	5.3
Two-model problems				
Believable model	89	4.9	46	5.8
Unbelievable model	92	6.5	28	6.7
Neutral model	80	5.6	47	5.0

Another noteworthy aspect of the results is that the data are also consistent with the hypothesis that only one model is constructed to solve the one- and two-model problems (Schaeken &Van der Henst, 2004; Vandierendonck et al., 2000). If two separate models had been constructed of the two-model problems, more working memory resources would have been needed to evaluate the valid conclusions of these problems than to evaluate the valid conclusions of the one-model problems. This would have been translated in a worse performance for the two-model problems. Yet, as can be seen in Table 6.4, the accuracy of the valid conclusions of both problems is at the same level.

However, the low accuracy of the two-model problems with an invalid conclusion also reveals that reasoners often fail to consider both possible orders of the premise terms. Closer inspection of the actual evaluations indeed showed that reasoners have the tendency to evaluate these conclusions on the basis of a simple model in which the third premise term is only represented before the fourth premise term instead of at the same level. Nonetheless, reasoners needed more time to process the last premise of the two-model problems--disclosing that the order is indeterminate—than they needed to process the last premise of the one-model problems. This suggests that reasoners seem to have noticed the indeterminacy of the two-model problems but failed to add a marker or to construct an isomeric model, or it suggests that this information must have been lost or ignored during conclusion evaluation.

THE DISRUPTING EFFECT OF BELIEF

These two experiments show an important influence of the believability of the problem on model construction and on model maintenance during conclusion evaluation. It proved to be harder to construct and to maintain a model representing an unbelievable relation in working memory than a model representing a believable relation. Although a few indications of facilitation were observed, this effect could almost entirely be characterized as a disrupting influence of the believability of the relation. The simultaneous activation of a script and of a model, representing a relation inconsistent with that script, seems to cause some kind of competition between both types of representations, making it hard to keep the correct representation active during conclusion evaluation.

So it seems that working memory limitations do not only limit the search for alternative models but also constrain the first two phases of the mental models theory. Moreover, these constraints seem to be caused both by the complexity of the information to be represented and by the content of the reasoning problem. Previous studies on content effects considered the role of belief on the interpretation of the premises (e.g., Revlin et al., 1980; Wason & Johnson-Laird, 1972) and the effect of the believability of the premises (e.g., Thompson, 1996) or of the conclusion on the acceptance rate of the conclusion (e.g., Evans, Newstead, Allen, & Pollard, 1994; Newstead, Pollard, Evans, & Allen, 1992; Roberts & Sykes, 2003), but they have never explicitly taken into account the believability of the model. One exception can be found in a study by Cherubini, Garnham, Oakhill, and Morley (1998) on categorical reasoning. In the latter study, the content of the models was considered more closely. These authors hypothesized that, before any model construction takes place, reasoners retrieve an LTM representation of the relation between the end-terms of the syllogism. This LTM-based model is by definition believable. If the premises describe information compatible with this model, the information is incorporated into the model. This results in a combined model, which is believable because it represents prior knowledge. If, however, the premises describe information incompatible with the LTM model, the data of Cherubini et al. (1998) suggest that reasoners are able to discard this model and start constructing a model solely on the basis of the premise information. This way, reasoners never experience large conflicts between the model constructed and their beliefs because they seem to be able to suppress their prior knowledge before they start modeling the premises.

In our study, however, the premises are presented sequentially, and the premise that renders the model unbelievable is displayed last in the row. Although the script does not explicitly interfere with model construction until an unbelievable premise is presented, it can be assumed that the information in the first premises will activate the script. When all the premises have been integrated, and inspection of the model reveals that the relation does not correspond to the script, it will be hard, if not impossible, to suppress this script knowledge. Consequently, the large influence of belief on model maintenance may have been caused by procedural details. It might be the case then, that the believability of the model will no longer affect model maintenance if reasoners are given the opportunity to suppress their script knowledge before model construction.

CONTROL OF SCRIPT KNOWLEDGE

To investigate whether reasoners are able to control the influence of their script knowledge, a further experiment was conducted using a slightly different procedure. In this experiment, a script header preceded each linear reasoning problem. This script header could either be printed in green or in red. The green script headers were paired with the previously used one- and two-model believable problems, and the red script headers were paired with the one- and two-model unbelievable problems. Reasoners were told beforehand that a green script header indicates that the reasoning problem will deal with information that does correspond to what they know, whereas a red script header means that the problem will present information that does not correspond to their knowledge of reality. This experimental condition was compared with a control condition in which all script headers were presented in white. If reasoners are able to completely control their script knowledge, the invalid conclusions of the believable and unbelievable problems should be evaluated equally accurately in the experimental condition. In the control condition, on the contrary, similar belief effects are expected, as were observed in the previous experiment discussed in this chapter.

The results partly confirm the predictions. As can be seen in Table 6.5, the colored script header did have an effect on the accuracy of the evaluation but for the one-model problems only. The difference in accuracy between the one-model believable and one-model unbelievable problems in the control condition proved to be significantly larger than the difference in accuracy between both problems in the experimental condition. Yet, even when reasoners knew beforehand that the problem would describe information inconsistent with reality, the one-model unbelievable problems were still solved less accurately than the one-model believable problems. In fact, the color of the script header did not affect performance on the believable problems but reduced the disturbing influence of the believability of the model.

Table 6.5
ACC and ET of the Invalid Conclusions and the Premise Processing Times of the Last Premise of Both the Valid and Invalid Conclusions (PPT) as a Function of Problem Type and the Color of the Script Header

	Colored Script Header			Uncolored Script Header		
	ACC(%)	ET (s)	PPT (s)	ACC(%)	ET (s)	PPT (s)
One-Model Problems						
Believable model	86	4.5	3.9	93	5.1	3.3
Unbelievable model	73	6.4	5.5	54	5.7	4.1
Two-model problems						
Believable model	57	7.1	4.8	47	7.1	4.6
Unbelievable model	36	6.8	6.4	28	7.9	5.6

The color of the script header did not alter performance on the two-model problems. Possibly this is due to the complexity of the problems. The invalid conclusions of the two-model problems are indeterminate, and evaluating these conclusions requires fleshing out an annotated model. Moreover, the previous experiment revealed that reasoners often fail to flesh out the model, which leads them to draw the incorrect conclusion irrespective of the believability of the model. The color of the script header did not influence the conclusion evaluation time either; the invalid conclusions of the unbelievable problems were evaluated more slowly than the invalid conclusions of the believable problems (see Table 6.5).

Another interesting finding in this experiment concerns the premise processing times of the last premise (see Table 6.5). Although this premise stated a believable relation between two actions, it was processed significantly slower if it belonged to an unbelievable problem than to a believable problem, both in the experimental and in the control condition. Hence, by presenting a script header, the corresponding script is explicitly activated and brought to the attention. Due to this explicit activation, the script again interferes with model construction. In this experiment, there were no neutral problems to compare performance with. However, because about the same amount of time was needed to process the last premise of the believable problems as in the previous experiment, it seems likely that the script again has only a disrupting influence on model construction.

The results of this experiment suggest that script knowledge is hard to suppress during model construction and maintenance. Although reasoners knew beforehand that some problems would not conform to reality, they were unable to totally suppress their knowledge. Even with a colored script header, unbelievable models were harder to construct than believable models, and conclusion evaluation on the basis of an unbelievable model happened less accurately and more slowly. However, reasoners were able to evaluate the one-model unbelievable problems more correctly when they knew beforehand that the problem would describe an unbelievable relation. This suggests that they are able to protect, to some extent, the model against interference of the script. Reasoners thus have some control of the script influence on model maintenance, but this control appears to be rather restricted and may depend on the working memory load of the model.

GENERAL DISCUSSION

Recent studies raised some doubts about the existence of a separate conclusion validation phase in the reasoning process of untrained reasoners (e.g., Evans et al., 1999; Polk & Newell, 1995; Schaeken & Van der Henst, 2004; Vandierendonck et al., 2000). Reasoners often seem to construct only one model and make a final inference on the basis of this initial model. Reasoning performance thus depends on the quality of this initial model and on the maintenance of this model during conclusion generation or evaluation. The present studies showed that the content of a reasoning problem is an important factor influencing model construction and model maintenance. More specifically, it is presumed that if a reasoning problem describes a meaningful relation, the LTM representation of this relation will be activated. This representation will be addressed to interpret the information in the premises and will probably bring about a more stable representation of the information. If, however, the premises or the model constructed of the premises conflicts with the LTM representation, a vast amount of working memory resources is required to avoid interference between both types of representations. However, because these resources are limited, it proves to be hard to protect the model from interference with the LTM representation. Working memory limitations thus not only curtail the search for alternative models, but they also limit the construction and maintenance of the initial model when this model conflicts with prior knowledge.

The findings of the third experiment also revealed that the disrupting influence of people's beliefs is quite robust and hard to control. Given the assumption that beliefs come into play automatically when a reasoning problem deals with meaningful relations, the only way to control this influence is by encoding the premise information without reference to its meaning (e.g., by constructing a model of only the first letters of the premises; Dierckx, Vandierendonck, & Pandelaere, 2003) or by using means that decrease working memory load. Apparently, in our experiment, reasoners were not able to spontaneously apply an alternative encoding method. They only partly succeeded in protecting the model from interference with the script.

The present studies testify to the importance of the content of the relation described in the problems on reasoning performance. Even when only believable or neutral premises are used to describe the relation, the model representing this relation may still be unbelievable and disrupt reasoning. This is not only true for linear reasoning problems. Also in categorical reasoning, the model constructed may be believable or unbelievable. Consider, for instance, the following problem:

> No animals are inhabitants of the island.
> Some tigers are inhabitants of the island.

The model of the first premise will represent a set of animals and a set of inhabitants of the island in such a way that it is clear that no animal and no inhabitant of the island is the same individual (see Johnson-Laird & Byrne, 1991):

> [a]
> [a]
>   [i]
>   [i]

To incorporate the information of the second premise into the model, the mental token for tiger should be added so that at least one individual in the model is a tiger that lives on the island:

> [a]
> [a]
>   [i]   t{a}
>   [i]   t{a}

However, people know that tigers are animals ($t\{a\}$) and this knowledge will be available during premise processing and modeling. The relation represented in this model is thus contradictory to their knowledge of the animal kingdom. Therefore, the model of this problem is unbelievable, and LTM knowledge may interfere with the reasoning process.

Categorical reasoning problems of this type have often been used in studies investigating the effect of the believability of the conclusion (e.g., Evans et al., 1994; Newstead et al., 1992). In these studies, such problems are paired with highly believable or unbelievable conclusions that can either be valid or invalid. However, closer inspection of the problems presented reveals that believable valid conclusions and unbelievable invalid conclusions go together with believable model problems, whereas unbelievable valid conclusions and believable invalid conclusions go with unbelievable model problems. To illustrate this, consider again the former example of the inhabitants of the island:

> No animals are inhabitants of the island.
> Some tigers are inhabitants of the island.

The valid conclusion "some tigers are not animals" is unbelievable, and the invalid conclusion "some animals are not tigers" is believable. Because both types of conclusions have to be evaluated on the basis of an unbelievable model (cf. supra), it can be expected that their evaluation will occur less accurately. In other words, the unbelievable valid conclusion should be less often accepted, and the believable invalid conclusion should be less often rejected. The opposite can be predicted for the believable model problems:

> Some animals are inhabitants of the island.
> No tiger is an inhabitant of the island.

The model constructed of this problem may have the following form:

$$
\begin{array}{ll}
a & [i] \\
a & [i] \\
 & [t]\,\{a\} \\
 & [t]\,\{a\}
\end{array}
$$

Because no tiger lives on the island and not every animal has to live on the island (if *some* is interpreted as meaning *not all*), the model is believable. The valid conclusion of this problem, "Some animals are not tigers," is believable whereas the invalid conclusion "some tigers are not animals" is unbelievable. Given that both types of problems have to be evaluated on a believable model, it may be expected that the evaluation should occur more accurately. So the valid conclusions should be more often accepted, and the invalid conclusions should be more often rejected.

The predicted data pattern is indeed found in many studies. Invalid believable conclusions are accepted more often than invalid unbelievable conclusions, and, albeit not in every study, valid believable conclusions are accepted more often than valid unbelievable conclusions.

With this reanalysis of the problems, we do not want to claim that the believability of the model is the only factor influencing reasoning performance. Based on the believability of the model alone, we cannot explain the equal performance on the valid believable and unbelievable problems as detected in some studies (e.g., Evans et al., 1994) or the disappearance of the belief bias effect when determinate problems are presented (e.g., Newstead et al., 1992). Nor can we explain why Roberts and Sykes (2003) have found similar belief bias effects with problems having an unbelievable model. We only want to point out that, in these studies, the believability of the model influencing reasoning performance, is entangled with the believability and the validity of the conclusion and that it may be important to control or manipulate this factor in future experiments. The challenge is to find ways to control or manipulate the believability of the premises, the believability of the model, the believability of the conclusion, and the validity of the conclusion, independently of one another.

ACKNOWLEDGMENT

This chapter presents research results of the Belgian program Interuniversity Poles of Attraction initiated by the Belgian State, Prime Minister's Office, Science Policy programming, Grants nr. P3/31 and nr. P4/19 from the Department of Science Policy, to the second author. The scientific responsibility is assumed by its authors.

REFERENCES

Bell, V. A., & Johnson-Laird, P. N. (1998). A model theory of modal reasoning. *Cognitive Science, 22,* 25–51.

Bower, G. H., Black, J. B., & Turner, T. J. (1979). Script in memory for text. *Cognitive Psychology, 11,* 177–220.

Bucciarelli, M, & Johnson-Laird, P. N. (1999). Strategies in syllogistic reasoning. *Cognitive Science, 23,* 247–303.

Cherubini, P., Garnham, A., Oakhill, J., & Morley, E. (1998). Can any ostrich fly? Some new data on belief bias in syllogistic reasoning. *Cognition, 69,* 179–218.

Dierckx, V., Vandierendonck, A. & Pandelaere, M. (2003). Is model construction open to strategic decisions? An exploration in the field of linear reasoning. *Thinking and Reasoning, 9,* 97–131.

Evans, J. St. B. T. (2000). Thinking and believing. In J. A. Garcia-Madruga, N. Carriedo & M. J., Gonzalez-Labra (Eds.), *Mental models in reasoning* (pp. 41–55). Madrid, Spain: UNED.

Evans, J. St. B. T., Handley, S. J., Harper, C. N. J., & Johnson-Laird, P. N. (1999). Reasoning about necessity and possibility: A test of the mental model theory of deduction. *Journal of Experimental Psychology: Learning, Memory and Cognition, 25,* 1495–1513.

Evans, J. St. B. T., Newstead, S. E., Allen, J. L., & Pollard, P. (1994).

Debiasing by instruction: The case of belief bias. *European Journal of Cognitive Psychology, 6,* 263–285.

Graesser, A. C., & Nakamura, G. V. (1982). The impact of schema on comprehension and memory. *The Psychology of Learning and Motivation, 16,* 59–109.

Johnson-Laird, P. N., & Bara, B. G. (1984) Syllogistic inference. *Cognition, 16,* 1–62.

Johnson-Laird, P. N., & Byrne, R. M. J. (1991). *Deduction.* Hove, UK: Psychology Press.

Johnson-Laird, P. N., Byrne, R. M. J., & Schaeken, W. (1992). Propositional reasoning by model. *Psychological Review, 99,* 418–439.

Knauff, M., Rauh, R., & Schlieder, C. (1995). Preferred mental models in qualitative spatial reasoning: A cognitive assessment of Allen's calculus. In J. D. Moore & J. F. Lehman (Eds.), *Proceedings of the 17th annual conference of the Cognitive Science Society* (pp. 200– 205). Hillsdale, NJ: Lawrence Erlbaum Associates.

Newstead, S. E., Handley, S. J., & Buck, E. (1999). Falsifying mental models: Testing the predictions of theories of syllogistic reasoning. *Memory and Cognition, 27,* 344–354.

Newstead, S. E., Pollard, P., Evans, J. St. B. T., & Allen, J. L. (1992). The source of belief bias in syllogistic reasoning. *Cognition, 45,* 257–284.

Polk, T. A., & Newell, A. (1995). Deduction as verbal reasoning. *Psychological Review, 102,* 533–566.

Rauh, R. (2000). Strategies of constructing preferred mental models in spatial relational inference. In W. Schaeken, G. De Vooght, A. Vandierendonck, & G. d'Ydewalle (Eds.), *Deductive reasoning and strategies* (pp. 177–190). Mahwah, NJ: Lawrence Erlbaum Associates.

Revlin, R., Leirer, V. O., Yopp, H., & Yopp, R. (1980). The belief bias effect in formal reasoning: The influence of memory on logic. *Memory and Cognition, 8,* 584–592.

Roberts, M. J. & Sykes, E. D. A. (in press). Belief bias and relational reasoning. *Quarterly Journal of Experimental Psychology.*

Schaeken, W., & Van der Henst, J.-B. (2004). Cognitive economy in relational reasoning: The role of isomeric mental models. Unpublished manuscript.

Schank, R. C., & Abelson, R. P. (1977). *Scripts, plans, goals, and understanding.* Hillsdale, NJ: Lawrence Erlbaum Associates.

Thompson, V. A. (1996). Reasoning from false premises: The role of soundness in making logical deductions. *Canadian Journal of Experimental Psychology, 50,* 315–319.

Vandierendonck, A., & De Vooght, G. (1996). Evidence for mental model–based reasoning: A comparison of reasoning with time and space concepts. *Thinking and reasoning, 2,* 249–272.

Vandierendonck, A., De Vooght, G., Desimpelaere, C., & Dierckx, V. (2000). Model construction and elaboration in spatial syllogisms. In W. Schaeken, G. De Vooght, A. Vandierendonck & G. d'Ydewalle (Eds.), *Deductive reasoning and strategies* (pp. 191–207). Mahwah, NJ: Lawrence Erlbaum Associates.

Vandierendonck, A., & Van Damme, R. (1988). Schema anticipation in recall: Memory process or report strategy? *Psychological Research, 50,* 116–122.

Wason, P. C. & Johnson-Laird, P. N. (1972). *Psychology of reasoning: Structure and content.* London: Batsford.

7

The Mental Models Theory of Relational Reasoning:
Premises' Relevance, Conclusions' Phrasing and Cognitive Economy

Walter Schaeken   –
Jean-Baptiste Van der Henst
Walter Schroyens

The mental models theory of relational reasoning postulates that individuals reason by constructing the possible models of the situation described by the premises. The present chapter reports three experiments, which focus on the fact that most multiple-model problems contain an irrelevant premise. Experiment 1 shows that problems with an irrelevant premise are easier than problems with only relevant information. Experiment 2 shows that the connective of the relevant premise of multiple-model problems with an irrelevant premise influences the connective used in the conclusion. Experiment 3 shows that a large proportion of reasoners do not construct fully explicit models, but what we call isomeric models, that is, models in which the indeterminacy is represented more or less implicitly. These experiments support the claim that reasoners do not blindly construct multiple models and that they pay special attention to the relevant information in the premises.

INTRODUCTION

Many daily deductions depend on relations between things. Suppose you want to pack your hand luggage for the plane. Your colleague gives you the following information:

Book *A* is heavier than book *B*.
Book *C* is lighter than book *B*.

On the basis of this information you can infer that book *A* is heavier than book *C*. Such inferences hinge on relations that are internal to propositions. Consequently, the propositional calculus cannot capture their validity; it handles only external connections between connections. Predicate calculus can capture such an inference.

It includes propositional calculus but additionally introduces machinery for dealing with the internal structure of propositions.

People, however, can often easily make such relational inferences. There are three sorts of relational deductions. First, some relations are transitive, as in the previous example. Second, some relations are intransitive and support valid deductions, as in the following example:

> Maddy is the mother of Maryse.
> Maryse is the mother of Anna.
> Therefore, Maddy is not the mother of Anna.

Third, some relations are nontransitive and support neither transitive nor intransitive inferences, as in the following example:

> Kristien is next to Niki.
> Niki is next to Wim.

If they are arranged in a circle, than Kristien is next to Wim, but, if they are arranged in a line, then Kristien is not next to Wim.

In this chapter, we focus on transitive inferences. Our plan is to begin with a short historical overview. Next, we describe in some detail the mental models theory of relational reasoning. Finally, we report three experimental studies, which might seem at first sight quite diverse but that have led us to reach a conclusion about the importance of cognitive economy in the mental models theory.

TRANSITIVE RELATIONAL REASONING: A BRIEF REVIEW

Early research on transitive relation inferences focused on what is called three-term series problems. These are problems in which three terms are introduced, such as the following:

> *A* is heavier than *B*.
> *B* is heavier than *C*.

Psychologists have sought to resolve the nature of the mental representation of the premises and the mental processes by which the conclusion is derived. There has been considerable controversy over whether those representations and processes are primarily verbal or visual.

According to the linguistic approach (e.g., Clark, 1969a, 1969b), reasoning relies on linguistic principles, and the type of relational terms used in the premises is the main factor of interest. One important principle is the principle of lexical marking: Premises with marked terms are harder to process and represent than premises with unmarked terms. Other principles postulated by Clark are the principle of the primacy of functional relations and the principle of congruency. The more difficult it is to represent the information in the problem, the harder the reasoning process is. This approach can be seen as an early precursor to inference-rule theories (e.g., Braine & O'Brien, 1998; Rips, 1994).

The competing view of the linguistic model is the analogical approach (De Soto, London, & Handel, 1965; Huttenlocher, 1968). According to this approach, people construct a representation of the premises, which is isomorphic to the situation portrayed in the premises. Characteristically, this representation takes the form of a mental spatial array that linearly orders the items mentioned in the premises in a way that corresponds to the situation described in the premises. For instance, the information in the previous problem could be mentally represented in the following manner:

A
B
C

All the information is integrated and stored in a single representation. Consequently, reasoning is nothing more than constructing such an integrated representation of the premises and describing it. The difficulty of the reasoning process is mainly determined by the difficulty of the construction of the integrated representation. This approach can be considered a precursor to the mental models theory (Johnson-Laird, 1983).

Both approaches proposed radically different representation and reasoning processes. However, it turned out that they made similar predictions. For instance, the principle of directionality of the analogical approach leads to the same predictions as the principle of lexical marking of the linguistic approach. In response to this impasse, some theorists adopted an ecumenical viewpoint and proposed that reasoners use both linguistic and analogical representations and processes (e.g., Ormrod, 1979; Shaver, Pierson, & Lang, 1974; Sternberg, 1980, 1981a, 1981b).

THE MENTAL MODELS THEORY AND TWO-DIMENSIONAL SPATIAL PROBLEMS

Byrne and Johnson-Laird (1989) decided to take another way around the impasse. On the one hand, they worked out a more complete analogical theory, that is, the mental models theory, based on the seminal work of Johnson-Laird (1983). On the other hand, they examined problems for which the theories are susceptible to make different predictions, that is, two-dimensional problems. We now present both aspects.

The theory based on the manipulation of mental models proposes that the logical properties of relations, such as transitivity, are not explicitly represented at all but are emergent from the meanings of relations (Johnson-Laird, 1983). This contrasts with rule-based theories (e.g., Hagert, 1984), in which a transitivity meaning postulate is included. According to Byrne and Johnson-Laird (1989), reasoners first construct a model of the meaning of the premises (the model construction stage). Next, they formulate a putative conclusion on the basis of this model (the conclusion construction stage). Finally, reasoners search for a falsifying model, that is, a model that is consistent with the information in the premises but inconsistent with the putative conclusion (the conclusion validation stage). If they find such a model, they return to the second stage. If they don't find such a model, the putative conclusion is accepted as a valid conclusion.

Three-term series problems, which are one-dimensional problems, have an important disadvantage: Single-model problems support a valid conclusion, whereas multiple-model problems support no valid conclusion. It is impossible to disentangle these two factors. Byrne and Johnson-Laird (1989) concentrated on a new sort of relational problem, that is, the two-dimensional problem, in which both factors can be disentangled. Furthermore, the two sorts of theories make different predictions for different versions of these problems.

We give a more detailed account of the mental models theory by describing some different two-dimensional problems. For instance consider the following problem:

(1) A is to the right of B.
    C is to the left of B.
    D is in front of C.
    E is in front of A.
    What is the relation between D and E?

According to mental model theory (Byrne & Johnson-Laird, 1989), the reasoner should construct the following model:

C   B   A
D   E

On the basis of this model, the reasoner can infer that "D is to the left of E" (or "E is to the right of D"). Next, the reasoner tries to falsify this initial conclusion by attempting to build another model compatible with the premises. However, there is no such a model; Problem 1 is then called a one-model problem and the initial conclusion can be considered as the final conclusion.

Consider now Problems 2 and 3 with the question in Problem 1:

(2)   B is to the right of A   (3)   B is to the right of A
       C is to the left of B   C is to the left of B
       D is in front of C   D is in front of C
       E is in front of B   E is in front of A

For Problem 2, a first model can be built,

C   A   B
D   E

This model supports the conclusion "D is to the left of E". In contrast with Problem 1, another model is compatible with the premises:

A   C   B
D   E

However, both models support the same conclusion—*D* is to the left of *E*—and there is no other model compatible with the premises. Problem 2 is a multiple-model problem. For Problem 3, there are also two models, but, in contrast to Problem 2, they lead to contradictory conclusions:

C   A   B   A   C   B
D   E   E   D

Consequently, there is no determinate answer and Problem 3 is called a nonvalid conclusion problem.

According to mental models theory, Problem 2 should be more difficult than Problem 1 because it is harder to deal with two models than with one model. Moreover, Problem 3 should be more difficult than *Problem 2* because it necessarily calls for the construction of two models to reach the correct answer.

However, according to Byrne and Johnson-Laird (1989), a rule-based approach as framed in Hagert (1984) should make the opposite prediction with respect to one-model and multiple-model problems. To solve Problem 1, reasoners must infer the relation between the pair of items to which *D* and *E* (the items in the question) are directly related. To make this inference, they must use a meaning postulate that captures the transitivity of the relations in the premises. Multiple-model problems, such as Problem 2, do not require the use of such a meaning postulate. The first premise is irrelevant, and the second explicitly shows the relation between the pair of items to which *D* and *E* are related. Therefore, according to the rule-based theory of Hagert (1984), Problem 2 should be easier than Problem 1; however, the results did not corroborate this prediction. In other words, one can distinguish both theories by their ability in taking into account the indeterminacy conveyed by the first two premises of Problem 2. According to mental models theory, indeterminacy in Problem 2 leads to the construction of two models; hence, this problem should be harder than a one-model problem like Problem 1. According to Hagert's model, indeterminate premises do not trigger any specific procedure; hence, the presence of indeterminacy does not result in an increase of difficulty.

The predictions of the mental models theory (one-model problems are easier than multiple-model problems; no-valid-conclusion problems are the hardest) have been supported in a number of studies using different types of relational premises, that is, spatial (Byrne & Johnson-Laird, 1989; Carreiras & Santamaria, 1997; Roberts, 2000; Vandierendonck & De Vooght, 1996), temporal (Schaeken, Girotto & Johnson-Laird, 1998; Schaeken & Johnson-Laird, 2000; Schaeken, Johnson-Laird & d'Ydewalle, 1996a,1996b; Vandierendonck & De Vooght, 1996), and abstract relational premises (Carreiras & Santamaria, 1997).

THE CRITICISM AGAINST THE MENTAL MODELS THEORY: RIPS
(1994)

In the domain of propositional reasoning, there has been a very sensitive debate between the proponents of rule-based theories and the proponents of mental models theory. Such a debate is practically nonexistent in the field of relational reasoning because there are almost no psychologists defending a rule approach for relational reasoning. However, one noticeable exception is Rips' (1994, note 3, p. 414-415) criticism against mental model theory.

First, Rips (1994) argued that the experiments of Byrne and Johnson-Laird (1989) were not carried out precisely. He claimed that the instructions specifically requested the participants to form spatial arrays in solving the problems. Consequently, reasoners might have been biased to use an imaginal strategy that favored the predictions of the mental model theory. It is not so difficult to refute this argument. On the one hand, how could participants respond in this way if they had never formed a spatial image? On the other hand, and more important, the studies of temporal reasoning (Schaeken et al., 1996a, 1996b) and abstract relational reasoning (Carreiras & Santamaria, 1997) gave no instruction about imagining arrays. Nevertheless, these studies showed exactly the same pattern as the studies on spatial reasoning: They support the main predictions of the mental models theory.

Second, Rips (1994) claimed that the method of counting the number of models in these problems was inconsistent with the method of counting for other types of inferences, for which a problem requires more than one model only if additional models rule out potential conclusions that are inconsistent with the initial model. This is a correct criticism: The mental models theory postulates that reasoners do not bother to construct alternative models that differ in ways that are irrelevant to the task at hand. However, one might argue that the procedure in most of the recent relational reasoning experiments makes it hard for reasoners to do this. Indeed, there is no difference between the first two premises of the multiple-model problems and the no-valid-conclusion problems. Only the fourth premise is different: It is this premise that turns the problems into no-valid-conclusion problems. Because most recent experiments use a sequential premise presentation procedure, the reasoner cannot know that it is unnecessary to construct the alternative model until they have solved the problem.

Third, Rips (1994) reflected on the version of the rule-based theories that was used by Byrne and Johnson-Laird (1989) to contrast their theory and predictions. Rips argued there is no reason to suppose that the final length of a derivation is the only pertinent factor in a rule-based theory. Searching for a correct proof can be sidetracked by the presence of irrelevant information, such as the first premise of the multiple-model problems. Indeed, one needs all premises to solve the one-model problem in the Byrne and Johnson-Laird study, but one can solve the multiple-model problem without reading the first premise.

It is indeed possible that an irrelevant premise could complicate the search for a derivation. On the one hand, Schaeken et al.'s (1996a) fifth experiment compared temporal one-model problems containing an irrelevant premise with one-model problems containing no irrelevant premise:

A before *B*	*A* before *B*
B before *C*	*B* before *C*
D while *B*	*D* while *A*
E while *C*	*E* while *C*

What is the relation between *D* and *E*?

For the problem on the left, you don't need the first premise; for the problem on the right, you need all premises. No difference was found between these two sorts of problems (in terms of accuracy and latency), so it would seem that an irrelevant premise does not lead reasoners astray. On the other hand, Vandierendonck and De Vooght (1996) observed that, for spatial reasoning (but not for temporal reasoning), one-model problems without an irrelevant premise were solved better than one-model problems with an irrelevant premise. Moreover, they observed faster reading times on both spatial and temporal one-model problems without an irrelevant premise than for one-model problems with an irrelevant premise. Therefore, the evidence is inconclusive and, very important, only based on one-model problems. Indeed, an even more adequate comparison would include multiple-model problems both with and without an irrelevant premise. Schaeken et al. (1998) made this comparison. We now describe this study in more detail, because we want to reinterpret the findings.

THE EFFECT OF AN IRRELEVANT PREMISE

To build multiple-model problems without irrelevant premises, Schaeken et al. (1998) designed a new sort of problem. We describe the spatial problems that were presented in the study in detail.

The participants were asked to imagine two kinds of cards. One kind had two cells, each of which contained a geometrical shape, as in the following cases:

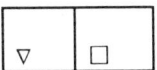

The other kind had only one cell, which contained a letter:

In addition to the shape or the letter, a symbol could also appear in the cells: * or $.

With this kind of materials, Schaeken et al. (1998) developed one-model and multiple-model problems with and without an irrelevant premise. Consider Problem 5, a one-model problem with no irrelevant premise:

(5)   The square is on the left of the triangle.

The triangle is on the left of C.
* is in the same cell as the square.
$ is in the same cell as C.
What is the relation between * and $?

This problem is consistent with one model:

The model supports the conclusion that the * is on the left of the $. If reasoners solve this problem using rules of inference, they must infer from the first two premises the relation between the items to which * and $ are directly related.

Consider Problem 6, a one-model problem with an irrelevant first premise:

(6)   The square is on the left of the triangle.
The triangle is on the left of C.
* is in the same cell as the triangle.
$ is in the same cell as C.
What is the relation between * and $?

This problem is consistent with one model:

The model supports the conclusion that the * is on the left of the $. If reasoners solve this problem using rules of inference, they can ignore the first premise because the second premise explicitly gives the relation between the two items to which * and $ are directly related.

Consider *Problem 7*, a multiple-model problem with no irrelevant premise:

(7)   The square is on the same card as the triangle.
The triangle is at the left of C.
* is in the same cell as the square.
$ is in the same cell as C.
What is the relation between * and $?

This problem is consistent with at least two distinct models:

Both of these models, however, support the conclusion that the * is on the left of the $. If reasoners use rules of inference, they must infer from the first pair of premises the relation between the items (*C* and square) to which * and $ are directly related.

Consider Problem 8, a multiple-model problem with an irrelevant premise:

(8)   The square is on the same card as the triangle.
The triangle is on the left of *C*.
* is in the same cell as the triangle.
$ is in the same cell as *C*.
What is the relation between * and $?

This problem is consistent with at least two distinct models:

Both models, however, support the conclusion that the * is on the left of the $. According to the rule-based model of Hagert (1984), reasoners should ignore the first premise, because the second premise explicitly gives the relation between the two items (*C* and triangle) to which * and $ are directly related. Schaeken et al. (1998) presented also temporal problems.

Eight versions of each problem were constructed. First, four versions were constructed by systematically manipulating the spatial or temporal relations (*before* and *after*) in the first two premises. In the first version, both premises contained *before*, and in the second version the first premise contained *before* and the second *after*. The first premise of the third version contained *after* and the second premise *before*, and in the fourth version both premises contained *after*. We then constructed two different variants of each of the four versions by manipulating the order of the third and fourth premises and the order of the two items in the final question.

The 280 participants were tested in one group. The participants received one spatial problem and one temporal problem. Half of the participants were given the spatial problem first; the other half began with the temporal problem. Before receiving the second problem, the participants had to solve four filler items (two categorical syllogisms and two propositional problems).

The number of correct responses for the problems were as follows:

One-model problem with an irrelevant premise: 64%
One-model problem without an irrelevant premise: 66%
Multiple-model problem with an irrelevant premise: 56%
Multiple-model problem without an irrelevant premise: 43%

These data show not only that one-model problems were reliably easier than multiple-model problems (65% vs. 50%) but also that one-model problems without an irrelevant premise were reliably easier than multiple-model problems without an irrelevant premise (66% vs. 43%). Moreover, there was no significant difference between the two sorts of one-model problems. Therefore, Schaeken et al. (1998) concluded that their findings were in accordance with the mental models theory and were very problematic for Rips' (1994) note: Contrary to his claim, multiple-model problems without an irrelevant premise were still harder than one-model problems without such an irrelevant premise.

What Schaeken et al. (1998), however, did not really discuss was the finding that, especially, the multiple-model problem without an irrelevant premise was harder to solve than the multiple-model problem with an irrelevant premise. In other words, these results seem to indicate the opposite of Rips' (1994) claim: An irrelevant premise with multiple-model problems seems to make reasoning easier. This would, however, imply that reasoners pay more attention to the relevant part of the problem. Or, in other words, one could interpret these results as evidence for the claim that there is no blind construction of multiple models.

In the next section, we describe another study that indicates that the relevant part of a problem has somehow a special status.

THE WORDING OF THE CONCLUSION

Almost all studies devoted to relational reasoning deal with the performance question: How good people are with relational inferences? Hence, the comparison of all theoretical hypotheses focused on performance results and the predictions were drawn from problem difficulty. Many factors linked to problem difficulty were studied, such as the number of models, the length of the formal derivation, the number of premises, the linguistic form of premises (affirmative, such as "John is taller than Paul", or negative, such as "Paul is not as tall as John"), or the markedness of adjectives (marked adjectives, such as *shorter* and unmarked adjectives, such as *taller*). However, no study has ever investigated the influence of these factors on the type of conclusions that people formulate. We do not know anything about the way relational premises influence the wording of the conclusion. It is rather surprising that psychologists of reasoning have ignored this question because in another field of syllogistic reasoning, namely reasoning involving quantifiers, such as *all, none, some, some-not*, this issue was one of the first to be investigated (Woodworth & Sells, 1935) and has been extensively explored in a number of studies (for a review, see Evans, Newstead, & Byrne, 1993). It is well known as the atmosphere issue. Empirical results show that universal premises ("all *A* are *B*") prompt universal conclusions, particular premises ("some *A* are *B*") prompt particular conclusions, affirmative premises prompt affirmative conclusions, and negative premises prompt negative conclusions.

What about relational reasoning? Does the linguistic form of the premises affect the linguistic form of the conclusion or not? Does the way to construct and inspect mental models influence the type of conclusions formulated? Does the question asked in a relational problem have an effect on the conclusion? Van der Henst and Schaeken (2005) tackled these important but traditionally unaddressed questions. Consider the following problems:

(10)   A is to the left of B.
        B is to the left of C.

(11)   B is to the right of A.
        C is to the right of B.

(12)   B is on the left of C.
        A is to the left of B.

The question is same for each: What is the relation between A and C? All these problems are logically equivalent and support the same logical conclusion. However, they are also linguistically distinct. Two problems use the comparative *left* and the other uses the comparative *right*. What could be the impact of this difference on the conclusion? Moreover, the model construction is also different: For Problems 10 and 11, the mental model will be built in a left-to-right direction, and for Problem 12, it will be built in a right-to-left direction. Will this difference be reflected by the conclusion expressed? Similarly, the question asked for these problems has a left-to-right direction (i.e. it first mentions the left-side element of the model and then the right-side element) but what would happen if it had a right-to-left direction, such as "What is the relation between C and A?"

In their study, Van der Henst and Schaeken (2005), manipulated a number of factors and tested a number of predictions. We do not go into the details of the predictions here, but we present the factors they manipulated and the results they obtained. They used two-dimensional spatial problems as Problem 1 and 2. The question asked in each problem always concerned the last two elements introduced: D and E. Item D was always to the left of E. The six following factors were manipulated:

The *relational term* of the first premise: *left* vs *right*
The *relational term* of the second premise: *left* vs *right*
The number of models: one vs two models (two-model problems always had an irrelevant premise)
The *type of presentation*: simultaneous presentation (the premises were all presented together) vs sequential presentation (the premises were presented separately)
The *direction of the question*: left to right ("what is the relation between D and E?") vs right to left ("what is the relation between E and D?")
The *direction of the integration* of the last two elements into the model: left to right (for instance, A left B, B left C, D front A, E front C; for this problem, D, which is on the left side of the model is integrated before E, which is on the right side) vs right to left (for instance, A left B, B left C, E front C, D front A; for this problem, E, which is on the right side of the model, is integrated before D, which is on the left side).

174 participants participated in the experiment and solved 16 problems each. A systematic manipulation of all independent variables led to 64 problems. However, in order to limit exhaustion and bore, participants received only 16 problems: Hence, two of the six factors were investigated in a between-subjects design.

The performance results were conformed to the standard results because more errors were observed with two-model problems than with one. However, the question of interest was the influence of the type of problem and the way the problems are represented in the wording of the conclusion. How do the six factors contribute to the incidence of *left* and *right* conclusions (i.e., "*D* is to the left of *E*" and "*E* is to the right of *D*")? Only correct answers were taken into account in the analysis.

First, at the most general level, participants manifested a clear preference for left conclusions. Indeed, out of the 64 problems, 51 were answered more with left conclusions than with right conclusions whereas 12 were answered more with right conclusions than with left conclusions and 1, with 50% right and 50% left conclusions. Moreover, when the preference for right conclusions was higher, at least a third of conclusions were left, whereas, when the preference for left was higher, the minimum amount of right conclusions was only 3%. These results strongly suggest that people are prone to inspect the mental model they built in a left-to-right way.

Second, the direction of the question had a strong influence on the conclusion. Out of the 32 problems including a left-to-right question, 32 were predominantly answered with a left conclusion. In contrast, out of the 32 problems including a right-to-left question, only 19 were solved predominantly with a left conclusion, 12 with a right conclusion, and 1 with 50% of right and 50% of left conclusions. These results show that a left-to-right question enhances the predisposition to inspect the model in a left-to-right way, whereas a right-to-left question reduces that predisposition. Thus, the question is an important factor in determining the way people inspect their model.

Third, the mode of premises' presentation (simultaneous vs. sequential) also had an influence on the incidence of left and right conclusions. Out of the 32 problems including a left-to-right question, 28 exhibited a pattern in which more left conclusions were found for problems in the sequential presentation order than for problems in the simultaneous order. Four problems exhibited a reversed pattern. Similarly, out of the 32 problems including right-to-left questions, 24 exhibited a pattern in which more right conclusions were found for problems in the sequential presentation order than for problems in the simultaneous order. Eight problems exhibited a reversed pattern. In other words, the sequential presentation enhances the directional scanning elicited by the question. This could be explained by the fact that with a sequential presentation, the question is the only item available whenever subjects are about to give their answer.

Fourth, the wording of the premises had also an influence on the wording of the conclusions. When the first two premises used the comparative *left* (left-left problems), more left conclusions and fewer right conclusions were formulated than when the first two premises used the comparative *right* (right-right problems): Whereas the difference between left and right conclusions for all left-left problems had a mean of 47.3%, for right-right problems it had a mean of 29.7%. However, the influence of the form of the premises was only present for the simultaneous presentation. For the sequential presentation, right-right problems did not elicit more right conclusions than left-left problems. This indicates that when the premises are not available participants are not using the comparative introduced by the premises. This also suggests that participants are more prone to construct a linguistic representation (which relies on the linguistic form of the premises) in the case of a simultaneous presentation and are more prone to construct a model-based representation in the case of a sequential presentation.

Moreover, for two-model problems, it appeared that the conclusion was more congruent with the relevant premise than with the irrelevant one. People were more prone to use the comparative of the relevant premise in formulating their conclusion: Whereas the difference between left and right conclusions for problems with a left relevant premise (and a right irrelevant premise) had a mean of 47.3%, for problems with a 'right' relevant premise (and left irrelevant premise), it had a mean of 24.2%. However, the influence of the relevant premise was especially present with the simultaneous presentation. This again suggests that the linguistic form of the premises has an influence in the case of a simultaneous presentation.

Fifth, it could have been expected that the order in which the items are integrated into the mental models would have an influence on the conclusion formulated. In particular, one could have expected that a left-to-right integration of the last two items would have induced more left conclusions and that a right-to-left integration of the last two elements would have induced more right conclusions. However, this prediction was not confirmed. This suggests that the order in which the elements are integrated in the model does not govern the inspection process of the model.

AN ISOMERIC MENTAL MODEL:
A COGNITIVE ECONOMICAL REPRESENTATION OF A MULTIPLE-MODEL PROBLEM

To explain our new proposal about the representation of multiple-model problems, we present some findings in previous experiments that are rather problematic for the mental models theory. On the basis of these problematic findings, we propose some revisions of mental model theory based on the notion of isomeric models. Finally, we describe an experiment that supports our claim.

Byrne and Johnson-Laird (1989) hypothesized that models were constructed sequentially: Reasoners build a first model, and afterwards they build a second model and so on. One problem for this approach can be found in the data reported by Carreiras and Santamaria (1997), Schaeken et al. (1996a, 1996b; see also Schaeken & Johnson-Laird, 2000), and Vandierendonck and De Vooght

(1996). They observed that the reading time of the premise that leads to the construction of the second model (Premise 2 in Problems 2 and *3*) was longer in comparison with the second premise of a one-model problem. According to the sequential model, it is only after reading the problem, constructing the first model, and formulating the putative conclusion that reasoners start constructing a second model. Consequently, this account should predict a difference in the total latencies but not in the latencies of the critical premise.

These findings were interpreted as evidence for a somewhat different mental model theory: Reasoners construct mental models incrementally by establishing a representational foundation as soon as possible, which is updated with the incoming information. In other words, reasoners construct multiple models simultaneously. However, there is also a serious problem with this account. If reasoners constructed models simultaneously, one would expect the reading times to be longer not only for the critical premise of the problem (in comparison with a similar one-model problem) but also for the subsequent premises. Reasoners have to incorporate the incoming information in two models instead of one. However, a number of studies comparing one-model problems and two-model problems observed only a reliable difference in reading times for the critical premise but not for the subsequent ones (Carreiras & Santamaria, 1997; Schaeken & Johnson-Laird, 2000; Schaeken et al., 1996a, 1996b; Vandierendonck & De Vooght, 1996).

Both the sequential and the simultaneous versions of the model theory have another problem with the data. The general prediction of the mental models theory—the more models compatible with a problem, the harder the problem—is not fully confirmed. First, the difference between one-model and two-model problems is in most studies very small. For instance, in the five experiments of Schaeken et al. (1996a), the differences are respectively 7%, 11%, 4%, 10%, and 10% (one exception is found in Roberts, 2000, but we explain it in Experiment 2). Such a small difference is a bit surprising because two-model problems require the representation of twice as much information than single-model problems. Second, Vandierendonck et al. (2000) did not observe a significant difference between two- and three-model problems, counter to the predictions of the mental models theory.

How can one cope with these findings? We believe one can cope rather easily, if one adheres to the principle of cognitive economy. The view that people attempt to economize their cognitive resources is widely accepted in cognitive psychology. Granted that human beings have limited cognitive resources, it is reasonable to argue that a principle of economy guides the resolution of many cognitive tasks. We think that the process of constructing and manipulating models could be better described in light of the cognitive economy principle.

One way of being economical is to not represent irrelevant information. There are two sorts of irrelevant information: information not pertinent to the question and redundant information. For instance in Problem 2, the second premise is not useful, and not representing it will lead to the construction of only one model. This should reduce effort because working memory load would be roughly halved (from two to one model). However, the participant cannot know in advance that it is irrelevant and has no reason to avoid taking it into account (Van der Henst, 1999). Is it possible to avoid representing redundant information? It might be if the same premise is presented twice, but this is not the case in the problems presented earlier. But consider now not the premises of Problem 2, which are not redundant, but the two models of Problem 2, which are clearly very similar. They differ only with respect to the position of C. Indeed, if one discards C, what is represented in Model 2 is clearly redundant to what it is represented in Model 1.

A very economical way to represent information conveyed in Problem 2 is to build a representation without redundancy. Our claim is that when an indeterminacy is encountered, as in Problem 2, rather than constructing two fully explicit models, people construct a single model that captures the indeterminacy. We call this new kind of mental model an isomeric mental model. (*Isomeric* is a term of organic chemistry that expresses that functional groups can have different positions with respect to the headchain, which results in the same molecule formula and mass but a different structure and properties.) The isomeric mental model of Problem 2 could be depicted in the following manner:

$$C$$

$$
\begin{array}{cc}
A & B \\
D & E
\end{array}
$$

A single model is constructed, and the two arrows, which correspond to an annotated part of the model, indicate inside this model that there is an indeterminacy between C and A. In accordance with mental model theory, we predict that isomeric mental models are harder to construct than nonisomeric ones. We think that this new account accommodates the problem we presented in the introduction. First, the greater difficulty of two-model problems over single-model problems is due to the construction of isomeric models but not to the construction of multiple models. Consequently, the difference in performance between these two sorts of problems is expected to be low because an isomeric model is nothing more than a single model for two-model problems. Second, the reading times of the premise that requires the construction of an isomeric model will be reliably longer because the construction of the isomeric part generates cognitive effort. Third, the reading times of subsequent premises should not be much longer because the same amount of information must be integrated in the existing model.

Reasoning With Paper and Pencil: Evidence for the Existence of Isomeric Models

In the previous paragraph, we described some problems with the previous mental models accounts, which led us to hypothesize the existence of isomeric mental models. Now, we describe a study that provides us some direct evidence for the existence of isomeric models.

Schaeken and Van der Henst (2004) gave participants spatial reasoning problems and allowed them to use external aids while they performed the task. They expected that participants would benefit from the availability of external aids by reducing working memory load. However, and more important, the outcome of the manipulation of external aids should teach us something about the internal representation. On the basis of several illustrative problems in mathematics and physics, Larkin and Simon (1987) argued convincingly that external and internal spatial representations can be viewed as equivalent. Larkin and Simon stated that the creation of a mental image employs inference processes similar to those that make information explicit in the course of drawing a diagram (for a similar argument, see also Evans, 2000, and Huttenlocher, 1968).

Consequently, Schaeken and Vander Henst (2004) predicted that people would have no difficulty in using paper and pencil while they solved spatial relational problems. They also predicted that what participants would write would more closely resemble isomeric spatial models than fully explicit multiple models. However, note the authors' prediction that the use of paper and pencil would reduce the load on working memory. Participants might therefore not see the need to adopt an economical representation and might not construct isomeric models. Consequently, if there were less need to economize, such models would be less likely to occur. Hence, our methodology, far from facilitating the incidence of these models, is more likely to prevent it. We predict that a one-model problem will be easier than a two-model problem because the latter is isomeric. We also predict that a two-model problem will be harder than a no-valid- conclusion problem because for the latter the role of the isomeric part is more important than for the former.

There were three sorts of problems (one-model problem, multiple-model problems with valid answers, and no-valid-conclusions problems) and two sorts of conditions in the present experiment. The two sorts of condition were as follows: In the control condition, premises were presented on a sheet of paper, and participants had to write the answer without writing anything else; in the paper-and-pencil condition, premises were presented as in the control condition, but, additionally, we gave participants the opportunity to write and draw whatever they wanted. Half the participants solved the problems in the control condition and then the problems in the paper- and-pencil condition, and half the participants carried out the two blocks in the opposite order. Participants were presented with 18 problems (9 in each condition).

Table 7.1 presents the percentages of correct responses in the two conditions for the three sorts of problems. In the control condition, one-model problems (77%) were easier than multiple-model problems (62%),and they were easier than the no-valid conclusion problems (65%). In the paper-and-pencil condition, we obtained the same pattern: One-model problems (87%) were easier than multiple-model problems (75%) and the no-valid-conclusion problems (69%). In general, reasoners solved more problems correctly in the paper-and-pencil condition (77%) than in the control condition (68%).

However, more important for the present discussion, are the paper-andpencil data. We divided the participants into groups on the basis of what they wrote for the multiple-model and the no-valid-conclusion problems (i.e., six problems for each participant). We used a very simple criterion for categorizing the participants: They had to write the same kind of model for at least four of the six problems. If participants didn't meet this criterion, they were put in the mixed group.

Twenty-six of the 60 participants were assigned to the category of isomeric models constructors. They wrote models such as the following:

A   B   C
D   E

Some of the participants drew arrows on one dimension (as in the example); others drew arrows on the two horizontal dimensions. Other participants drew only one arrow (e.g., from B to A). A final group of participants wrote A and B next to each other, while placing the C much farther away. Eleven participants constructed two fully explicit models. Nine participants constructed only one model. Eleven participants were not consistent in what they wrote and formed the mixed group. Finally, three participants wrote nothing. It is possible that the data somewhat

Table 7.1
Percentages Correct Responses in the Two Conditions on the Three Sorts of Problems

	One-Model Problems	Multiple-Model Problems	No-Valid-conclusion Problems
Control	77	62	65
Paper-and-Pencil	87	75	69

Table 7.2
Percentages of Correct Responses in the Two Conditions for Each of the Five Categories

Category	Paper-and-Pencil Condition	Control Condition
Isomeric models	85	73
Fully explicit models	89	80
Mixed models	64	58
Only 1 model	65	51
Nothing	63	63

underestimate the incidence of isomeric models. In 25% of the no-valid-conclusion problems, reasoners constructed only one model, but they produced the correct conclusion. Such cases suggest that they placed in imagination some kind of sign in the written model, which makes clear that the premises did not determine the relation between two of the elements.

What is as important as the previous point is the relation between the accuracy data on the one hand and the paper-and-pencil data on the other hand. In Table 7.2 the relation between accuracy and paper-and-pencil data is presented.

Reasoners who wrote isomeric or fully explicit models solved significantly more problems correctly in the paper-and-pencil condition than reasoners who were in the other categories (87% vs. 64%). Interestingly, this effect was not limited to the paper-and-pencil condition. The same pattern arose in the control condition, in which the participants could not write anything down: Reasoners who wrote isomeric models or fully explicit models solved significantly more problems than reasoners in the other categories (76% vs. 57%). That the patterns of data in the control and the paper-and-pencil condition were the same strengthens our claim that the reasoning in both conditions did not really differ. The results also suggest that those participants who had a poor paper-and-pencil report (the one-model and the mixed categories) also had poorer or noisier internal representations than participants who had a relatively good paper-and-pencil report.

The present experiment corroborated the predictions of the model theory about the relative difficulty of different spatial problems. In general, one-model problems were easier than multiple-model problems, and the latter were easier than the no-valid-conclusion problems. More important, the paper-and-pencil data provided relatively direct evidence for the existence of isomeric mental model construction. The isomeric group was the largest group in the experiment. There was also a substantial but smaller group of participants who constructed fully explicit multiple models. However, as we have argued, external aids reduced the load on working memory. Hence, some participants who used isomeric models when no external aids were provided may construct fully explicit mental models when external aids are provided. For the same reason, those people who constructed isomeric models in the paper-and-pencil test would probably not construct fully explicit internal models under no-external-aid circumstances.

GENERAL DISCUSSION

The three experiments described in this chapter looked at first sight for different things: accuracy in Experiment 1, the wording of the conclusion in Experiment 2, and what was written by participants during reasoning in Experiment 3. Nevertheless, the three experiments are clearly connected around one central theme, that is, cognitive economy in reasoning. People aim at maximizing cognitive efficiency by lowering cognitive effort. On the one hand, they focus somewhat more on the relevant problem information, as Experiments 1 and 2 show. On the other hand, they often construct isomeric models. The construction of such models avoids the representation of redundant information (which is the case if one constructs fully explicit multiple models), but, at the same time, it gives reasoners the opportunity to avoid mistakes, at least if they flesh out the initial isomeric model.

We want to emphasize the importance of Experiments 1 and 2 because it softens one of the main arguments against rule-based theories. On the one hand, mental model theorists argued in the past that if a reasoner were to use formal inference rules, he or she would know what information is irrelevant (i.e., the indeterminate relation) and what information is relevant (i.e., the determinate relations). It is assumed that reasoners would use only relevant premises and disregard the indeterminacy conveyed by the irrelevant premise. Reasoners would try to apply inference rules only to relevant premises. On the other hand, the same mental model theorists argued that to construct the mental model(s) of the premises reasoners take into account all information, both the relevant and the irrelevant. Our research shows that the relevant information has a special status; in other words, it is not the case that reasoners pay as much attention to the irrelevant information as to the relevant information. Subsequent research must clarify how reasoners find out which information is more and which is less relevant.

A potential route for this research is more research about isomeric models. Experiment 3 shows that for multiple-model and no-valid-conclusion problems, a large group of reasoners does not construct fully explicit models (as the models theory predicts in the case of a good working memory), nor just one model (as the model predicts in the case of a worse working memory). This large group constructs an isomeric model, that is, a model in which the indeterminacy between two elements is implicitly represented.

The idea that cognitive effort constrains reasoning has often been advocated in the literature on reasoning (Ormerod, 2000; Payne, 1993; Schroyens, Schaeken, Fias, & d'Ydewalle, 2000). However, we think that we have provided a more detailed picture of the processes taking place in relational reasoning by arguing that people pay more attention to the relevant part and that they avoid representing redundant information. Our main argument can also be interpreted as support for recent claims that reasoners prefer to consider only one possibility at a time (see also Evans, 2000; Mynatt, Doherty, & Dragan, 1993) and that the conclusion validation stage is optional (Evans, 2000; Evans, Handley, Harper, & Johnson-Laird, 1999; Ormerod, 2000; Van der Henst, 2000, 2002; Schaeken, De Vooght, Vandierendonck, & d'Ydewalle, 2000) In other words, although reasoners are in principle capable of searching for counterexamples, in practice they are often satisfied with a plausible model of the situation. This is in perfect accordance with our cognitive economy account.

ACKNOWLEDGMENT

The research in this chapter was supported by grants from the Fund for Scientific Research-Flanders (FWO) and the Research Council of the University of Leuven.

REFERENCES

Braine, M. D. S., & O'Brien, D. P. (1998). *Mental logic.* Mahwah, NJ: Lawrence Erlbaum Associates.

Byrne, R. M. J., & Johnson-Laird, P. N. (1989). Spatial reasoning. *Journal of Memory and Language, 28,* 564–575.

Carreiras, C., & Santamaria, C. (1997). Reasoning about relations: Spatial and nonspatial problems. *Thinking and Reasoning, 3,* 309–327.

Clark, H. H. (1969a). Influence of language on solving three-term series problems. *Journal of Experimental Psychology, 82,* 205–215.

Clark, H. H. (1969b). Linguistic processes in deductive reasoning. *Psychological Review, 76,* 387–404.

De Soto, C. B., London, M., & Handel, S. (1965). Social reasoning and spatial paralogic. *Journal of Personality and Social Psychology, 2,* 293–307.

Evans, J. St. B. T (2000). What could and could not be a strategy in reasoning? In W. Schaeken, G. De Vooght, A. Vandierendonck, & G. d'Ydewalle (Eds.), *Deductive reasoning and strategies* (pp. 1–22). Mahwah, NJ, US: Lawrence Erlbaum Associates.

Evans, J. St. B. T., Handley, S. J., Harper, C. N. J., & Johnson-Laird, P. N. (1999). Reasoning about necessity and possibility: A test of the mental model theory of deduction. *Journal of Experimental Psychology: Learning, Memory and Cognition, 25,* 1495–1513.

Evans, J. St. B. T., Newstead, S. E., & Byrne, R. M. J. (1993). *Human reasoning: The psychology of deduction.* Hillsdale, NJ: Lawrence Erlbaum Associates.

Hagert, G. (1984). Modelling mental models: Experiments in cognitive modelling spatial reasoning. In T. O'Shea (Ed.), *Advances in artificial intelligence* (pp. 389–398). Amsterdam: North-Holland.

Huttenlocher, J. (1968). Constructing spatial images: A strategy in reasoning. *Psychological Review, 75,* 550–560.

Johnson-Laird, P. N. (1983). *Mental models.* Cambridge: Cambridge University Press.

Larkin, J. H., & Simon, H. A. (1987). Why a diagram is (sometimes) worth ten thousand words. *Cognitive Science, 11,* 65–100.

Mynatt, C. R., Doherty, M. E., & Dragan, W. (1993). Information relevance, working memory, and the consideration of alternatives. *Quarterly Journal of Experimental Psychology, 46A,* 759–778.

Ormerod, T. C. (2000). Mechanisms and strategies for rephrasing. In W. Schaeken, G. De Vooght, A. Vandierendonck, & G. d'Ydewalle (Eds.), *Deductive reasoning and strategies* (pp. 131–151). Mahwah, NJ: Lawrence Erlbaum Associates.

Ormrod, J. E. (1979). Cognitive processes in the solution of three-term series problems. *American Journal of Psychology, 92,* 235–255.

Payne, S. J. (1993). Memory for mental models of spatial descriptions: An episodic-construction-trace hypothesis. *Memory and Cognition, 21,* 591–603

Rips, L. J. (1994). *The psychology of proof. Deductive reasoning in human thinking.* Cambridge, MA: MIT Press.

Roberts, M. J. (2000). Strategies in relational reasoning *Thinking and Reasoning, 6,* 1–26.

Schaeken, W., De Vooght, G., Vandierendonck, A., & d'Ydewalle, G. (2000). *Deductive reasoning and strategies.* Mahwah, NJ: Lawrence Erlbaum Associates.

Schaeken, W., Girotto, V., & Johnson-Laird, P. N. (1998). The effect of irrelevant premise on temporal and spatial reasoning. *Kognitionswissenchaft, 7,* 27–32.

Schaeken, W., & Johnson-Laird, P. N. (2000). Strategies in temporal reasoning. *Thinking and Reasoning, 6,* 193–219.

Schaeken, W., Johnson-Laird, P. N., & d'Ydewalle, G. (1996a). Mental models and temporal reasoning. *Cognition, 60,* 205–234.

Schaeken, W., Johnson-Laird, P. N., & d'Ydewalle, G. (1996b). Tense, aspect and temporal reasoning. *Thinking and Reasoning, 2,* 309–327.

Schaeken, W., & Van der Henst, J.-B. (2004). *Cognitive economy in relational reasoning: The role of isomeric mental models.* Unpublished manuscript.

Schroyens, W., Schaeken, W, Fias, W., & d'Ydewalle, G. (2000). Heuristic and analytic processes in propositional reasoning with negatives. *Journal of Experimental Psychology: Learning, Memory and Cognition, 26,* 1713–1734.

Shaver, P., Pierson, L., & Lang, S. (1974). Converging evidence for the functional role of imagery in problem solving. *Cognition, 3,* 359–375.

Sternberg, R. J. (1980). Representation and process in linear syllogistic reasoning. *Journal of Experimental Psychology, 109,* 119–159.

Sternberg, R. J. (1981a). A proposed resolution of curious conflicts in the literature on linear syllogisms. In R. Nickerson (Ed.), *Attention and Performance* (Vol. 8, pp. 719–744). Hillsdale, NJ: Lawrence Erlbaum Associates.

Sternberg, R. J. (1981b). Reasoning with determinate and indeterminate linear syllogisms. *British Journal of Psychology, 72,* 407–420.

Van der Henst, J.-B. (1999). The mental model theory of spatial reasoning re-examined: The role of relevance in premise order. *British Journal of Psychology, 90,* 73–84.

Van der Henst, J.-B. (2000). Mental model theory and pragmatics. *Behavioral and Brain Sciences, 23,* 283–284

Van der Henst, J.-B. (2002). Mental model theory versus the inference rule approach in relational reasoning. *Thinking and Reasoning, 8,* 193–203.

Van der Henst, J.-B., & Schaeken, W. (2005). The wording of the conclusions in relational reasoning. *Cognition, 97,* 1–22..

Vandierendonck A., & De Vooght, G. (1996). Evidence for mental-model-based reasoning: Comparison of reasoning with time and space concepts. *Thinking and Reasoning 2,* 249–272.

Woodworth, R. S., & Sells, S. B. (1935). An atmosphere effect in syllogistic reasoning. *Journal of Experimental Psychology, 18*, 451–460.

8

Extensional Reasoning about chances

Vittorio Girotto
Michel Gonzalez

In this chapter, we discuss an almost natural extension of the model theory: probabilistic reasoning. According to the theory, deductive reasoning is an extensional process. Reasoners draw deductive inferences on the basis of the models of what the premises refer to (their extensions). From mental models, they may also derive probability evaluations, without relying on the rules of the probability calculus. After an analysis of the different modes of naive probabilistic reasoning, we discuss an important implication of the theory. If the theory is correct, then we should find traces of extensional reasoning in individuals who do not know the probability calculus. We report historical evidence that, well before the advent of the modern probability theory, individuals could solve extensionally problems of chance. Moreover, we present results showing that children evaluate chances on the basis of an elementary combinatorial analysis, in which they enumerate the possible ways in which an event may occur. These results contravene some recent account of reasoning under uncertainty, according to which the human mind is intrinsically unable to deal with probabilities.

INTRODUCTION

Whene'er is broken up the game of Zara,
He who has lost remains behind despondent,
The throws repeating, and in sadness learns;
The people with the other all depart. (Dante, *Purgatorio*, Canto VI. 1–4; translated by Henry Wadsworth Longfellow)

In this chapter, we discuss an important extension of the model theory: probabilistic reasoning. According to the theory, deductive reasoning is an extensional process. Reasoners draw deductive inferences on the basis of the models of what the premises refer to (their extensions). From mental models, they may also derive probabilities, without relying on the rules of the probability calculus. They have simply to enumerate and compare the possibilities represented in the models. In the first part of the chapter, we briefly review the main forms of naive probabilistic

151

inferences. We then introduce the notion of naive extensional reasoning about probability and the model-theoretical account of it. In the following section, we discuss an important implication of the theory. If the theory is correct, then we should find traces of extensional reasoning in individuals who are unfamiliar with the probability calculus. We report historical evidence that, long before the advent of the probability calculus, individuals could solve problems of chance extensionally. Moreover, we present results showing that children evaluate chances on the basis of an elementary combinatorial analysis, in which they enumerate the possible ways in which an event may occur. We also review some evidence that naive reasoners can successfully apply extensional procedures to numerical probability problems. However, we also point out some limits of naive extensional reasoning. Finally, we discuss the consequences of the reported results for an alternative theory of naive probability.

NONEXTENSIONAL AND EXTENSIONAL INFERENCES ABOUT UNCERTAIN EVENTS

In daily life, individuals often encounter situations in which they have to express their beliefs about an uncertain event, such as the result of an exam. Sometimes, individuals make judgments verbally: "It is likely that I'll pass the exam," sometimes, they make them in numerical form: "There are two chances in three that I'll pass the exam." Many studies have investigated the way in which numerical expressions of uncertainty are formed, and the extent to which they respect the rules of mathematical probability. A large body of evidence shows that individuals who are unfamiliar with the probability calculus often make incorrect probability judgments (e.g., Kahneman, Slovic, & Tversky, 1982). In particular, they appear to violate the fundamental additivity rule (i.e., given two exclusive events, or two incompatible propositions, A and B, the probability that either A or B occur equals the sum of their respective probabilities: $p(A$ or $B) = p(A) + p(B))$, and its consequences, that is the complementarity rule (i.e., $p(A) + p(\neg A) = 1$) and the conjunction rule (i.e., $p(A) = p(B)$, if A implies B). Moreover, they do not comply with the conditional probability rule (i.e., the probability of event A, given the occurrence of event B, equals the probability of their conjunction divided by the probability of event B: $p(A|B) = p(A\&B)/p(B)$). These findings are relevant both for the theoretical debate about human rationality (e.g., Stanovich & West, 2000) and for more practical reasons. Indeed, it has been demonstrated that decisions under uncertainty are coherent, if and only if they express beliefs compatible with mathematical probability (de Finetti, 1937/1964; Ramsey, 1926/1964; Savage, 1954). Therefore, one may conclude that incorrect probability judgments may lead individuals to make incoherent decisions.

Memory-Based and Arithmetic-Based Erroneous Inferences

In previous psychological literature extensional reasoning has been opposed to intuitive reasoning (e.g., Tversky & Kahneman, 1983). Many studies showed that naive probability judgments are based on nonextensional reasoning and do not respect the elementary properties of mathematical probability. From these results, however, one should not conclude that naive reasoning is always nonextensional. In this chapter, we show that in many situations naive individuals do reason extensionally; that is, they draw inferences based on an enumeration of possibilities.

What are the typical situations in which naive reasoners exhibit erroneous probability reasoning? On the one hand, some situations require reasoners to make a probability judgment by retrieving from long-term memory data associated with a specific content. For example, Tversky and Kahneman (1983) asked a group of participants to predict how many words having the form ....*ing* (i.e., seven-letter words ending with *ing*) could be found in a four-page sample (about 2.000 words) of a novel. A second group of participants had to predict the expected number of words having the form ".....*n*. (i.e., seven-letter words with *n* as penultimate letter).Because all ....*ing* words are .....*n*. words, one has to conclude that a text sample will contain at least as many .....*n*. words as ....*ing* words. Yet, the expected number of ....*ing* words predicted by participants in the first group was significantly greater than the expected number of .....*n*. words predicted by participants in the second group. These judgments violate the conjunction rule, which dictates that $p($.....*n*. word) be greater than $p($....*ing* word). What is the source of these erroneous judgments? If they are not provided with numerical information, individuals are likely to predict the expected frequency of a given class of events on the basis of the frequency with which these events are retrieved from memory. The easier the process of item retrieval, the higher the predicted frequency of the class. Tversky and Kahneman asked two other groups of participants to produce as many ....*ing* words, or as many .....*n*. words, as possible, in 60 seconds. On average, participants produced twice as many ....*ing* words as .....*n*. words. Thus, the greater availability of the exemplars of the former class yields participants to violate the conjunction rule.

In sum, some situations do not provide reasoners with numerical information so that to make numerical evaluations, they must use information retrieved from memory. The resulting inferences do not always respect the rules of mathematical probability (for a description of how the memory retrieval process may produce many biases in probability judgments, see, e.g., Dougherty, Gettys, & Ogden, 1999; Hintzman, 1988).

On the other hand, naive individuals err even if they are presented with all the numerical values they need to solve a probability problem. For instance, most reasoners fail the following version of the test-disease problem (see Hammerton, 1973):

> A screening test of an infection is being studied. Here is the information about the infection and the test results.
> There is a 4% chance that a person who is tested has the infection.
> If the person is infected, there is a 75% chance that he or she will have a positive reaction to the test.
> If the person is not infected, there is still a 12.5%

chance that he or she will have a positive reaction to the test.
Imagine that Pierre is tested now. If Pierre has a positive reaction, what is the probability that he actually is infected? ___ %

In this case, reasoners do not need to base their probability judgment on information retrieved from memory. The problem provides numerical values of probabilities (i.e., p(infected) = 4%, p(positive|infected) = 75%, p(positive|not infected) = 12.5%), which are sufficient to infer the required probability. Reasoners could compute p(infected|positive) by applying the conditional probability rule:

$$p(\text{infected|positive}) = p(\text{infected \& positive})/p(\text{positive}).$$

To compute the two terms of the ratio, that is p(infected & positive) and p(positive), reasoners need to apply both the the additivity rule (i.e., p(positive) = p(infected & positive) + p(not infected & positive)), and the conditional probability rule (i.e., p(infected & positive) = p(infected) x p(positive|infected), and p(not infected & positive) = p(not-infected) x p(positive|not-infected)). Therefore, the required probability—that is, p(infected|positive), equals the following:

$$(75\% \times 4\%) / [(75\% \times 4\%) + (12.5\% \times (100\% - 4\%))] = 20\%$$

In fact, most reasoners fail this problem. Typically, reasoners give as the answer either one value taken from the text problem, for example, the inverse conditional probability p(positive|infected), which is the most frequent erroneous answer (see Villejoubert & Mandel, 2002), or the result of some elementary arithmetic operation performed on two values at most, for example, p(positive|infected) – p(positive|not infected) = 75% – 12.5% (for a detailed analysis of errors, in this sort of problem, see Gigerenzer & Hoffrage, 1995). It is likely that reasoners produce their answers by means of contingent treatments. Indeed, the activation of a given operation seems to depend on the specific pattern of data provided in the problem. For example, in problems in which information about p(positive|infected) is expressed as "all infected people are positive" rather than as a numerical value (i.e., 100%), reasoners do not make the inference p(infected|positive) = p(positive|infected) = 100%, as they typically do when the problem is presented in the earlier version. Rather, they compute the complement of p(positive|not-infected), that is 1 – p(positive|not infected) (see Casscells, Schoenberger, & Grayboys, 1978; Cosmides & Tooby, 1996).

In sum, when the problems require the application of probabilistic rules, naive reasoners fail by using elementary procedures, the application of which depends on the specific values of the probabilities provided in the problem.

Extensional Inferences

Although naive reasoners err even in numerical problems, they do not always make incorrect probability judgments. Consider the following problem:

> You cast two dice simultaneously. You do not see how they land. If your friend tells you that the sum of the numbers is 7, what is the probability that one of the two dice landed 5?

This problem asks for the evaluation of a conditional probability, that is p(one5|sum7), where "one5" represents the event "one die lands 5," and "sum7" represents the event "the sum is 7." You could solve it by applying the conditional probability rule—that is, p(one5|sum7) = p(one5 & sum7)/p(sum7). The point is that the problem does not provide you with the relevant numerical values: What is the probability of the conjunctive event "one die lands 5 and the sum is 7"? What is the probability that two dice sum to 7? Unlike the test-disease problem, in the dice problem one cannot infer these probabilities from other, provided probabilities.

A way to solve the problem consists of making a precise calculation of a series of probabilities by means of the rules of the probability calculus, under the assumption that all possible throws are equiprobable. Given that each die can produce six different results, two dice can produce 6 x 6 = 36 different combinations. Assuming that all combinations are equiprobable, one deduces from the additivity rule that the probability of each combination is 1/36. There are three possibilities to obtain a sum of 7: 1 + 6, 2 + 5, and 3 + 4. As each sum corresponds to two possible combinations (e.g., 1 + 6 corresponds to 1 and 6, and 6 and 1) there are six possible combinations producing a sum of 7. According to the additivity rule, the probability of having a sum of 7 equals the sum of the probabilities of these six combinations, that is, p(sum7) = 6/36. The conjunctive event "one5 & sum7" corresponds to two combinations (i.e., 2 and 5, 5 and 2). According to the additivity rule, the probability of this event equals the sum of the probabilities of these two combinations, that is p(one5 & sum7) = 2/36. Finally, by applying the conditional probability rule one infers that p(one5|sum7) equals (2/36)/(6/36) = 1/3.

This complex procedure is certainly correct, given that it relies on the rules of the probability calculus. However, there is another, much simpler way to solve the problem. If you consider that there are three ways of obtaining a sum of 7 (i.e., 1 + 6, 2 + 5 , and 3 + 4), and in one of them (i.e., 2 + 5) the die lands 5, you conclude that the probability of this event is 1/3. In other words, you may reason extensionally, by enumerating and counting the ways in which an event may occur. In this case, you may evaluate the conditional probability p(one5|sum7) by enumerating the possibilities in which a die lands 5 out of the possibilities of producing a sum of 7. Evaluations of this sort correspond exactly to probabilities based on the assumption that the considered elementary events are equiprobable and form a finite set. In sum, an extensional procedure warrants the accuracy of probability evaluations, despite the fact that it is not based on an explicit application of the rules of the probability calculus.

Do naive individuals really use extensional procedures in judging uncertain events? Do they draw correct inferences by applying these procedures? In the following sections, we show that models theory gives an affirmative answer to both questions, and we present evidence that naive individuals (including children) make coherent probability evaluations by means of extensional reasoning.

THE MODEL THEORY OF NAIVE EXTENSIONAL REASONING ABOUT PROBABILITIES

The mental models theory of reasoning appears as a natural candidate for a cognitive account of naive extensional reasoning. According to the models theory, individuals draw deductive inferences not by applying formal rules but by constructing and manipulating mental models that represent the possibilities described in the assertions, that is, their extension (Johnson-Laird & Byrne, 1991). Probabilistic inferences too can be explained in a similar way (Johnson-Laird, 1994; Johnson-Laird, Legrenzi, Girotto, Legrenzin & Caverni, 1999): Individuals represent possibilities as sets of models from which they may derive probabilities, without relying on the probability calculus. For example, consider the following problem:

> There is a box in which there is a yellow marble or a red marble, or both. What is the probability of having a yellow marble and a red marble in the box?

most reasoners answer one third chance (Johnson-Laird et al., 1999). According to the theory, reasoners construct the following representation of the premise:

> yellow
>   red
> yellow red

The three lines indicate three models, each representing a true possibility. The first model represents the possibility that the box contains a yellow marble, the second one the possibility that the box contains a red marble, and the third one the possibility that the box contains both marbles. Given that one of the three models represents the possibility that both marbles are in the box, reasoners infer that the probability of this event is one out of three. In other words, they infer the probability of an event from the proportion of models in which it occurs, out of the entire set of models. In a series of studies, Johnson-Laird et al. (1999) showed that most participants produce the evaluations predicted by the model theory (for a review, see Legrenzi, Girotto, Johnson-Laird, & Legrenzi, 2003). These evaluations are extensional because they are based on the enumeration of the various possibilities in which the assertions are true. They are also naive because they do not need any knowledge of the probability calculus.

If the model theory is correct—that is, if naive reasoners draw extensional inferences on the basis of their representation of the premises—we should find traces of extensional inferences in the reasoning of individuals who totally ignore the existence of a probability calculus. In other words, we should find evidence of extensional inferences both in adults who never encountered the probability calculus and in children. In the following section, we present data supporting this prediction.

EARLY EXTENSIONAL REASONING

Historical Evidence

The model theory's prediction that naive individuals may reason extensionally about uncertain events, and derive correct chance evaluations, is at odds with a prediction derived from an alternative view. According to the frequentist hypothesis, naive individuals may correctly predict frequencies, because natural selection has provided the human mind with an innate module to make inferences about frequencies but not about probabilities, given that probabilities are not encountered in natural environments. This should explain why naive reasoners solve numerical problems, such as the test-disease one, when the problems present information in terms of natural frequencies but not when they present information in terms of single-case probabilities (Cosmides & Tooby, 1996; Gigerenzer & Hoffrage, 1995). The advocates of this view have emphasized the recent emergence of the notions of probability and percentage, as a further proof of the artifactual character of reasoning about probabilities:

> The notion of "probability" did not gain prominence in probability theory until one century after the mathematical theory of probability was invented ... Percentages became common notations only during the 19th century ... Thus, probabilities and percentages took millennia of literacy and numeracy to evolve; organisms did not acquire information in terms of probabilities and percentages until very recently. How did organisms acquire information before that time?" (Gigerenzer & Hoffrage, 1995, p. 686)

This question is theoretically relevant. According to the advocates of the frequentist hypothesis, organisms (i.e., human beings) living before the invention of the mathematical theory of probability could not acquire information about probabilities and percentages. However, they did acquire information in a sequential way by updating event frequencies so that they could reason extensionally only about absolute frequencies. In contrast, if the model theory is correct that naive individuals have common intuitions about numerical probability, we should find evidence that before the 17th or 18th century human beings did reason extensionally about probabilities.

Indeed, evidence exists that long before the advent of the probability calculus individuals solved problems of decision under uncertainty in an extensional way, that is, by enumerating the possible ways in which some outcomes could occur. A striking example of early extensional reasoning is given by Jacopo della Lana, one of the first commentators of Dante's *Divine Comedy*. In Canto VI of the *Purgatorio*, Dante mentions a popular medieval game, the *"zara"*. It consisted of guessing the outcome of a throw of three dice. As early as 1324, Della Lana (our translation; see Della Lana, 1324|1866) commented on it as follows:

> Reasonably, the number that can be obtained in more ways must occur more often. For instance, in this game of dice, three is the lowest number and it can occur in only one way, that is, when all three dice land one; four can be obtained with three dice in only one way, that is, one die lands two and two dice land one. Since these numbers can occur in only one way, they are not computed in the game, in order to avoid such an annoyance and in order to avoid having to wait too long, and they are called *azari*. The same is true for XVII and XVIII, which are similarly called *azari*, and are the highest possible numbers. The numbers in the middle can be obtained in more than one way; and the number that can be obtained in more ways is called the best bet. Sometimes, however, the dice land with the number that can be obtained in less ways.

This excerpt clearly indicates that Della Lana (1324|1866) understood that the expectation of an outcome depends on the number of dice combinations that produce it, so players should guess the outcomes produced by more combinations. Apparently, the unknown individuals who established the game rules had the same intuitions, given that they excluded the numbers produced by only one combination from the possible guesses. This extensional evaluation of chance, however, was partially correct. In particular, Della Lana did not take into account all the permutations of a given throw. For example, he did not realize that 4 is obtained when the dice land as 2, 1, 1, but also when they land as 1, 2, 1, and as 1, 1, 2. (Leibniz made a similar error in a letter to Louis Bourguet, dated 1714.) Correct solutions of the *zara* game, based on the consideration of permutations, were given, among others, by the anonymous author of the 13th century poem "De Vetula" (see Kendall, 1956), by Cardano in his book on gambling *Liber de ludo aleae* (circa 1563; see Ore, 1965) and by Galileo in a letter written circa 1613 (see Galileo, 1898/1962). In all these cases, enumerating and comparing sets of possibilities produced numerical evaluations of chance. Galileo's solution stands out from the others, because of its conciseness, clarity, and completeness. However, it does not depart from the other ones in terms of mathematical complexity. Galileo had to answer a question that a person (probably Cosimo de Medici, grand duke of Tuscany) asked him about the best numbers to guess. He answered it, by performing a combinatorial analysis of the game that, apart from its completeness, relied on the same extensional intuitions as those of present day naive reasoners:

The fact that in a dice-game certain numbers are more advantageous than others has a very obvious reason, i.e. that some are more easily and more frequently made than others, which depends on their being able to be made up with more variety of numbers. (translated by E. H. Thorne in David,1962, p. 192)

Developmental Evidence

Children's reasoning about chance provides another way of testing the model theory predictions. If an extensional evaluation of chance is based on the enumeration and counting of possibilities, then even children should be able to do it correctly. Indeed, counting appears to be one of the fundamental cognitive abilities of even young children (Dehaene, 1997).

According to the traditional Piagetian view, the development of probability concepts parallels the development of deductive reasoning abilities (Piaget & Inhelder, 1951/1975). In particular, young children do not compute correct probability ratios (consisting of relating the number of favorable outcomes to the number of all outcomes) because they do not master part-whole relationships. It is difficult to draw firm conclusions from the observations related by Piaget and Inhelder. More recent studies, however, suggest that even young children have some intuitive knowledge of probability (for a review, see Reyna & Brainerd, 1994). For example, Brainerd (1981) asked a group of 5-year-olds to put seven chips representing monkeys and three chips representing birds in an opaque box. After shaking the box, the experimenter asked "If I close my eyes and take one chip from the box, do you think I will get a monkey or a bird?" Most children answered "monkey"—the animal represented by most chips. In the condition in which they were asked "did we have more monkeys or more birds?" all children who answered "more monkeys" predicted that the experimenter would get a monkey rather than a bird. Thus, 5-year-olds predict that the more likely of two events is the one represented by the larger number of possibilities. Moreover, Acredolo, O'Connor, Banks, and Horobin (1989) asked children of various ages to judge the likelihood that a bug would land on a flower (good outcome) rather than on a spider (bad outcome). They found that even 7-year-olds evaluate a box containing five flowers and five spiders as a more favorable situation than one containing two flowers and four spiders.

These results are important. They show that young children make correct extensional evaluations, at least in situations in which they have simply to count possibilities, each corresponding to a perceptual unit. To test the model theory prediction, we conducted a study in which we proved that children are able to make correct evaluations of chance even in situations in which they have to mentally construct possibilities, rather than count perceptually given units. Four groups of 11-year-olds (with approximately equal numbers of boys and girls in each group), all attending a middle school in a small Northern Italian town, read the following, simplified version of the *zara* game:

A die has six faces. Each face has a number: 1, 2, 3, 4, 5, and 6. Paolo and Maria are playing with two dice. They throw them, and then they check whether they have correctly guessed the sum of the two numbers turning up. Now they are throwing the dice again. Paolo says, "In my opinion, this time the sum is 10." Maria says, " In my opinion, this time the sum is 12." According to you, who has more chances to win, Paolo or Maria?

A group of children had to answer this probability question by designating Paolo or Maria, or both. Another group, before answering it, had to enumerate the different possibilities for the two guessed numbers ("How many ways are there for the two dice to sum to 10?" and "How many ways are there for the two dice to sum 12?"). Two other groups of children (with and without the initial enumeration question) received a version of the problem in which Paolo and Maria guessed the numbers 8 and 10.

On the probability question, correct answers were those in which children attributed more chances to the player who guessed the sum made up with more throws. On the enumeration question, correct answers mentioned "4 + 6 and 5 + 5" versus "6 + 6", for the 10 and 12 problem and "3 + 5, 2 + 6, and 4 + 4" versus "4 + 6 and 5 + 5", for the 8 and 10 problem. Mentions of permutations, like (5, 5), (4, 6), and (6,4) for a sum of 10, were not taken into account, given that very few children (5%) considered them. In any case, as we showed earlier, even adult reasoners do not have a clear intuition about the ordered arrangements of the elements of a set. Most children correctly answered the probability question for the 10 and 12 problem (84% across conditions). Fewer children solved the same question for the 8 and 10 problem (55% across conditions). We attribute this difference to the different combinatorics required by the two problems: In the 10 and 12 problem, one of the sums (12) is produced by only one throw. Moreover, it is also a special number, being the sum of the highest possible number of each die. By contrast, in the 8 and 10 problem, both sums are produced by more than one throw. Indeed, children in the 10 and 12 problem solved the enumeration question better than children in the 8-10 problem (77% vs. 40% correct enumeration, respectively).

We proposed the same problem (without the initial request to enumerate the possibilities) to two groups of young adults (psychology undergraduates at Padua University). One group read the 10 and 12 version. The other group read the 8 and 10 version. The results were similar to those obtained with children: Whereas most undergraduates (71%) correctly answered the probability question for the 10 and 12 version, only 45% solved the same question for the 8 and 10 version (in which most participants considered that Paolo and Maria had the same chance to win). These findings suggest that children at the age of 11 years have reached the same combinatorial ability as adults, at least in this sort of problem.

These and other results obtained in our studies show that children reason about chances by considering combinations. They base their evaluations of chance on elementary combinatorics and judge as more likely the event produced by more possibilities.

EXTENSIONAL REASONING IN NUMERICAL PROBLEMS

Johnson-Laird et al. (1999) argued that naive reasoners can solve conditional probability problems presenting numerical information if they can apply intuitive principles of extensional reasoning. Girotto and Gonzalez (2001) found that 85% of participants solved the following version of the test-disease problem:

> A person who was tested had 4 chances out of 100 of having the infection.
> Three of the 4 chances of having the infection were associated with a positive reaction to the test.
> Twelve of the remaining 96 chances of not having the infection were also associated with a positive reaction to the test.
> If Pierre has a positive reaction, there will be ___ chance(s) that the infection is associated with his positive reaction vs. ___ chance(s) that no infection is associated with his positive reaction.

In this case, reasoners may represent the data as a partition of a set of 100 chances. This set is made up of two subsets (i.e., 4 chances of having the disease vs. 96 chances of not having it), each containing another subset (i.e., 3 chances of being positive in the first subset and 12 chances in the second one). This version of the problem asks for a distributive evaluation of chance, that is, a form of evaluation that is common in daily life, for example in betting contexts (e.g., "I bet twenty to one that ..." or "the odds are twenty to one that ..."), and, apparently, predated the advent of the theory of probability, as suggested, for example, by the following verses:

> Twenty to one then he is shipped already. (Shakespeare, *The Two Gentlemen of Verona*, I.1)

> Good gods? what happines has Palamon?
> Twenty to one, hee'le come to speake to her. (Shakespeare, *The Two Noble Kinsmen*, II.3)

Of course, these verses do not imply that individuals at the time of Shakespeare adhered to the subjectivist view of probability, according to which a probability of 20/21 corresponds to the odds of 20 to 1 (e.g., de Finetti, 1937/1964; Ramsey, 1926/1964). These verses, however, indicate that individuals who did not know the probability calculus spontaneously attributed numerical chances to two alternative events.

To make a distributive evaluation, naive reasoners have simply to count the chances associated to the evidence (e.g., being positive) for both hypotheses (e.g., being infected vs. not infected). In this way, they give a correct evaluation of probability, without applying any rule of the probability calculus. In model-theoretical terms, reasoners construct the following representation of the situation:

    infected   positive 3
    not infected   positive 12
    ...

The first model represents the 3 chances of being infected and positive, the second one represents the 12 chances of being not infected and positive, and the three dots represent the implicit models in which the evidence does not occur. Given the distributive question, they may easily extract the chances associated, respectively, to infected and not-infected hypotheses. (For a demonstration of how distributive questions may improve chance evaluation in other problems, see Girotto & Gonzalez, 2000.)

Gigerenzer and Hoffrage (1995) found that participants solved versions of the test-disease problems presenting data as absolute frequencies in a sample of observations, that is, versions similar to the following one:

> Four of the 100 people tested were infected.
> Three of the 4 infected people had a positive reaction to the test.
> 12 of the 96 uninfected people also had a positive reaction to the test.
> Imagine that this test is given to a new group of people. Among those who have a positive reaction, how many will actually have the infection? ___ out of ___

According to Gigerenzer and Hoffrage (1995), this result corroborates the hypothesis that naive individuals are specifically able to deal with frequencies, rather than with single-event probabilities. However, Girotto and Gonzalez (2001, 2002) found that performance does not depend on the type of information. Participants solved problems activating a representation of a unique set of possibilities (frequencies or chances) and asking for a distributive question, that is problems in which they could reason extensionally by enumerating and counting possibilities. By contrast, participants failed problems referring to multiple sets of frequencies or chances or presenting data as percentages (Girotto & Gonzalez, 2001; Lewis & Keren, 1999; but see, e.g., Macchi, 2000). In other words, they failed problems that did not activate the representation of a unique set of possibilities. This suggests that, regardless of the information type, correct inferences in numerical problems depend on the possibility to apply extensional reasoning.

We stated earlier that extensional reasoning warrants the accuracy of probability evaluations. This does not mean, however, that naive extensional procedures always yield accurate probability judgments. Consider the following problem:

> Suppose that only one of the following assertions is true about a specific hand of cards:
> If there is a jack in the hand, then there is a 2 in the hand.
> If there is an ace in the hand, then there is a 2 in the hand.
> Which is more likely to be in the hand: the 2 or the jack?

Most participants answered that the 2 is more likely than the jack (Johnson-Laird & Savary, 1996). This answer is an illusion, given that, if the first assertion is true, then the second is false, so that in the hand there is an ace and not a 2. Similarly, if the second assertion is true, then the first is false so that in the hand there is a jack and not a 2. In both cases, therefore, the 2 cannot occur in the hand, so the jack is more likely than the 2. The model theory predicted this illusion by positing that naive reasoners tend to represent true, but not false, possibilities. In this case, the mental models of the disjunction of the two conditionals are as follows:

        jack   2
        ace   2
        ...

From this set of models, reasoners infer that the 2 is more likely than the jack, given that the former is represented in more models than the latter. The fully explicit models, however, are

        not jack   ace   not 2 (second conditional false)
        jack   not ace   not 2 (first conditional false)

From these models, one has to conclude that the jack is more likely than the 2, given it is impossible that there is a 2 in the hand. In sum, given an incorrect representation of the possibilities, extensional procedure may lead to erroneous probability judgments.

CONCLUSIONS

In this chapter, we discussed a new and relevant extension of the model theory, that is, reasoning about probabilities. According to the theory, naive reasoners infer the probability of an event from the possible ways in which it could occur. We analyzed previous results indicating that naive reasoners solve correctly conditional probability problems presenting numerical information, without relying on the application of the rules of the probability calculus. We also reported new results suggesting that individuals who are totally unfamiliar with this calculus, such as children and individuals who lived before its advent, could reason extensionally about probabilities.

Developmental and historical evidence of an early emergence of extensional intuitions about probability corroborates the model theory of naive reasoning. In contrast, these findings are difficult to explain by the frequentist view, according to which natural selection shaped an innate module in the mind to make inferences about frequencies but not about probabilities. The advocates of this view have emphasized the recent emergence of the theory of probability (Gigerenzer & Hoffrage, 1995). We agree with these authors. Mathematical theory of probability did emerge only recently. However, the mathematical treatment of probability should not be confused with the intuitive sense of probability. The latter does not need the rules of the calculus of probabilities. As the reported historical evidence suggests, even individuals living in the Middle Ages had a sense of numerical probability.

Studies of naive physics show that naive individuals' reasoning about the way in which the world works is essentially pre-Galilean. For example, naive individuals (whether present-day psychology undergraduates or the 17th century Aristotelian critics of Galileo) think that a wide-swing pendulum oscillates much more slowly than one with a narrow swing (e.g., Bozzi, 1958). In contrast, the present results suggest that naive probability is essentially Galilean: Eleven-year-olds' solutions of a decision-under-uncertainty problem are not really different from Galileo's solution of a similar problem. Apart from the systematic nature of Galileo's combinatorics, in both cases, probabilities are extensionally inferred from mental models of possibilities.

ACKNOWLEDGMENTS

We thank Alice McEleney and Aline Pélissier for their helpful comments. We also thank Lara Pavan for her help in collecting data and the children and staff of Lorenzo da Ponte school in Vittorio Veneto.

REFERENCES

Acredolo, C., O'Connor, J., Banks, L., & Horobin, K. (1989). Children's ability to make probability estimates: Skills revealed through application of Anderson's functional measurement methodology. *Child Development, 60,* 933–945.

Bozzi, P. (1958). Analisi fenomenologica del moto pendolare armonico [Phenomenological analysis of pendular harmonic motion]. *Rivista di Psicologia, 52,* 281–302.

Brainerd, C. J. (1981). Working memory and the developmental analysis of probability judgment. *Psychological Review, 88,* 463–502.

Casscells, W., Schoenberger, A., & Grayboys, T. (1978). Interpretation by physicians of clinical laboratory results. *New England Journal of Medicine, 299,* 999–1000.

Cosmides, L., & Tooby, J. (1996). Are humans good intuitive statisticians after all? Rethinking some conclusions from the literature on judgment under uncertainty. *Cognition, 58,* 1–73.

Dante, A. (1867). The divine comedy. Boston, US: Ticknor and Fields. (Translated by Henry Wadsworth Longfellow)

David, F. N. (1962), *Games, gods and gambling. A history of probability and statistical ideas.* London: Griffin and Co.

Dehaene, S. (1997). *The number sense: How the mind creates mathematics.* New York: Oxford University Press.

de Finetti, B. (1964). Foresight: Its logical laws, its subjective sources. In H. E. Kyburg Jr, & H. E. Smokler (Eds. and Trans.), *Studies in subjective probability* (pp. 93–158). New York: Wiley. (Original work published 1937)

Della Lana, J. (1866). *Comedia di Dante degli Allagherii col commento di Jacopo della Lana bolognese [The Comedy of Dante, with the commentary by Jacopo della Lana from Bologna].* Bologna, Italy: Tipografia Regia. (Original work published 1324)

Dougherty, M. R. P., Gettys, C. F., & Ogden, E. E. (1999). MINERVA-DM: A memory processes model for judgments of likelihood. *Psychological*

Review, 106, 180–209.

Galileo, G. (1962). Sopra le scoperte dei dadi. In F. N. David (Trans.), *Games, gods and gambling. A history of probability and statistical ideas* (pp. 192–195). London: Griffin and Co. (Original work published 1898).

Gigerenzer, G., & Hoffrage, U. (1995). How to improve Bayesian reasoning without instruction: Frequency format. *Psychological Review, 102,* 684–704.

Girotto, V., & Gonzalez, M. (2000). Strategies and models in statistical reasoning. In W. Schaeken, G. De Vooght, A. Vandierendonck, & G. d'Ydewalle (Eds.), *Deductive reasoning and strategies* (pp. 267–285). Mahwah, NJ: Lawrence Erlbaum Associates.

Girotto, V., & Gonzalez, M. (2001). Solving probabilistic and statistical problems: A matter of information structure and question form. *Cognition, 8,* 247–276.

Girotto, V., & Gonzalez, M. (2002). Chances and frequencies in probabilistic reasoning: Rejoinder to Hoffrage, Gigerenzer, Krauss and Martignon. *Cognition, 84,* 353–359.

Hammerton, M. (1973). A case of radical probability estimation. *Journal of Experimental Psychology, 101,* 252–254.

Hintzman, D. L. (1988). Judgments of frequency and recognition memory in a multiple-trace memory model. *Psychological Review, 95,* 528–551.

Johnson-Laird, P. N. (1994). Mental models and probabilistic thinking. *Cognition, 50,* 189–209.

Johnson-Laird, P. N., & Byrne, R. M. J. (1991). *Deduction.* Hillsdale, NJ: Lawrence Erlbaum Associates.

Johnson-Laird, P. N., Legrenzi, P., Girotto, V., Legrenzi, M. S., & Caverni, J. P. (1999). Naive probability: A mental model theory of extensional reasoning. *Psychological Review, 106,* 62–88.

Johnson-Laird, P. N., & Savary, F. (1996). Illusory inferences about probabilities. *Acta Psychologica, 93,* 69–90.

Kahneman, D., Slovic, P., & Tversky, A. (Eds.). (1982). *Judgment under uncertainty: Heuristics and biases.* Cambridge, UK: Cambridge University Press.

Kendall, M. G. (1956). The beginnings of the probability calculus, *Biometrika, 43,* 1–14.

Legrenzi, P., Girotto, V., Johnson-Laird, P. N., & Legrenzi, M. S. (2003). Possibilities and probabilities. In L. Macchi & D. Hardman (Eds.), *Reasoning and decision-making* (pp. 147–164). London: Wiley.

Lewis, C., & Keren, G. (1999). On the difficulties underlying Bayesian reasoning: A comment on Gigerenzer and Hoffrage. *Psychological Review, 106,* 411–416.

Macchi, L. (2000). Partitive formulation of information in probabilistic problems: Beyond heuristics and frequency format explanations. *Organizational Behavior and Human Decision Processes, 82,* 217–236.

Ore, O. (1965). *Cardano, the gambling scholar.* New York: Dover.

Piaget, J., & Inhelder, B. (1975). *The origin of the idea of chance in children.* New York: Norton, 1975. (Original work published 1951)

Ramsey, F. P. (1964). Truth and probability. In H. E. Kyburg Jr, & H. E. Smokler (Eds.), *Studies in subjective probability* (pp. 61–92). New York: Wiley.

(Original work published1926)

Reyna, V. F., & Brainerd, C. J. (1994). The origins of probability judgment: A review of data and theories. In G. Wright & P. Ayton (Eds.), *Subjective probability* (pp. 239–272). New York: Wiley.

Savage, L. J. (1954). *The foundations of statistics.* New York: Wiley.

Stanovich, K. E., & West, R. F. (2000). Individual differences in reasoning: Implications for the rationality debate? *Behavioral and Brain Sciences, 23,* 645–665.

Tversky, A., & Kahneman, D. (1974). Judgment under uncertainty: Heuristics and biases. *Science, 185,* 1124–1131.

Tversky, A., & Kahneman, D. (1983). Extensional versus intuitive reasoning: The conjunction fallacy in probability judgment. *Psychological Review, 90,* 293–315.

Villejoubert, G., & Mandel, D. R. (2002). The inverse fallacy: An account of deviation from Bayes theorem and the additivity principle. *Memory and Cognition, 30,* 171–178.

9

Models of Cause and Effect

P. N. Johnson-Laird
Eugenia Goldvarg-Steingold

This chapter presents a theory of cause and effect. According to the theory, the meanings of causal assertions depend on a temporal constraint between sets of possibilities, and there is a difference in meaning (and hence logic) between causes and enabling conditions. Thus, "C will cause E" corresponds to three possibilities:

c e
not c e
not c not e

Here there is the temporal constraint that E does not precede C. If C is the unique cause of E, then the second possibility is ruled out. In contrast, "C will allow E" is consistent with any possibility unless C is the unique enabler of E, in which case the assertion corresponds to the three possibilities:

c e
c not e
not c not e

Individuals do not normally represent these fully explicit possibilities but rather rely on mental models. We report a series of experiments corroborating the model theory. The theory implies that the meaning of causation is not probabilistic, that it does not depend on causal powers or mechanisms, and that causal deductions do not depend on schemas or rules.

INTRODUCTION

In many homes, the light over the stairs is controlled by two switches, one at the top and one at the bottom of the stairs. Throwing a switch turns the light on if it is off and off it is on. Everyone understands this simple causal mechanism. There are four possible configurations of the switches, and in two of them the lights are on and in the other two the lights are off. If you have such a system in your house, ask yourself, what are the two configurations in which the lights are on? The authors have yet to meet any householder who knows the answer. Equally rare are those individuals who can draw the wiring diagram of this happy contrivance.

Nevertheless, we all understand the basic causal situation: We all have a mental model of cause and effect, albeit the model is rudimentary for most of us. Indeed, reasoning in daily life, as Hume (1748/1988) remarked, usually depends on causal relations. Similarly, individuals prefer explanations for phenomena couched in terms of cause and effect (Legrenzi, Legrenzi, Girotto, & Johnson-Laird, 2001; Tversky & Kahneman, 1980).

Scholars in many disciplines have studied causation, but they have yet to reach a consensus. They disagree about its philosophical foundations, about the meaning of causal assertions, and about causal reasoning. We do not worry about the philosophical problems— with whether, for instance, causal relations are objective or subjective. And we also do not worry about what exactly causal relations hold between—facts, actions, events, objects, or states of affairs. Certainly, causes can be actions, such as throwing a switch, but as Benjamin Franklin wrote, "for want of a nail the shoe was lost," and so they can also be states of affairs too. We therefore use the neutral expression *states* to include physical events, psychological actions, states of affairs, facts, and any other potential cause or effect. We say no more about these philosophical matters because our goal is to advance a psychological theory of what naive individuals understand when they grasp causal relations. By *naive* we mean merely individuals who have not studied philosophy, logic, or psychology.

So what does it mean to say that throwing a switch causes the light to go on? And how do people reason on the basis of such causal assertions? Our aim in the present chapter is to answer these two questions using the theory of mental models. But our answer conflicts with a number of alternative proposals, so the chapter also explores these alternatives. We begin by outlining the theory of mental models. We show how the theory readily extends to causal relations, and we report two experiments corroborating its account. The theory draws a principled distinction between the meaning—and hence the logical implications—of causes and enabling conditions. If the theory is right, then the following two assertions differ in meaning:

> Throwing the switch at the bottom of the stairs will cause the light to come on.
> Throwing the switch at the bottom of the stairs will allow the light to come on.

To the best of our knowledge, no other current theory in psychology, philosophy, or artificial intelligence makes this distinction. On the contrary, following John Stuart Mill (1874), these theories postulate that there is no difference between the meaning of the two relations. We accordingly show why Mill's view is so seductive, but we establish experimentally that naive individuals do draw a distinction in meaning between causes and enabling conditions and that this distinction is the one that the model theory predicts.

The model theory is also contrary to another popular vein in philosophical and psychological analysis that posits a probabilistic meaning for causation (e.g., Cheng, 1997; Suppes, 1984). We show that this approach also runs into severe difficulties in accounting for the performance of naive individuals. Likewise, we present evidence showing that individuals reason about causal relations using mental models rather than formal rules of inference or causal schemas. Finally, we discuss the general nature of causal relations in the light of the model theory.

THE THEORY OF MENTAL MODELS

How do naive individuals reason? One theory goes back to the Enlightenment and still has many proponents (e.g., Braine & O'Brien, 1998; Rips, 1994). According to this theory, reasoners follow the laws of thought. These laws are made explicit in formal logic, and the psychologists' task is to pin down the particular version of these laws that are embodied as rules of inference in the mind. No doubt people can acquire such rules when they take a course in formal logic, and then they can use them to make inferences. What is at issue, however, is whether naive individuals, who have never studied logic, unconsciously rely on formal rules of inference. They certainly are not aware of following such rules. They cannot describe them. And they make errors in reasoning. Errors here or there hardly refute the doctrine of the laws of thought, but what is embarrassing are systematic and predictable errors. The laws of thought, by definition, do not allow for them. Hence, the rules of inference in current theories yield only valid inferences, so whatever errors occur should be sporadic and haphazard—a consequence of an accident in the mind rather than of basic principles (see Braine & O'Brien, 1998; Rips, 1994). In fact, studies show that people do make systematic and predictable mistakes in reasoning. But before we describe these studies, we outline the theory of mental models because this theory predicted the errors.

More than 50 years ago the great Scottish psychologist Kenneth Craik (1943) proposed that the mind builds small-scale models of the world, which it uses to anticipate events and to guide its decisions. The modern theory of mental models postulates that they are also the normal outcome of understanding discourse and the basis of reasoning (Johnson-Laird, 1983; Johnson-Laird & Byrne, 1991). The modern theory makes three important assumptions:

1. Each mental model represents a possibility, and its structure mirrors the structure of what it represents. For example, a model of a set of individuals, such as some Belgian cyclists, consists in a set of mental tokens, where each token corresponds to an individual.
2. Mental models represent what is true but not what is false. This postulate has some surprising consequences, and it is known as the principle of truth. In certain circumstances, to which we return later, individuals can flesh out their models so that they represent both what is true and what is false. That is, they convert mental models into fully explicit models.
3. Models can represent what is physically possible, what is

deontically possible (permissible), or what is logically possible.

Reasoning can start with verbal premises, general knowledge, perceptions, assumptions for the sake of argument, or some mixture of them. We refer to the starting point as the premises but they may come from any of these sources. An inference is logically valid if its conclusion must be true given that its premises are true. The model theory provides a unified account of various sorts of reasoning. A valid conclusion is necessary—it must be the case—if it holds in all the models of the premises; it is possible—it may be the case—if it holds in at least one of the models; and its probability—assuming that each model is equiprobable—depends on the proportion of models in which it holds.

We can illustrate the theory with a simple example. Consider the following problem:

> Either there was a power cut or else the switch wasn't down.
> In fact, the switch was down.
> What follows?

The first premise, which is an exclusive disjunction, is consistent with two possibilities:

> power cut
> ¬down

Each line in this diagram denotes a mental model representing a separate possibility, so *power cut* denotes a model of the possibility in which there was a power cut. The symbol ¬ denotes negation, *down* denotes a model of the switch as down, and so ¬*down* denotes a model of the switch as not down. Mental models can take the form of visual images, spatial representations, or more abstract structures, but we do not represent their details here. What is much more important is that the first model represents the truth of the proposition "there was a power cut," but it does not represent explicitly that in this possibility it is false that "the switch was not down"(i.e., the switch was down). Individuals try to make mental footnotes about what is false, but, as we show later, they soon forget them. The second premise eliminates the second of the two models, so the conclusion that follows corresponds to the first model: "There was a power cut." This conclusion is valid because it holds in all the models—in this case, the single model —of the premises.

Suppose that one were to construct fully explicit models, which represent both what is true and what is false given the premises. The computer program implementing the theory constructs both mental models and fully explicit models for any premises, and the fully explicit models tell us what the correct conclusions are from a set of premises. The fully explicit models of the exclusive disjunction stated earlier are as follows:

> power cut   down
> ¬power cut   ¬down

These models also correspond to the fully explicit models of the biconditional assertion: "There is a power cut if and only if the switch is down." This equivalence is not obvious, a phenomenon that bears out our claim that individuals normally abide by the principle of truth, so they do not automatically construct fully explicit models.

A conditional assertion, such as "if the switch is down, then the light is on" has the following mental models:

        down   on
        ...

where *on* denotes the light as on, and the ellipses is an implicit model representing those possibilities in which the antecedent of the conditional "the switch is down" is false. Thus, the ellipses is really a place holder representing possibilities that people do not normally think about. But, in principle, they can make them fully explicit if they can remember the mental footnotes about what is false (Barrouillet & Lecas, 1999; Johnson-Laird & Byrne, 2002). The fully explicit models of the conditional are as follows:

        down   on
        ¬down   on
        ¬down   ¬on

The mental models of the converse conditional "if the light is on, then the switch is down"are as follows:

        on   down
        ...

The theory accordingly predicts that individuals readily confuse a conditional with its converse unless they have knowledge that helps them flesh out the possibilities explicitly.

All the model theory's predictions about reasoning with sentential connectives derive from the preceding account. In recent years, there has been an accumulation of experimental evidence corroborating the theory (for references, see the Web page developed by Ruth Byrne and her colleagues at Trinity College, http://www.tcd.ie/Psychology/People/Ruth_Byrne/mental_models). Inferences that depend on a greater number of mental models are more difficult, taking longer and leading to more errors. Erroneous conclusions tend to correspond to individual mental models of premises. And because reasoners soon forget about what is false, especially with complex premises, they make egregious errors. They draw conclusions that seem compelling but that are illusory. Such illusions occur in sentential reasoning (Johnson-Laird & Savary, 1999), probabilistic reasoning (Johnson-Laird, Legrenzi, Girotto, Legrenzi, & Caverni, 1999), modal reasoning (Goldvarg & Johnson-Laird, 2000), reasoning about consistency (Johnson-Laird,

Legrenzi, Girotto, & Legrenzi, 2000), and quantified reasoning (Yang & Johnson-Laird, 2000). The illusions are a litmus test for the use of mental models because they are contrary to theories of reasoning based on formal rules of inference or on schemas for reasoning.

MODELS AND THE MEANING OF CAUSAL RELATIONS

Causal assertions are of three main sorts:

> 1. General causal assertions, such as "closing a circuit causes a current to flow."
> 2. Singular causal assertions where the outcome is known, such as "closing the circuit caused the current to flow."
> 3. Singular causal assertions where the outcome is not known, such as "closing the circuit will cause the current to flow."

The main assumption of the model theory of causal relations is that they concern possibilities: Given two states of affairs, C and E, the meaning of a causal relation between them concerns what is possible and what is impossible in their cooccurrence. A second assumption introduces a temporal constraint: If C has a causal influence on E, then E does not precede C in time. This principle allows that a cause can be contemporaneous with its effect. As Kant (1781/1934) observed, the weight of a billiard ball causes a depression in a cushion, but the weight doesn't seem to precede its effect. The meanings of causal relations do not call for physical contact because causal claims can relate distant states of affairs: "The sun's mass causes the earth's orbit."

A general causal assertion, "C causes E," has a single fully explicit model of the different possibilities that can all occur, albeit as different states within the same situation or universe of discourse:

$$
\begin{array}{cc}
c & e \\
\neg c & e \\
\neg c & \neg e
\end{array}
$$

The temporal constraint is that E cannot precede C. The assertion is false if it is possible to have C without E. In contrast, a singular causal assertion with an unknown outcome, "C will cause E," has three fully explicit models, which each represent different alternative possibilities within the situation. Only one of these possibilities will actually occur at a given time:

$$
(1) \quad
\begin{array}{cc}
c & e \\
\neg c & e \\
\neg c & \neg e
\end{array}
$$

This again includes the temporal constraint that E cannot precede C. These possibilities also correspond to those for the proposition that "C is sufficient for E." Hence, the causal relation is a weak one that allows for other causes of the effect, E. An example of this sort of weak causation is "throwing the upstairs switch will cause the light to come on" because the downstairs switch can also cause the light to come on. The claim "C will cause E" is false in case C occurs without E:

> c   ¬e

If a singular causal assertion has a known outcome, "C caused E," then it has a model of the factual situation and alternative models representing counterfactual possibilities:

c	e	(the factual case)
¬c	e	(a counterfactual possibility)
¬c	¬e	(a counterfactual possibility)

A counterfactual possibility is a state that was once possible but that did not, in fact, occur (see e.g., Byrne, 1997; Johnson-Laird & Byrne, 1991; McEleney & Byrne, 2001). "C caused E" is false, of course, if either C or E did not occur. But it can be false even when both of them did occur, if they violated the temporal constraint or if the relation between them was not causal. Here the counterfactual possibilities are critical. If they include a case in which C occurred without E, then C did not cause E. Hence, the assertion "throwing the upstairs switch caused the light to come on" is false if throwing the upstairs switch merely allowed the light to come on under the control of another circuit:

throw	on	(the factual case)
throw	¬on	(a counterfactual possibility)
¬throw	¬on	(a counterfactual possibility)

Several other causal relations exist, and each of them can occur in general and singular assertions. For simplicity, however, we consider only their occurrences as singular causal relations with unknown outcomes. The relation "C will prevent E" means that the occurrence of C will cause E not to occur. It has the following fully explicit models:

(2)	c	¬e
	¬c	e
	¬c	¬e

An assertion of the form "C will allow E," such as "mending the fuse will allow the light to come on" has a strong implicature that not mending the fuse will not allow the light to come on (see Grice, 1975). It would not be informative to make the claim if you knew that the light would come on without mending the fuse. Hence, the implicature amounts to a claim that mending the fuse is the unique enabling condition. Thus, the models of "C will allow E," where C is the unique enabler are as follows:

(3)	c	e
	c	¬e
	¬c	¬e

In other words, C is necessary for E to occur. Where C is only one enabler and others do exist, then the assertion has models of all four possibilities. An assertion of the form "C will allow not E" and its analogous implicature have the following models:

(4) c $\neg e$
    c e
    $\neg c$ e

If C is the unique cause of E—that is, "C and only C will cause E"—then the causal relation is a strong relation compatible with only two possibilities. It has the following models:

c e
$\neg c$ $\neg e$

Similarly, "C and only C will prevent E" has the following models:

c $\neg e$
$\neg c$ e

An example of unique causation is the following: "Closing an electrical circuit will cause current to flow because current flows in no other case."

The preceding analyses have used fully explicit models. However, the principle of truth predicts that naive individuals will tend to rely on mental models. An assertion of the form "C will cause E" like the conditional assertion "if C then E" calls for the following mental models:

c e
...

Here the implicit model represents the possibilities in which the antecedent, C, is false. Given a mental footnote that captures this information, it is possible to flesh out the models fully explicitly.

Individuals normally reason on the basis of mental models, which can embody temporal relations (Schaeken, Johnson-Laird, & d'Ydewalle, 1996). With simple assertions such as "C will cause E," reasoners appreciate that effect could have other causes, and they should be able to list the fully explicit possibilities. Unique causation as expressed, say, by "C and only C will cause E" has the same mental models as causation, where other causes are possible but the mental footnote implies that the implicit case is one in which neither C nor E occur.

Table 9.1 summarizes the mental models of the singular causal relations together with their fully explicit models both for unique and nonunique senses. The existence of these various sorts of causal relations may come as a surprise to the reader. Philosophers have often assumed that there is only a single relation of cause and effect (see Hesslow, 1988). If state E is bound to occur regardless of whether C occurs, or bound not to occur, then there is no causal relation, and experiments corroborate that participants make such judgments (Cheng & Nisbett, 1993). If E is bound to occur if C occurs, then there may not be any causal relation between them. For instance, E may also be bound to occur even if C does not occur—that is, there are only the following possibilities:

$$
\begin{array}{ll}
c & e \\
\neg c & e
\end{array}
$$

We carried out two experiments to test the model theory of the meaning of causal relations. In an unpublished study, the participants had to write what was possible and what was impossible given general causal assertions of three sorts (see Table 9.2). In a second experiment (Goldvarg & Johnson-Laird, 2001), the participants carried out the same task for singular causal assertions of the four weak sorts (see Table 9.3):

1. A will cause B.
2. A will prevent B.
3. A will allow B.
4. A will allow not B.
5. A or not A will cause B or not B (a control tautology).

The control tautology is compatible with all four possibilities. The contents of the assertions in both experiments concerned everyday matters, such as "having a spinal implant will prevent Vivien from being in pain."

Table 9.1
The Models for Singular Causal Relations.

Connective	Mental Models		Fully Explicit Models of Unique Antecedents		Fully Explicit Models of Nonunique Antecedents	
1. C will cause E	c	e	c	e	c	e
	...				$\neg$c	e
			$\neg$c	$\neg$e	$\neg$c	$\neg$e
2. C will prevent E	c	$\neg$e	c	$\neg$e	c	$\neg$e
	...		$\neg$c	e	$\neg$c	e
					$\neg$c	$\neg$e
3. C will allow E	c	e	c	e	c	e
	...		c	$\neg$e	c	$\neg$e
					$\neg$c	e
			$\neg$c	$\neg$e	$\neg$c	$\neg$e
4. C will allow not E	c	$\neg$e	c	$\neg$e	c	$\neg$e
	...		c	e	c	e
			$\neg$c	e	$\neg$c	e
					$\neg$c	$\neg$e

Note: The models in the left column are the mental models normally used by human reasoners, the middle column shows the fully explicit models for unique antecedents (e.g., the unique cause of an event), and the right-hand column shows the fully explicit models in cases where the antecedent is not unique (e.g., there is another possible cause). "$\neg$" denotes negation and ". . ." denotes a wholly implicit model. The mental models for the unique and nonunique relations differ only in their mental footnotes (see text).

Table 9.2

The Patterns of Response to Three General Causal Relations in the First Experiment and the Number of Participants (n = 20) Generating Each of Them on at Least Three Trials Out of Five.

	Participants' Interpretations						
Listed as possible	c e c ¬e ¬c e c ¬e	c e ¬c e ¬c ¬e	c e ¬c ¬e	c e c ¬e ¬c ¬e	c e c ¬e ¬c e ¬c ¬e	c ¬e ¬c e ¬c ¬e	c ¬e
Listed as impossible	—	c ¬e	c ¬e ¬c e	¬c e	c e	c e c ¬e	c e c ¬e
C causes E		15	2				
C allows E	11	5		4			
C prevents E						10	5

Note: The remaining responses were idiosyncratic.

Table 9.3.

The Patterns of Response to Four Specific Causal Relations and a Control Tautology in the Second Experiment, and the Number of Participants (n = 20) Generating Each of Them on at Least Three Trials Out of Five.

	Participants' Interpretations						
Listed as possible	c e c ¬e ¬c e c ¬e	c e ¬c e ¬c ¬e	c e ¬c ¬e	c e c ¬e ¬c ¬e	c e c ¬e ¬c e ¬c ¬e	c ¬e ¬c e ¬c ¬e	c e c ¬e ¬c e
Listed as impossible	—	c ¬e	c ¬e ¬c e	¬c e	c e	c e c ¬e	c e c ¬e
Tautology	13	6					
C will cause E		9	10				
C will allow E	4		10	5			
C will prevent E					3	14	
C will allow not E						10	7

Note: The remaining responses were idiosyncratic.

Table 9.2 shows the most frequent interpretations in the first experiment, and Table 9.3 shows the most frequent interpretations in the second experiment (i.e., the number of participants who made each interpretation three or more times out of five trials). The participants reliably generated both true and false possibilities for the causal relations in both experiments. They also showed a significant bias to starteach list with the possibility corresponding to the explicit mental model of the causal relation. They tended to make unique interpretations of the singular causal claims, that is, to minimize the number of possibilities that are true. This bias was less apparent for the general claims with the exception of "*C* prevents *E*." Overall, the interpretations coincided with the model theory's predictions. There are 16 possible interpretations, so the chance probability of making a predicted unique or nonunique interpretation is one out of eight. There were significant tendencies to make the predicted interpretations of *causes, allows*, and *prevents* in Table 9.2; and, likewise, of *will cause, will allow, will prevent*, and *will allow not* in Table 9.3. The only unexpected result was the tendency of *will allow* and *will allow not* to elicit interpretations compatible with only two possibilities.

CAUSES, ENABLING CONDITIONS, AND CIRCUMSTANCES

Suppose you observe the following sequence of events: The downstairs switch was pushed down and the light in the hall came on. What is the causal relation, if any, between the two events? The observation rules out two of the eight possible causal relations (see Table 9.1): Pushing the switch down did not prevent the light coming on in either the unique or nonunique sense. But the observation is compatible with any of the remaining relations and, of course, with the lack of any causal relation. It follows that the mere observation of a particular sequence of states is not sufficient to establish the causal relation, if any, that holds between them. Causal relations are not merely about what occurred but also about what might have occurred. But what might have occurred cannot be determined from observation alone. It depends on knowledge of what is possible. The model theory accordingly postulates a principle of circumstantial interpretation: Causal interpretation depends on how people conceive the circumstances of states, that is, on the particular states that they consider to be possible.

Other theorists have invoked similar ideas (see, e.g., Hart and Honoré's, 1959/1985, and McGill's, 1989, context of a cause, Mackie's, 1980, causal field, and Cheng and Novick's, 1991, focal set of events). The circumstantial principle, however, implies that individuals use their general knowledge and their knowledge of the state at issue to generate a set of mental models. Each model represents a possibility, and, in the case of a singular causal claim about a fact, one model represents the actual state of affairs. The models represent what a person takes to be the relevant possibilities in the circumstances, and they determine what the person judges to be the appropriate causal relation.

Consider if the circumstances of the example about the hall light are as follows:

down	on	(the factual case)
¬down	on	(a counterfactual possibility)
¬down	¬on	(a counterfactual possibility)

Then an appropriate description is as follows: "Pushing the switch down caused the light to come on."

Consider if the circumstances are as follows:

down	on	(the factual case)
down	¬on	(a counterfactual possibility)
¬down	¬on	(a counterfactual possibility)

Then an appropriate description is as follows: "Pushing the switch down allowed the light to come on."

And consider if the circumstances are as follows:

down	on	(the factual case)
down	¬on	(a counterfactual possibility)
¬down	on	(a counterfactual possibility)

Then an appropriate description is as follows: "Pushing the switch down might have allowed the light not to come on."

Unfortunately, there may be no way to decide the circumstances of events. They bedevil analyses of causation. For example, inferences of the form known as strengthening the antecedent are valid in many circumstances:

> A causes C.
> ∴ A and B cause C.

This inference, for example, is unexceptional:

> Pushing the upstairs switch up will cause the light to come on.
> ∴ Pushing the upstairs switch up and the downstairs light up will cause the light   to come on.

But the following inference is invalid:

> Pushing the upstairs switch up will cause the light to come on.
> ∴ Pushing the upstairs switch up and breaking the bulb in the light will cause the   light to come on.

The circumstances of the conclusion are no longer those of the premise. The conclusion is false even if the premise is true.

As we have shown, the model theory distinguishes between causing an effect and allowing it to occur. Yet theorists have followed Mill (1874) in denying that there is any logical or semantic distinction between the two. So what does distinguish causes from enabling conditions? According to Hart and Honoré (1985), the cause is the unusual state, and the enabling condition is the usual state.

According to Cheng and Novick (1991), the cause is what is inconstant and the enabling condition is what is constant. According to others, the cause violates a norm assumed by default, whereas the enabling condition does not (see, e.g., Einhorn & Hogarth, 1986; Kahneman & Miller, 1986; Kahneman & Tversky, 1982). And according to still another group of theorists, the cause is the factor that is conversationally relevant in explanations (Mackie, 1980; Turnbull & Slugoski, 1988). Hilton and Erb (1996) therefore suggest a two-stage process: "explanations are first cognitively generated by building mental models of the causal structure of events, from which particular factors are identified in conversationally given explanations" (p. 275).

Why have theorists followed Mill (1814) on this matter? The answer, we believe, depends on subtleties in the circumstances of events. Suppose you know that good sunlight and a certain new fertilizer cause poor flowers to grow remarkably well. You may envisage the following circumstances:

```
sunlight  fertilizer  growth
sunlight  ¬fertilizer             ¬growth
¬sunlight            fertilizer ¬growth
¬sunlight            ¬fertilizer            ¬growth
```

Here the causal roles of sunlight and fertilizer are equivalent. They are the jointly the unique cause of the growth, and in the absence of either of them there is no growth. Other circumstances, however, are possible. Consider, for instance, these circumstances:

```
sunlight  fertilizer  growth
sunlight  ¬fertilizer            growth
sunlight  ¬fertilizer            ¬growth
¬sunlight            fertilizer ¬growth
¬sunlight            ¬fertilizer            ¬growth
```

Here the relation between the sunlight and growth is as follows:

```
sunlight  growth
sunlight  ¬growth
¬sunlight            ¬growth
```

That is, sunlight allows growth to occur. In contrast, fertilizer and growth occur in all the possibilities:

```
fertilizer  growth
fertilizer  ¬growth
¬fertilizer            growth
¬fertilizer            ¬growth
```

Fertilizer and growth are not equivalent causal factors, and the previous full circumstances show that the presence of sunlight enables the fertilizer to cause growth. In other words, the circumstances correspond to the description: "Given that there is good sunlight, if a certain new fertilizer is used on poor flowers, then they grow remarkably well. However, if there is not good sunlight, poor flowers do not grow well, even if the fertilizer is used on them."

Another set of circumstances swaps the causal roles of sunlight and fertilizer:

```
sunlight  fertilizer  growth
¬sunlight            fertilizer  growth
¬sunlight            fertilizer  ¬growth
sunlight  ¬fertilizer            ¬growth
¬sunlight            ¬fertilizer            ¬growth
```

These circumstances correspond to the following description: "Given the use of a certain new fertilizer on poor flowers, if there is good sunlight, then the flowers grow remarkably well. However, if the new fertilizer is not used on poor flowers, they do not grow well, even if there is good sunlight."

If the model theory is correct, then naive individuals ought to be able to identify which is the cause and which is the enabling condition in descriptions such as the previous contrasting pair. We carried out an experiment to test this prediction (Goldvarg & Johnson-Laird, 2001). In an earlier study, Cheng and Novick (1991) presented descriptions of circumstances without using any causal expressions, and the participants were able to identify the causes and the enabling conditions within these descriptions. But Cheng and Novick used descriptions of constant enabling conditions and of inconstant causes. In the preceding descriptions, however, neither the causes nor the enabling conditions are constant. Our experiment also counterbalanced the order of mention of cause and enabling condition. The participants acted as their own controls and read in random orders eight descriptions that each concerned a cause, an enabling condition, and an effect. The descriptions also included two filler items—one in which there were two joint causes and one in which there were no causes. The participants encountered just one version of a particular content but two instances of the four sorts of description in the experiment as a whole. Their task was to identify the enabling condition and the cause in each scenario. They were told that the cause of an event "brings about the event," and the enabling condition "makes the event possible," but these clauses did not occur in the scenarios themselves.

The participants correctly identified the enabling conditions and causes on 85% of trials, and every participant was correct more often than not. Hence, individuals given descriptions of scenarios that make no reference to causation can distinguish enabling conditions from causes. Contrary to a long-established tradition beginning with Mill (1874), we conclude that causes and enabling conditions do differ in meaning, that naive individuals can distinguish between them, and that they can base their distinction on descriptions of the relevant circumstances. These results are highly pertinent to an alternative theory of causation to which we now turn.

PROBABILISTIC THEORIES OF CAUSATION

Certain 20th century philosophers proposed that causation is a probabilistic notion. This idea would probably have astounded philosophers of early epochs: Hume (1748/1988) argued for a constant conjunction of cause and effect, Kant (1781/1934) argued for a necessary connection between them, and Mill (1874) argued for an invariable cause and effect. We surmise that probability entered into conceptions of causation as a result of quantum mechanics (see, e.g., von Mises, 1957, sixth lecture). On the one hand, Russell (1912) suggested that the concept of causation should be expurgated from philosophy because it had been replaced by probabilistic correlations in science. On the other hand, some philosophers modified their conception of causality to fit the new world. Reichenbach (1956) argued that "C causes E" if the conditional probability of E given C is greater than the conditional probability of E given not C (see also Salmon, 1980; Suppes, 1970, 1984; cf. Legrenzi & Sonino, 1994). Cheng and her colleagues have proposed a similar psychological theory based on probabilities (e.g., Cheng & Novick, 1990; Cheng, 1997). Cheng assumes that when the contrast between the two conditional probabilities is noticeably positive "C causes E," and, when it is noticeably negative "C prevents E."

The chief evidence for a probabilistic semantics is that people judge that a causal relation holds in cases in which the cause is neither necessary nor sufficient to bring about the effect. Most people, for instance, will assent to the proposition: "HIV causes AIDS," even though they know that not every one with HIV develops AIDS. Loose generalizations are common in daily life. A more accurate assertion is, accordingly "HIV usually causes AIDS." Readers who agree that this assertion is more accurate have conceded the main point: If causes were intrinsically probabilistic, then the two assertions would not differ in accuracy. The probabilistic approach may be justified for scientific conceptions of causation, especially since the development of quantum mechanics. But, as we try to show, a probabilistic meaning is implausible for causal relations in everyday life.

The two preceding experiments in this paper count against a probabilistic meaning for causation. If a general causal claim "C causes E," is construed probabilistically, then nothing is impossible. The effect E can occur both with the cause C and without it. All that matters is that the effect should occur more often with the cause than without it. Yet none of the participants in our first experiment concurred with this principle (see Table 9.2). They all judged that "C causes E" ruled out as impossible the case in which the cause occurs without the effect.

Singular causal claims are still more problematic for probabilistic analyses. They raise the problem of interpreting the probabilities of unique events. They imply—at least at face value—that an assertion such as "Pushing the switch down caused the light to come on" does not mean that the light came on. It probably did, but it may not have. And, once again, the results of our second experiment showed that naive individuals take assertions of the form "C will cause E," to rule out the possibility of C without E (see Table 9.3).

Our third experiment showed that naive individuals do distinguish between causes and enabling conditions. But consider the following equal distribution of frequencies:

```
sunlight  fertilizer  growth              20
sunlight  ¬fertilizer        growth            20
sunlight  ¬fertilizer              ¬growth       20
¬sunlight           fertilizer ¬growth       20
¬sunlight           ¬fertilizer        ¬growth        20
```

In this distribution, the conditional probability of growth given sunlight ($p = 2/3$) is greater than the probability of growth given no sunlight ($p = 0$), and so sunlight should be judged as a cause of growth. But the distribution also shows that the conditional probability of growth given fertilizer ($p = 1/2$) is greater than the probability of growth given no fertilizer ($p = 1/3$), so fertilizer should be judged as a cause of growth. Hence, both sunlight and fertilizer are causes of growth according to the probabilistic account, and sunlight is the stronger candidate. Yet, as the model theory predicts, individuals judge sunlight to be the enabling condition and fertilizer to be the cause. In short, the probabilistic theory has the unfortunate consequence of obliterating the distinction between causes and enabling conditions.

Why do people so commonly assent to loose causal generalizations? One factor may be that they are aware that many causes in everyday life yield their effects only if the required but unknown enabling conditions are present and potentially disabling conditions are absent. It follows that when people assent to loose generalizations such as "HIV causes AIDS," they are granting the effect, other things being equal. They mean that the causal relation holds unless some enabling condition is absent or some disabling condition is present.

If causes and enabling conditions differ in meaning, then they should also differ in their logical consequences. For example, suppose that the following proposition is true: "Taking bichloride of mercury will cause her to die," and assume that the causal antecedent is true: "She takes bichloride of mercury." It follows validly that "she will die." In contrast, suppose that the following proposition is true: "Not taking bichloride of mercury will allow her to live," and that the enabling antecedent is true: "She does not take bichloride of mercury." It does not follow validly that "she will live." We have observed exactly this pattern and other such patterns in deductive inference (Goldvarg & Johnson-Laird, 2001), thereby corroborating the model theory's claim that the two sorts of relation are logically distinct.

DEDUCTIVE REASONING FROM CAUSAL RELATIONS

Some theorists suppose that causes can be neither observed nor deduced, that they are only induced. But the causal status of an observation can be deduced from knowledge of its circumstances. Knowledge makes available explicit possibilities, which can modulate the interpretation of conditionals (Johnson-Laird & Byrne, 2002) and which can be used to resolve inconsistencies among assertions (Legrenzi et al., 2001). Similarly, if you observe that someone throws the switch and the lights come on, then the explicit possibilities in your knowledge can yield the deduction that throwing the switch caused the lights to come on.

How do individuals make causal deductions? One answer is that they rely on the laws of thought, that is, formal rules of inference of some sort (see, e.g., Braine & O'Brien, 1998). Indeed, Rips (1994, p. 336) suggested that formal rules could be extended to deal with causal reasoning. A similar proposal is that causal deductions depend on axioms (or meaning postulates) of the following sort: "If C causes D, and D prevents E, then C prevents E," where C, D, and E are variables that take states as their values (see, e.g., von Wright, 1973). Another answer is that causal deduction depends on pragmatic reasoning schemas (e.g., Cheng, Holyoak, Nisbett, & Oliver, 1986). That is, the preceding axiom is framed instead as a rule of inference:

> C causes D.
> D prevents E.
> ∴ C prevents E

This idea goes back to Kelley's (1973) theory of causal attribution, which postulated such schemas for checking causal relations. Similarly, Morris and Nisbett (1993) proposed a schema including the following two rules:

> (1) If cause C is present then effect E occurs.
> Cause C is present.
> ∴ Effect E occurs.

> (2) If cause C is present then effect E occurs.
> Effect E does not occur.
> ∴ Cause C is not present.

Still another answer, however, is that you reason using mental models. Consider the following set of possibilities satisfying the temporal constraint:

> c   d   e
> ¬c   ¬d   e
> ¬c   d   ¬e

You infer the following: "C will cause E." You infer this because the set contains each of the possibilities required for this relation.

To try to decide among these three alternative theories, we carried out several experiments examining causal reasoning (Goldvarg & Johnson-Laird, 2001). In one experiment, the task was to draw conclusions from pairs of causal premises. The first premise interrelated two states of affairs, C and D, using one of the four causal relations, and the second premise interrelated D and E, also using one of the four causal relations (see Table 9.1). The experiment examined all 16 possible pairs of relations, and the model theory predicts that naive reasoners should draw conclusions from all of them. Half of these conclusions are valid, but half of them are invalid. For example, consider a problem of the following form:

> C prevents D.
> D causes E.
> What, if anything, follows?

The model theory predicts that the premises should yield the following mental model:

> c   ¬d
>   d   e
>   ...

So reasoners should tend to draw the conclusion "C prevents E," because C occurs without E. The fully explicit model of the premises, however, is as follows:

c	¬d	e
c	¬d	¬e
¬c	d	e
¬c	¬d	e
¬c	¬d	¬e

And, as this model shows, C does not prevent E. In fact, there is no causal relation between them. Neither formal rules nor pragmatic schemas, as they are currently formulated, make any predictions about these deductions.

The results of the experiment corroborated the model theory. In the previous example, for instance, 19 out of the 20 participants drew the predicted conclusion. And, in general, they tended to draw the conclusions predicted by the mental models of the premises.

Another experiment examined the occurrence of illusions in causal reasoning. As we remarked at the beginning of the chapter, mental models do not represent what is false, and they yield grossly erroneous conclusions from certain premises. If such illusory inferences occur in causal reasoning, then they would provide further support for the model theory, which is at present the only theory to predict them. As an example, consider the following problem:

> One of these assertions is true and one of them is false:
> Marrying Pat will cause Viv to relax.
> Not marrying Pat will cause Viv to relax.
> The following assertion is definitely true:
> Viv will marry Pat.
> Will Viv relax?

The mental models of the disjunction of the first two premises are as follows:

> marry   relax
> ¬marry   relax

So it seems that Viv is bound to relax. But these models fail to represent what is false (i.e., when the first premise is true, the second premise is false, and vice versa). If it is false that marrying Pat will cause Viv to relax, then Viv won't relax even after she marries Pat. If it is false that not marrying Pat will cause Viv to relax, then she won't relax even though she doesn't marry Pat. On a unique interpretation of cause, the premises imply nothing whatsoever about whether or not Viv will relax, and on a nonunique interpretation of cause the premises imply that Viv won't relax. The conclusion that Viv will relax is therefore an illusion. In our experiment, nearly everyone succumbed to the illusory inferences but drew the correct conclusions to the control problems.

GENERAL DISCUSSION

The model theory postulates a minimal semantics for causation: The cause is sufficient for the effect, which does not precede the cause. The semantics does not invoke physical contact (cf. Geminiani, Carassa, & Bara, 1996; Leslie, 1984; Michotte, 1946/1963) because people often make causal assertions that violate physical contiguity. And it does not invoke a probabilistic relation or one based on causal powers or mechanisms (cf. Harré & Madden, 1975; Koslowski, 1996). Mechanisms can be crucial in inferring causation from correlations or other observations (see, e.g. Miyake, 1986; White, 1995), but mechanisms themselves embody causal relations, and they are not part of the meaning of a causal assertion. However, contrary to the tradition dating back to Mill (1874), the model theory does draw a semantic distinction between causes and enabling conditions. Naive individuals, as our experiments showed, concur with this distinction.

Is there nothing more to the meaning of causal relations than possibilities and the temporal constraint that an effect does not precede its cause or enabling condition? One doubt is that the mere existence of the relevant set of possibilities satisfying the temporal constraint does not suffice for a causal relation. Consider the following two alternative possibilities, for example:

divisible by two	even
not divisible by two	not even

One does not assert that being divisible by two causes a number to be even but rather that being divisible by two necessarily implies that a number is even. The domain is one of logical possibilities rather than physical possibilities. Likewise, the following alternative possibilities exist in some countries:

over the age of 18	drinks alcohol
over the age of 18	does not drink alcohol
not over the age of 18	does not drink alcohol

Yet one does not assert that being over the age of 18 enables a person to drink alcohol but rather that being over the age of 18 makes it permissible for a person to drink alcohol. The domain is one of deontic possibilities rather than physical possibilities; that is, someone under the age of 18 years may, in fact, drink alcohol, but it would violate what is permissible. Causal, logical, and deontic claims all relate to possibilities, but the domain within which they hold (physical vs. inferential vs. deontic) yields the difference between them.

Yet even in domains concerning physical possibilities, could there be cases that satisfy the model theory but that are not causal? Consider, for example, the relation between day and night. It is not possible to have day without night following closely on its heels. Or so it seems. Yet day does not cause night. Surely more is at stake than mere possibilities, and something is missing from our analysis? One candidate might be a causal mechanism that explains the circumstances—day is a consequence of the sun shining on the earth, and, as the earth rotates, day on one part of the earth gives way to night. Thus, the correlation between day and night is explained in terms of a common underlying cause. A corollary of this account is that there is a possibility in which day is not followed by night: You need only orbit the earth at a speed that counteracts the effects of the earth's rotation, and you will live in perpetual day. This possibility refutes the causal claim that day causes night. Thus, the invocation of explanatory principles and generalizations is a useful way—perhaps the only way in many cases—to infer causation from correlation, but the resulting conclusion of a causal relation means no more than the model theory postulates.

The model theory provides accounts of what causal relations mean, of how they are mentally represented, and of how people make deductive inferences from them. Causal relations refer to sets of temporally ordered possibilities. Naive individuals envisage these possibilities in mental models, and they make causal interpretations using their knowledge to envisage the circumstances of states of affairs. They infer the consequences of causal claims from what holds in their models of the premises. The theory draws a sharp distinction between the meaning of causal relations and the evidence that supports them. It also distinguishes between unique causation in which a state is necessary and sufficient to bring about an effect and nonunique causation in which a state is sufficient, but not necessary, to bring about an effect because it can have other causes. The principal consequence of the theory is that the meanings of causal relations are determinate, not probabilistic. The assertion "A caused B" can accordingly be paraphrased as "A made it impossible for B not to occur." A corollary is that cause is a transitive relation. The assertion that "A allowed B" can be similarly paraphrased as "A made it possible for B to occur." The case for a causal relation depends on observation, background knowledge, and common sense. None of these components, however, concern the meaning of the relation but merely help individuals to determine whether or not that meaning is satisfied by states of affairs. The best test to establish a general causal relation is a scientific experiment.

ACKNOWLEDGMENTS

Preparation of this article was supported by a grant to the first author from the National Science Foundation (Grant BCS 0076287) to study strategies in reasoning.

REFERENCES

Barrouillet, P., & Lecas, J.-F. (1999). Mental models in conditional reasoning and working memory. *Thinking and Reasoning, 5,* 289– 02.

Braine, M. D. S., & O'Brien, D. P. (Eds.). (1998). *Mental logic.* Mahwah, NJ: Lawrence Erlbaum Associates.

Byrne, R. M. J. (1997). Cognitive processes in counterfactual thinking about what might have been. In D. K. Medin (Ed.), *The psychology of learning and motivation: Advances in research and theory* (Vol. 37, pp. 105– 54). San Diego, CA: Academic Press.

Cheng, P. W. (1997). From covariation to causation: A causal power theory. *Psychological Review, 104,* 367–405.

Cheng, P. W., Holyoak, K. J., Nisbett, R. E., & Oliver, L. M. (1986). Pragmatic versus syntactic approaches to training deductive reasoning. *Cognitive Psychology, 18,* 293–328.

Cheng, P. W., & Nisbett, R. E. (1993). Pragmatic constraints on causal deduction. In R. E. Nisbett (Ed.), *Rules for reasoning* (pp. 207–227). Hillsdale, NJ: Lawrence Erlbaum Associates.

Cheng, P. W., & Novick, L. R. (1990). A probabilistic contrast model of causal induction. *Journal of Personality and Social Psychology, 58,* 545–567.

Cheng, P. W., & Novick, L. R. (1991). Causes versus enabling conditions. *Cognition, 40,* 83–120.

Craik, K. (1943). *The nature of explanation.* Cambridge, UK: Cambridge University Press.

Einhorn, H. J., & Hogarth, R. M. (1986). Judging probable cause. *Psychological Bulletin, 99,* 3–19.

Geminiani, G. C., Carassa, A., & Bara, B. G. (1996). Causality by contact. In J. Oakhill & A. Garnham (Eds.), *Mental models in cognitive science* (pp. 275–303). Hove, UK: Psychology Press.

Goldvarg, Y., & Johnson-Laird, P. N. (2000). Illusions in modal reasoning. *Memory and Cognition, 28,* 282–294.

Goldvarg, E., & Johnson-Laird, P. N. (2001). Naive causality: A mental model of causal meaning and reasoning. *Cognitive Science, 25,* 565–610.

Grice, H. P. (1975). Logic and conversation. In P. Cole & J. L. Morgan (Eds.), *Syntax and semantics, vol. 3: Speech acts.* New York: Academic Press.

Harré, R., & Madden, E. H. (1975). *Causal powers.* Oxford, UK: Blackwell.

Hart, H. L. A., & Honoré, A. M. (1985). *Causation in the law* (2nd ed.). Oxford, UK: Clarendon Press.

Hesslow, G. (1988). The problem of causal selection. In D. J. Hilton (Ed.), *Contemporary science and natural explanation: Commonsense conceptions of causality* (pp. 11–32). Brighton, UK: Harvester Press.

Hilton, D. J., & Erb, H-P. (1996). Mental models and causal explanation: Judgements of probable cause and explanatory relevance. *Thinking and Reasoning, 2,* 273–308.

Hume, D. (1988). An enquiry concerning human understanding. La Salle, IL: Open Court. (Original work published 1748)

Johnson-Laird, P. N. (1983). *Mental models: Towards a cognitive science of language, inference and consciousness.* Cambridge, UK: Cambridge University Press.

Johnson-Laird, P. N., & Byrne, R. M. J. (1991). *Deduction.* Hillsdale, NJ: Lawrence Erlbaum Associates.

Johnson-Laird, P. N., & Byrne, R. M. J. (2002). Conditionals: A theory of their meaning, pragmatics, and role in inference. *Psychological Review, 109,* 646–678..

Johnson-Laird, P. N., Legrenzi, P., Girotto, P., & Legrenzi, M. S. (2000). Illusions in reasoning about consistency. *Science, 288,* 531–532.

Johnson-Laird, P. N., Legrenzi, P., Girotto, P., Legrenzi, M. S., & Caverni, J.-P. (1999). Naive probability: A mental model theory of extensional reasoning. *Psychological Review, 106,* 62–88.

Johnson-Laird, P. N., & Savary, F. (1999). Illusory inferences: A novel class of erroneous deductions. *Cognition, 71,* 191–229.

Kahneman, D., & Miller, D. T. (1986). Norm theory: Comparing reality to its alternative. *Psychological Review, 93,* 75–88.

Kahneman, D., & Tversky, A. (1982). The simulation heuristic. In D. Kahneman, P. Slovic, & A. Tversky (Eds.), *Judgment under uncertainty: Heuristics and biases* (pp. 201–210). Cambridge: Cambridge University Press.

Kant, I. (1934). *Critique of pure reason.* J.M.D. Meiklejohn (Trans.). New York: Dutton. (Original work published 1781)

Kelley, H. H. (1973). The processes of causal attribution. *American*

Psychologist, 28, 107–128.

Koslowski, B. (1996). *Theory and evidence: The development of scientific reasoning.* Cambridge, MA: MIT Press.

Legrenzi, M., Legrenzi, P., Girotto, V., & Johnson-Laird, P. N. (2001). *Reasoning to consistency: A theory of naïve nonmonotonic reasoning.* Unpublished manuscript.

Legrenzi, P., & Sonino, M. (1994). Psychologistic aspects of Suppes's definition of causality. In P. Humphreys (Ed.), *Patrick Suppes: Scientific philosopher* (Vol. 1, pp. 381–399). The Netherlands: Kluwer.

Leslie, A. M. (1984). Spatiotemporal contiguity and perception of causality in infants. *Perception, 13,* 287–305.

Mackie, J. L. (1980). *The cement of the universe: A study in causation.* Oxford, UK: Oxford University Press.

McEleney, A., & Byrne, R. M. J. (2001). *Counterfactual thinking and causal explanation.* Unpublished manuscript.

McGill, A. L. (1989). Context effects in judgments of causation. *Journal of Personality and Social Psychology, 57,* 189–200.

Michotte, A. (1963). *The perception of causality.* London: Methuen. (Original work published 1946)

Mill, J. S. (1874). *A system of logic, ratiocinative and inductive: Being a connected view of the principles of evidence and the methods of scientific evidence* (8th ed.). New York: Harper.

Miyake, N. (1986). Constructive interaction and the iterative process of understanding. *Cognitive Science, 10,* 151–177.

Morris, M. W., & Nisbett, R. E. (1993). Tools of the trade: Deductive schemas taught in psychology and philosophy. In R. E. Nisbett (Ed.), *Rules for reasoning* (pp. 228–256). Hillsdale, NJ: Lawrence Erlbaum Associates.

Reichenbach, H. (1956). *The direction of time.* Berkeley: University of California Press.

Rips, L. J. (1994). *The psychology of proof.* Cambridge, MA: MIT Press.

Russell, B. A. W. (1912). On the notion of cause. *Proceedings of the Aristotelian Society, 13,* 1–26.

Salmon, W. C. (1980). Probabilistic causality. *Pacific Philosophical Quarterly, 61,* 50–74.

Schaeken, W., Johnson-Laird, P. N., & d'Ydewalle, G. (1996). Mental models and temporal reasoning. *Cognition, 60,* 205–234.

Suppes, P. (1970). *A probabilistic theory of causality.* Amsterdam: North-Holland.

Suppes, P. (1984). *Probabilistic metaphysics.* Oxford, UK: Basil Blackwell.

Turnbull, W., & Slugoski, B. R. (1988). Conversational and linguistic processes in causal attribution. In D. Hilton (Ed.), *Contemporary science and natural explanation: Commonsense conceptions of causality* (pp. 66–93). Brighton, UK: Harvester Press.

Tversky, A., & Kahneman, D. (1980). Causal schemas in judgments under uncertainty. In M. Fishbein (Ed.), *Progress in social psychology.* Hillsdale, NJ: Lawrence Erlbaum Associates.

von Mises, R. (1957). *Probability, statistics and truth* (2nd ed.). London:

Allen and Unwin.

von Wright, G. H. (1973). On the logic and epistemology of the causal relation. In P. Suppes (Ed.), *Logic, methodology and philosophy of science, IV* (pp. 293–312). Amsterdam: North-Holland.

White, P. A. (1995). Use of prior beliefs in the assignment of causal roles: Causal powers versus regularity-based accounts. *Memory and Cognition, 23*, 243–254.

Yang, Y., & Johnson-Laird, P. N. (2000). Illusions in quantified reasoning: How to make the impossible seem possible, and vice versa. *Memory and Cognition, 28*, 452–465.

10

A Mental Model Theory of Informal Argument

David W. Green

The theory of mental models is extended to cover informal argument. I propose that in comprehending arguments individuals create a representation of the structure of presented arguments and an argument mental model. Both representations are involved in reaching a decision. Arguments vary in their strength and the relative strength of arguments pro and con an option determines the decision reached. Relevant data are considered and further developments and predictions identified.

INTRODUCTION

Individuals and groups reach decisions through talk, so we need a theory that covers both individual and distributed cognition if our psychological accounts are to be complete and relevant. This chapter proposes that an integrated theory is possible if we extend the theory of mental models by making explicit use of the notion of an argument. We define an argument as minimally comprising a claim and a reason (see Kuhn, 1991; Oestermeier & Hesse, 2000; Rips, 1999; Toulmin, 1958; van Eemeren, et al., 1996; Voss & Means, 1991). The notion of an argument is central for two reasons. First, decisions in everyday life are often reached in circumstances of considerable ignorance. In consequence, individuals cannot simply value one course of action over another, so the classical theories of choice are inapplicable (Fox, 1994; Hogarth & Kunreuther, 1995; Oatley, 1996; Shafir, Simonson & Tversky, 1993). Instead, individuals argue with themselves about the appropriate course of action (Billig, 1987; Green, 1995, 1996; Moshman & Geil, 1998; Rips, 1999). They seek reasons, pro and con, for some course of action. Indeed, in the absence of compelling reasons, individuals may refuse to take any action at all (Shafir et al., 1993). Decision and actions are argument based (see also Lipshitz, 1993). Second, the notion of argument provides a bridge between the realms of individual thinking and the thinking of groups of individuals (see, e.g., Billig, 1987; Kuhn, 1991). Argument is critical to the conduct of the law. It is central to the conduct of science and to the exercise of individual freedom in democracies (Habermas, 1984). It is also critical to the conduct of business (Mason & Mitroff, 1981). Argument is typically understood in the sense of an opposition between points of view entertained by different participants in a conversation. As Kuhn (1991) notes, resolution requires the weighing of alternatives by each participant.

An identical process of weighing must also occur when individuals argue with themselves. The focus of the present proposal is argumentation within individuals. Such a focus cannot deliver a full account of the cognitive processes involved when two or more individuals argue together because other psycholinguistic and discursive processes are involved (see, e.g., Rips, 1999), but it can consider key cognitive processes in representing and resolving arguments.

THE SPRINGS OF ACTION

The case for developing a psychological theory of argument may seem self-evident but a number of researchers have contested the role of arguments in human conduct both narrowly and more generally. Answering such objections can help define what kinds of data the theory must explain.

Evans and Wason (1976) argued in the context of the selection task (Wason, 1968) for the view that the reasons individuals give for their selections are merely rationalizations. Individuals select those cards to which they attend, and their selections reflect implicit (unconscious) attentional processes rather than explicit (conscious) analytic processes (Evans, 1996). Reasons are generated post-hoc. In rationalizing a decision in this task, individuals need only find a reason that fits or make sense of it. Because a given decision can be justified in various ways, the reasons individuals offer for rejecting cards should not be affected by which cards they do select. However, Green (1995, pp. 181–182) reported that the reasons individuals give for not selecting a particular card do depend on which cards they select. The reasons individuals propose are more constrained than the rationalization position allows. Individuals think about all the cards (if ever so briefly), and their selections can be seen as an outcome of a process of argumentation constrained by their ability to envisage alternative values on the cards (see Green, 1997). Interestingly, Moshman and Geil (1998) showed that groups of individuals arguing together about the merits of selecting cards reached the logically correct solution, even though none of the participants initially envisaged selecting the correct cards.

Zajonc (1980) contested more generally (but he had to argue to do so!) that we rarely weigh the pros and cons of a course of action and invariably choose on the basis of affective preferences and rationalize our choices (p. 155). Oatley (1996) concurred that emotions and feelings are needed to make decisions in an uncertain world, and Slovic, Finucane, Peters, and MacGregor. (2001) claimed further that reliance on affect and emotion is a quicker, easier, and more efficient way to navigate in a complex, uncertain, and sometimes dangerous world. Our feelings about an issue may in turn derive from images associated with it. In the area of consumer choice, for instance, Kim, Allen, and Kardes (1996) showed that the imagery associated with a particular product not only leads individuals to draw inferences about the product but also induces a direct affective response to it. In a number of studies, Slovic et al. established that judgments are guided by positive and negative feelings associated with images linked to the issue at hand (see also

Damasio, 1994). In one study, positive and negative images associated with a particular city predicted the actual choice of the city as a holiday destination. Images also seem to markedly affect public attitudes to new technologies or sociopolitical issues. For instance, images of the devastated Chernobyl reactor confirmed for many the risks of nuclear power generation. Sensitivity to such images may reflect a general tendency to focus on the extremeness of available evidence, whether imaginal or propositional, with perhaps too little regard to sample size (Griffin & Tversky, 1992).

Granted that an individual's feelings form the neural and psychological substrate of utility (Slovic et al., 2001), emotional factors are not necessarily the only ones involved in a decision. Indeed, to deny this possibility is tantamount to denying any capacity for reflective thought, or hypothetical thinking, or to so limit its use that one may question its adaptive value. Individuals may decide in the way they do for broadly cognitive reasons as well. Green, McClelland, Muckli, and Simmons (1999) showed that both cognitive and affective factors are important. They extended an earlier study by Macrae (1992). In that study, individuals read about Lucy, who went to a restaurant and got food poisoning. Individuals had to decide how much the restaurant should pay in fines. Macrae found that the amount of the fine was predicted by an affective factor: the amount of sympathy expressed for Lucy, where sympathy was assessed on a 9-point scale labeled *none at all* at one end and *a great deal* at the other end. Green et al. (1999) required individuals to give reasons for their decisions in addition to rating their sympathy for Lucy. Two types of reason were distinguished. Some individuals treated the episode of food poisoning as a one-off accident. Others considered that the restaurant had failed in its duty of care. Higher fines were associated with the generation or endorsement of the latter reason. Multiple regression analyses of the data in one experiment (Experiment 2) showed that the affective reason (rated sympathy) explained 2.8% of the variance in the fines ($p < .05$) and cognitive reasons explained 17.7% of the variance ($p < .001$).

Many factors may affect the extent to which individuals reflect on the pros and cons of a decision. The social psychological literature on persuasion and attitude change provides an important source of information on these factors. It led Petty and Cacioppo (1984) to distinguish two different routes in their account of persuasion: a peripheral route and a central route. For certain kinds of decisions, such as buying a low-cost product, the peripheral route dominates, and individuals purchase on the basis of familiarity of the brand and imagery associated with the product or the sheer number of arguments about it. In the case of more expensive products, a central route dominates, and individuals consider the import of the arguments. Their account nicely incorporates the fact that human judgment and decision making is adaptive. However, it leaves open the nature of the mental representations involved and tells us little about the processes involved in the central route when individuals reflect on an issue. Basing an account around the theory of mental models allows us to articulate a number of possibilities and to accommodate existing evidence (e.g., Petty, Priester, & Wegener, 1994). The basic premise is that informal arguments are fundamentally about actual or possible states of affairs in the world and the actions we can take with respect to them. The precise nature of the representations constructed depends on the task in hand.

A MENTAL MODEL THEORY OF INFORMAL ARGUMENT

Preliminaries

The theory of mental models (Johnson-Laird, 1983; Johnson-Laird & Byrne, 1991) proposes that individuals represent states of affairs in the world by allowing mental tokens and their relations to stand for entities and their relations in the world. A mental model can incorporate information conveyed both by language and by perception. Mental tokens not only point to possible entities in the world, but also point to information in long-term memory about these entities. We can therefore extend the theory by allowing tokens to be affectively tagged (cf. Damasio, 1994). Such tagging provides one way in which feelings can enter informal argument.

An important feature of the theory is that individuals are held to minimize what they represent explicitly but can elaborate these initial representations (e.g., Johnson-Laird &Byrne, 1991; Legrenzi, Girotto & Johnson-Laird, 1993; Byrne, et al. 2000). Informal argument shows effects of both an initial representation and its elaboration. For instance, in the study by Green et al. (1999, Experiment 1) individuals reached more extreme decisions when they were free to envisage a single reason for their decision compared with when they had to decide between two presented reasons (the one-off accident reason and the duty of care reason) and had to endorse one of them (see also Lord, Lepper, & Preston, 1984). Experiment 2 in that study showed that decisions were sensitive to the argumentative actions individuals carried out. Individuals in a control condition were presented with the two possible reasons for a fine. They were free to endorse either one if it fitted their thinking on the matter or could write down another reason that did fit their thinking. Individuals in a rebuttal condition were presented with the same choice, but if they endorsed one or other of the presented reasons (e.g., the duty of care reason), they had to write an explicit rebuttal of the other reason (i.e., the one-off accident reason). As predicted, the difference in fines associated with the one-off accident reason and the duty of care reason was greater in the rebuttal condition: the mean difference was £1373 in the rebuttal condition compared with £374 in the control condition. Explicitly rebutting an alternative reduced its impact on the decision.

The circumstances leading to a more elaborate representation are not fully known. On emotive issues, there is some evidence to suggest that individuals ignore arguments counter to their position (Baron, 1995). Individuals certainly vary considerably in their skills in challenging the extent to which a reason supports a claim (Kuhn, 1991; Shaw, 1996) and on the extent to which they spontaneously consider all the relevant arguments (e.g., Kuhn, Weinstock, & Flaton, 1994). It may be, as the social psychological literature suggests, that individuals high in need for cognition are more likely to elaborate representations spontaneously (Petty, Priester, & Wegener, 1995). These data on informal argument are consistent with the expectations of the basic theory, but the theory must be extended to represent the fact that arguments have structure, are of different types, and have to be combined. The following section makes a specific proposal.

Principal Processes And Representations

As a way of introducing the proposal (see Green, 1996, for some initial thoughts) consider the following excerpt:

> Sanctions are in place to stop Saddam Hussein producing the means to wantonly destroy other people's lives. If sanctions were lifted, Saddam would not turn into a champion of international human rights, nor would he start spending his extra revenue on medicines and food for his people. He would immediately impose his control over the north of the country by all means at his disposal and would mass troops on the border of Syria, thereby making threatening overtures to Israel (Letters, *Independent* Feb 20 2001).

The writer goes on to assert that an Israeli preemptive strike on Saddam's weapons factories would risk all-out war in the region and that suffering not only to the Iraqi people but to millions of others in the region will be greater.

We can note first that arguments relate in various ways to other arguments. Arguments have a structure. This argument on sanctions seeks to argue against the claim of a previous letter rather than to support it. It does so, and this is the second point we can note, by inviting the reader to imagine a counterfactual situation in which sanctions are lifted. In comprehending this argument, individuals we suggest construct a mental model of this alternative state of affairs. Such a mental model justified by mental simulation supports the claim that sanctions should not be lifted, given the yardstick that a policy is to be preferred if it minimizes suffering. Other yardsticks are possible. An economic yardstick, for instance, might consider the costs and benefits of restrictions on oil flow.

Any theory of informal argument must answer a number of questions: how are arguments represented? How do these arguments affect the decision reached? The core of the present proposal is that a comprehension process generates an argument structure and builds one or more mental models of the states of affairs relevant to the issue (see Figure 10.1).

If individuals are to be able to represent arguments for one position or another in their own minds, or to argue for a course of action with others, they must be able to reference the presented arguments and know who made them. The notion of a mental token is a general one, so mental tokens and their relations can stand for arguments and their relations. Each token points to a claim and a reason, and relations among tokens capture the way each argument bears on the issue at hand and relates to other arguments (see, later examples of the kinds of argument structures). Argument tokens can also be labeled by the source of the argument such as the person who made them.

The heart of the present proposal is that, when individuals reflect on a problem, they construct a specific kind of mental model based on the presented arguments. For instance, in the previous example, the presented arguments trigger a mental simulation (Kahneman & Tversky, 1982) of a counterfactual state of affairs. The resulting model is justified or warranted by the mental simulation (Figure 10.2 illustrates) and will be termed an argument mental model or argument model, for short.

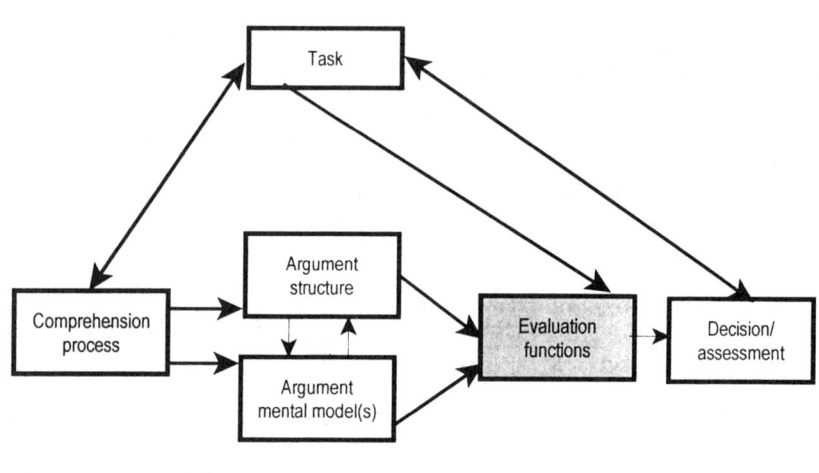

FIG. 10.1 A diagram of the main processes and representations in processing an argument.

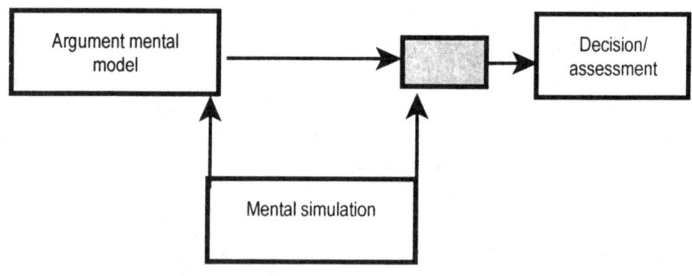

FIG. 10.2 A diagram of an argument mental model. The shaded oblong depicts the evaluation function.

The nature of the task establishes the decision requirements (e.g., quick or deliberate), the nature of the argument representations constructed, and the yardsticks or evaluations applied to them. An argument can be evaluated qua argument—the top route in Figure 1. For instance, the evaluation could be in terms of the sheer number or complexity of the arguments expressed in favor of a given position irrespective of their quality. Alternatively, the extremeness of the argument (e.g., the vividness of the associated imagery or its affective value), the source of the argument, or the quality of the data cited in the argument may be used to evaluate it. Note that in this regard this argument route differs from the peripheral route in the Petty and Cacioppo (1984) proposal. The evaluation of the argument mental model is in terms of the extent to which it supports one or other claim in terms of a specific yardstick relevant to the issue at hand, for instance, the number of lives saved.

The problem of combining conflicting arguments is handled by choosing the decision or course of action with the highest relative strength. In the event that no one argument is decisive, a further argumentative cycle occurs. Individuals can explicitly undercut or rebut presented arguments. They may, of course, do so in the course of comprehending the arguments initially, if they are oriented to do so. Computationally, reaching a decision based on conflicting arguments can be modeled as a process of constraint satisfaction, as Holyoak and Simon (1999) showed, but it is important theoretically to consider the actual nature of the representations constructed and how these contribute to the judgments of argument strength. A critical assumption is that decisions reflect the relative strength of arguments for one side or another, so we consider evidence for this assumption in the next section.

Table 10.1

Sample Materials in Argumentation Study 1

Background information
Quest is a computer software company in a competitive sector of the market. Futura is an investment company specializing in high technology companies. **On its Internet site, Futura criticized Quest's management. Two weeks later, Quest filed for bankruptcy and is now suing Futura claiming that Futura's message caused investors to lose confidence in Quest. The key arguments of the case are summarised below. Your task is to reach a verdict on the case given these arguments.**

1. Quest argued that their shares were trading at the average price of the shares in their sector prior to Futura's message
2. Futura argued that Quest's shares had already lost three quarters of their value over the previous two weeks and were still falling sharply at the time of their message.
3. Quest argued that their new product was likely to be profitable and would have boosted their share price if they had been able to launch it.
4. Futura argued that Quest's new product was still a year away from being launched at the time of their message and was too late to improve the company's prospects.

Argument Strength

In a recent experiment (Green & McCloy, 2003), based on work by Holyoak and Simon (1999), individuals were asked to reach a verdict in a mock legal case in which one company (Quest) was suing another (Futura) on the grounds that Futura's message posted over the Internet led to Quest's bankruptcy. Two arguments were presented on each side, with those on one side potentially undercutting arguments on the other. Table 10.1 provides a sample of the materials.

In contrast to other studies, where argument strength was either inferred (e.g., Osherson, Smith, Wilkie, Lopez, & Shafir, 1990) or was normatively established prior to the experiment (e.g., Bohner, Rank, Reinhard, Einwiller, & Erb, 1998), individuals rated the strength of each argument on a 10point scale. We take rated strength to index the strength of argument computed by an evaluation function. Consistent with expectations, the rated strength of the arguments pro plaintiff (Quest) and pro defendant (Futura) independently predicted the verdict, $p < 0.001$, in both cases. In other words, it is the relative strength of these arguments that determines the verdict. We consider later what factors affect rated argument strength.

Argument Structure and Argument Mental Models

Individuals are held to construct a dual representation in reflecting on arguments: They mentally represent the interrelationships of arguments with respect to a given issue, and they construct an argument mental model. We now consider the nature of the representations and their impact on decisions.

Arguments bear different relations to one another (see Baron, 1995; van Eemeren et al., 1996; Rips, 1999; and Table 10.2 for examples of possible structures). An argument might support another by providing a further reason for the claim it makes. Alternatively, it may undercut the reason motivating the claim or else present an opposing claim (a counterargument or rebuttal).

Table 10.2.
Informal arguments: examples of possible structures

Support
Bill is irresponsible (*claim*) because he fails to show up on time (*reason 1*) and because he does not hand in assignments on time (*reason 2*).
Undercut
Jack: You can't buy good coffee here I've tried all the coffee shops
Jill: Coffee shops aren't the only place. You should try the cafeterias (Rips, 1999).
Rebuttal
Jack has normal blood cholesterol; therefore he is unlikely to die of CHD.
Jack smokes and takes no exercise; therefore he is likely to die of CHD.

What evidence is there that individuals recognize, and mentally represent, the relationships of different arguments—their macrostructure? The evidence is partial and incomplete. Individuals can certainly identify arguments in texts (e.g., Oestermeier & Hesse, 2000; S haw, 1996;). They may also be said to display sensitivity to the structure of arguments indirectly. They rate a conclusion as more plausible, or more probable, if several distinct arguments converge on the same conclusion compared with when just one argument does so (George, 1999; McDonald, Samuels & Rispoli, 1996; Osherson et al.,1990). But the extent to which naive individuals explicitly recognize the structure of arguments is unknown. For example, there are no studies to my knowledge that examine whether or not individuals sort arguments (such as those in Table 10.2) according to their structural relations.

Is there then any empirical evidence supporting the principle of a dual representation? The social psychological literature (Petty et al., 1995) mentioned earlier is broadly consistent with the notion of a dual representation, but to address the matter more specifically we asked individuals in the study described previously to record the reasons for their verdicts. Individuals' decisions could reflect an appraisal of the quality of arguments in a domain independent way (the top route in Fig. 10.1). For instance, individuals might consider an argument to be weak if it lacks any independent data to support it. Alternatively, individuals could base their decision on an argument mental model—the lower route in Fig. 10.1. Their verdict should then reflect their judgment on whether or not Futura's action caused the bankruptcy.

Pennington and Hastie (1993), in their work on how individuals reach a verdict, proposed that they construct a story of the events. Such a story functions to generate the event in question— it functions in Peirce's terms (Feibleman, 1960; Green, 1994; Legrenzi, Legrenzi, Girotto, & Johnson-Laird, 2000) as an abductive explanation of the outcome (here Quest's bankruptcy). Individuals construct a mental model of the original state of affairs and mentally simulate the outcome (e.g., Green, 2001). If their simulation can generate the obtained outcome (e.g., Quest's bankruptcy), then they can treat it as an explanation of that outcome and as the cause of the outcome (Goldvarg & Johnson-Laird, 2001). They can select the verdict in terms of the yardstick that if the defendant caused the outcome (Quest's bankruptcy) they are to blame, whereas if they did not cause the outcome, they are not to blame. On one (hypothetical) mental simulation the share price falls in line with the market but Futura's message pushes the price down to a critical level and precludes the price picking up with the introduction of the new product. Such a simulation incorporates information from the two distinct pro Quest arguments and effectively maps components of the argument structure onto a single mental model.

Based on the resulting mental model, individuals would offer a reason such as "Futura caused Quest's collapse". Alternatively, individuals might explicitly entertain the counterfactual possibility (e.g., Johnson-Laird & Byrne, 1991) that if there had been no Internet message the company would have survived because of its new product. The reason offered would then be a counterfactual one (e.g., "if Futura had not posted its message, Quest would not have gone bankrupt"). Finally, they might assess the extent to which the event would have occurred anyway without the Internet message. The reason offered would then be a semifactual one (e.g., "even if Futura had not posted its message, Quest would have become bankrupt"). Causal and counterfactual causal accounts should be associated with a verdict finding in favor of the plaintiff Quest, whereas semifactual accounts should be associated with a verdict in favor of the defendant, Futura.

Table 10.3 supports the notion that there are two ways in which a verdict can be reached. Approximately 70% of participants explained their verdict in terms of states of affairs and 30% in terms of the quality of the arguments (e.g., the lack of independent evidence for the claims). As expected, the types of reasons offered varied as a function of the verdict reached $\chi^2 = 30.01$, $p < .001$. Counterfactual reasons were associated with a verdict in favor of the plaintiff (Quest), and semifactual reasons were associated with a verdict in favor of the defendant (Futura), $\chi^2 = 20.13$, $p < .001$. Of the participants who did not refer to the state of affairs described but to the nature of arguments, the majority found in favor of the defendant ($p < .01$, binomial test) perhaps because it is up to the plaintiff to prove that the defendant is at fault rather than up to the defendant to prove their innocence (Bailenson & Rips, 1996).

As a check on the proposal that the causal, counterfactual, and semifactual reasons offered for the verdict reflect the construction of a mental model, we also asked individuals to assess explicitly the extent to which Quest would have survived if Futura had not posted its message. They made their counterfactual judgments by circling one number on a scale running from *very improbable* (1) to *very probable* (20). Judgments varied as a function of verdict. As expected, they were higher when subjects found in favor of the plaintiff [mean = 13.41(2.62), n = 17] than when they found in favor of the defendant, mean = 7.97(3.61), $n = 42$, $t = 5.63$, $p < .0001$.

More specifically, individuals ($n = 23$) giving a semifactual reason rated the counterfactual probability as quite low, 7.26(3.16), whereas individuals ($n = 8$)

Table 10.3
Types of Reason (%) Offered as a Function of Verdict

Type of reason	Study 1 (minimal background)		Study 2 (enriched background)	
	Pro Plaintiff (N = 17)	Pro Defendant (N = 42)	Pro Plaintiff (N = 42)	Pro Defendant (N = 42)
Causal	29	7	52	17
Counter-factual	47	5	29	0
Semi-factual	0	55	0	74
Argument	18	33	0	5
Motivation/Other	6	0	19	5

giving a counterfactual reason and finding in favor of the plaintiff rated the probability twice as high, 14.25 (3.06).

The majority of individuals appear to envisage a mental model of the states of affairs, and this model drives their verdict. Argument quality may make an independent contribution or affect the extent to which individuals construct more than one mental model of the states of affairs. In fact, in the present study, the rated strength of the defendant's arguments predicted verdict with counterfactual probability partialled out, $r = .338$, $p < .01$, but the rated strength of the plaintiff's arguments was not a significant predictor, $r = .127$, ns, when rated counterfactual probability was partialled out. This suggests, but does not prove, that causal assessments were the principal basis of the strength ratings of the arguments for the plaintiff Quest, whereas other factors determined the strength ratings of the arguments for the defendant Futura.

Overall the data of this study support the notion of two different argument routes. The tendency to evaluate the quality of arguments rather than to assess the merits of different causal stories may arise because the background information is minimal (cf. Brem & Rips, 2000). In a follow-up study, we presented the same arguments but enriched the background information to a greater or lesser extent. In one condition, individuals read the following before reading the background information in common with the first study (the text in bold, Table 10.1):

> As you may know a company's current share price reflects the views of many investors and investment companies on the stream of profits the company will make in the future. Share prices rise if the market as a whole believes that there will be a strong stream of profits. Share prices fall in the expectation that profits will fall. The present case concerns Quest—a computer software company with an excellent track record and with a strong range of well-tested and innovative products. Innovation is important in

the sector, but a new product must also be well tested. At the time of the case, overall share prices within its sector had fallen dramatically *and lost between 70% to 80% of their value. Four out of 5 companies had suffered such declines.* At such a time, a company's share price can be extremely sensitive to negative information. Futura is an investment company specializing in high technology companies *but with no specific expertise in Quest's sector of the market.*

In two other conditions either the first or the second italicized text in the passage was omitted. There were no substantive differences among these three conditions, so we report the overall data and use the passage to illustrate. The enriched background should increase the number of individuals constructing a causal scenario because it allows them to flesh out their representation of the presented arguments. It should also increase the number of individuals finding in favor of Quest. The background suggests that the fall in Quest's share price was not a management failure but reflected market conditions in the sector as a whole as exemplified by the specific information on base rate (Evans, Handley, Perham, Over & Thompson, 2000; Girotto & Gonzalez, 2001). It also casts doubt on the validity of Futura's views. In fact, as Table 10.3 shows, with the enriched background, many more participants favored Quest, and very few explained their verdict in terms of the quality of arguments. Individuals favoring Quest were much more likely than those favoring Futura to mention at least one datum from the background information in their reasons (81% vs. 31%). Those favoring Futura presumably construed the presented arguments as consistent with the background. They could reason that Quest was likely to fail anyway given the market conditions. If they had entirely ignored the background, then many more would have cited the quality of argument as key to their decision.

Argument Construction and Resolution

These data are suggestive of a process of argument construction. All individuals may initially appraise the quality of arguments. Some curtail processing at this point in the absence of background information. Others go on to construct a mental model in which case complexity in the structure of arguments is parsimoniously represented by one or more mental models. Individuals use background information to endorse one model of the state of affairs over another or, perhaps, to reject states of affairs expressed by counterarguments. The data suggest that alternative models (e.g., causal and semifactual models) are not eliminated but jointly determine the outcome. This seems reasonable because in many everyday instances there are good reasons for some course of action and good reasons for some other course of action, and these reasons do not go away.

One can think of the alternative models as being ordered in terms of the likelihood of generating the outcome. The strength ratings provide an index of this ordering. For instance, a mental simulation of a change in share price may vary the rate at which it declines or stabilizes. The likelihood of a given outcome will then reflect the proportion of simulations in which one outcome occurs rather than another, and this will be encoded via the evaluation function in terms of a strength value and expressed behaviorally in a strength rating. Individual differences in strength ratings reflect which factors are considered in these mental simulations and the sensitivity of the evaluation function to these factors.

An alternative possibility is that individuals entertain a single explicit mental model (e.g., a causal or a semifactual model) linked to a verdict, and any alternative model is left implicit. But, if this is so, the implicit model nonetheless has a strength value. This possibility raises a theoretical question: According to the present proposal, it should make a difference if the representation is implicit or explicit. One solution is that in this task explicit representations also affect an individual's confidence in the verdict. In the second study, a subset of individuals, after choosing a verdict and rating their confidence in it, were asked whether they considered that Futura's actions caused Quest's bankruptcy and whether they considered that Quest's collapse was the result of another factor or factors. Just over half of the participants (53%) ticked both possibilities, and, as expected, these participants were, on average, less confident in their verdicts than those who ticked just one, $t(57) = 1.925$, $p < .05$, one-tailed test. However, entertaining two explicit models should not invariably decrease confidence. Individuals who explicitly rebut the alternative model should tend to be more confident than those who entertain the alternative but who do not rebut it (cf. the effects of rebuttal in Green et al., 1999). This prediction remains to be tested.

The process of argument resolution outlined here expands the range of mechanisms for reaching a conclusion in the theory of mental models. In the deductive case, the principle mechanism for reaching a conclusion has been one of accepting a conclusion if no alternative model of the premises yields a counterexample to it (e.g., Johnson-Laird, 1999, 2001; Johnson-Laird & Byrne, 1991). However, it would be wrong to suppose that the search for counterexamples is irrelevant in everyday reasoning. Individuals may search for possible counter-arguments to a presented argument as a way to achieve a more plausible or decisive outcome or to achieve greater confidence in their decision. In the case of judgments of probability, individuals are held to assess the proportion of models in which some states of affairs occurs (Johnson-Laird, Legrenzi, P., Girotto, Legrenzi, M.S., & Caverni, 1999) and in the case of reasoning with inconsistent premises, individuals either eliminate premises inconsistent with a given state of affairs or construct a causal scenario that will explain the inconsistency (Legrenzi et al., 2000).

FURTHER DEVELOPMENTS AND PREDICTIONS

Individuals can reach a verdict on the basis of arguments in various ways. They may consider just their number, the source of the arguments, or their quality. Alternatively, they may construct one or more causal models that generate a given state of affairs. Clearly, the process of reaching a verdict is just one instance where decisions are sensitive to competing models of state of affairs. In other circumstances, individuals must reach prospective decisions about future states of the world. In these circumstances, they must decide whether one course of action or another is likely to lead to the desired state of affairs. Here, too, individuals may engage in mental simulation to reach a decision.

Everyday problems typically raise a number of issues rather than just a single issue, such as did X cause Y? We can reorganize Fig. 10.2 to depict this possibility. Each issue can be linked into the decision and each link justified by a mental model backed by a mental simulation (see Fig. 10.3).

Each issue comes with a possible yardstick, and an evaluation in terms of this yardstick yields a strength value. Individuals' views on each issue can combine to determine opinion because argument strength provides a common currency (see Green, 2000, Experiment 2, for use of a diagram technique to explore individuals' representations of a problem with many issues). Two immediate questions arise. First, do individuals consider all issues in the same way? Prior thought on an issue, or received opinion on it, may lead them to retrieve a specific thought rather than reflect on the possibilities. Second, which issues should be considered? Individuals and groups presumably identify relevant issues in terms of the state of the affairs they desire. They may also consider some issues more important, or more salient, than others and thus attribute greater weight to them in reaching their decision.

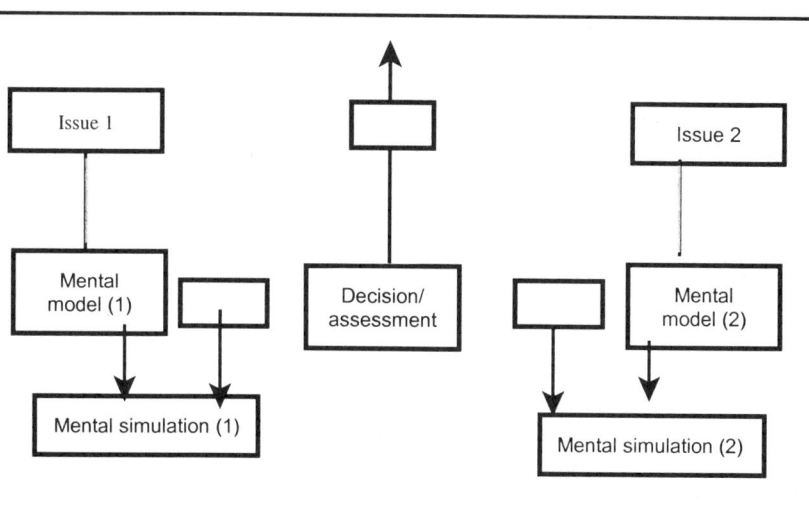

FIG. 10.3 A variant of an argument mental model. The shaded oblongs depict evaluation functions.

The current proposal emphasizes that decisions or conclusions are often uncertain. Degrees of certainty or belief in a decision (whatever the domain) should then be predictable from the ratings of argument strength. These ratings in turn reflect the outcomes of mental simulation. Such simulations are sensitive to the kinds of factors others have identified in the study of conditional inference, such as the presence of disabling conditions or the absence of necessary conditions, for a given outcome to occur (e.g., Byrne, 1989; Cummins, 1995; Stevenson & Over, 1995). Ratings of argument strength should be predictable from estimates of these conditions.

A fundamental issue is the extent to which individuals elaborate their initial model. Many factors are relevant: instructions, type of problem, background knowledge, and motivation. As noted earlier, the persuasion literature indicates that individuals with a high need for cognition are more likely to elaborate their representation of messages than individuals with a low need for cognition (see Petty et al., 1994). This individual difference variable suggests that the process of constructing a mental model will tend to vary as a function of the need for cognition. Individuals with a high need for cognition should construct the argument model incrementally and thus be able to argue against later counterarguments. In contrast, those low in need for cognition may avoid model construction and be influenced by later, rather than by earlier, arguments—in other words they will tend to show a recency rather than a primacy effect (see Petty et al., 1994, p. 92, for pertinent evidence).

The process of constructing an argument model based on a causal scenario, or thinking about different possible models, should take longer than making a judgment based on some feature of the arguments (e.g., their number). Social psychological evidence suggests that participants who have to scrutinize presented arguments take longer to read argumentative passages compared with those oriented toward making a more cursory analysis (Mackie & Worth, 1989). A more specific prediction can be made: Individuals initially oriented to make relatively peripheral assessments of argument quality should take longer subsequently to make judgments that require the construction of a causal model.

If individuals use arguments and background knowledge to generate an argument model embodying, for example, different causal claims, then these claims are potentially dissociable from the reasons that gave rise to them. Individuals may recall for instance that Futura's message caused Quest's bankruptcy (the mental model) but fail to recall the details of the mental simulation that led to it. In real life, the precise nature of expressed arguments may be rapidly forgotten, but parties in a conversation must at least keep track of the argumentative positions held by different individuals. It follows that individuals must have the ability to hold more than one argument mental model in mind and represent the relations among them. At a minimum, they must be able to tag where these argument models differ.

I have argued that affective responses are important and proposed that these can be treated as reasons. Such responses can guide decisions. Affective responses may also be incorporated tacitly. For instance, somatic markers (Damasio, 1994) attached to mental tokens may not achieve explicit representation in the model but may nonetheless guide strength ratings. An argument model therefore provides a way to interrelate explicit and implicit knowledge (see Evans & Over, 1996, for a discussion of this contrast). It allows both types of knowledge to guide opinion and action. The precise role of affective processes needs to be clarified. Affective reactions may dominate snap judgments but may also be generated in the course of constructing an argument mental model. For instance, affective responses will be generated if a causal scenario leads to the conclusion that a person previously assumed to be guilty is innocent.

CONCLUSION

Argumentation is fundamental to everyday decision making and action. Extending the theory of mental models by incorporating the notion of argument provides a way to create an integrated theory of individual and distributed cognition. Individuals create a dual representation in the course of comprehending an argument: a representation of the structure of presented arguments and an argument mental model. Both representations are potentially involved in reaching a decision. Arguments vary in their strength and the relative strength of arguments pro and con for a course of action determines the decision reached. An argument mental model not only expresses explicit information but also incorporates information that is tacit, such as the affective value of a mentioned object.

REFERENCES

Bailenson, J., & Rips, L. J. (1996). Informal reasoning and the burden of proof. *Applied Cognitive Psychology, 10,* S3–S16.

Baron, J. (1995). Myside bias in thinking about abortion. *Thinking and Reasoning, 1,* 221–235.

Billig, M. (1987). *Arguing and Thinking: A Rhetorical Approach to Social Psychology.* Cambridge: Cambridge University Press.

Bohner, G., Rank, S., Reinhard, M-A., Einwiller, S., & Erb, H-P. (1998). Motivational determinants of systematic processing: expectancy moderates effects of desired confidence on processing effort. *European Journal of Social Psychology, 28,* 185–206.

Brem, S. K., & Rips, L. J. (2000). Explanation and evidence in informal argument. *Cognitive Science, 24,* 573–604.

Byrne, R. M. J. (1989). Suppressing valid inferences with conditionals. *Cognition, 31,* 61–83.

Cummins, D. D. (1995). Naïve theories and causal deduction. *Memory and Cognition, 23,* 646–658.

Damasio, A. R. (1994). *Descartes= error: Emotion, reason, and the human brain.* New York: Avon.

Eemeren, F. H. van, Grootendurst, R., Henkemans, F. S., et al. (1996) .

Fundamentals of Argumentation Theory: A Handbook of Historical Backgrounds and Contemporary Developments. Mahwah, N.J.: Lawrence Erlbaum Associates.

Evans, J. St. B. T. (1996). Deciding before you think: relevance and reasoning in the selection task. *British Journal of Psychology, 87,* 223–240.

Evans, J. St. B. T., & Over, D. (1996). *Rationality and reasoning.* Hove, UK: Lawrence Erlbaum Associates.

Evans, J. St. B. T., & Wason, P. C. (1976). Rationalization in a reasoning task. *British Journal of Psychology, 63,* 205–212.

Evans, J. St. B. T., Handley, S., Perham, N., Over, D. E., & Thompson, V.A. (2000). Frequency versus probability formats in statistical word problems. *Cognition, 77,* 197–213.

Feibleman, J. K. (1960). *An Introduction to Peirce's Philosophy.* George Allen & Unwin: London.

Fox, J. (1994). On the necessity of probability: reasons to believe and grounds for doubt. In G.Wright & P. Ayton (Eds.), *Subjective probability* (pp.75–103). New York: John Wiley & Sons.

George, C. (1999). Evaluation of the plausibility of a conclusion derivable from several arguments with uncertain premises. *Thinking & Reasoning, 5,* 245–281.

Girotto, V., & Gonzalez, M. (2001). Solving probabilistic and statistical problems: a matter of information structure and question form. *Cognition, 78,* 242–276.

Goldvarg, Y., & Johnson-Laird, P. N. (2001). Naive causality: a mental model theory of causal meaning and reasoning. *Cognitive Science, 25,* 565–610.

Green, D. W. (1994). Induction: representation, strategy and argument. *International Studies in the Philosophy of Science, 8,* 45–50.

Green, D. W. (1995). The abstract selection task: thesis, antithesis and synthesis. In S. Newstead & J. St. B. T. Evans (Eds.) *Perspectives on thinking and reasoning.* Hove and London: Lawrence Erlbaum Associates.

Green, D. W. (1996). Models, arguments and decisions. In J. Oakhill & A. Garnham (Eds.), *Mental Models in Cognitive Science: A Festschrift for Philip Johnson-Laird* (pp. 119–137). Hove: Psychology Press.

Green, D. W. (1997). Hypothetical thinking in the selection task: amplifying a model-based approach. *Current Psychology of Cognition, 16,* 93–101.

Green, D. W. (2000). Argument and opinion. In J. García-Madruga, N. Carriedo, & M. J. González-Labra (Eds.), *Mental Models in Reasoning* (pp. 57–67). Madrid: UNED.

Green, D. W. (2001). Understanding microworlds. *Quarterly Journal of Experimental Psychology, 54A,* 879–901.

Green, D. W., & McCloy, R. (2003). Reaching a verdict. *Thinking and Reasoning, 9,* 307–333.

Green, D. W., McClelland, A., Muckli, L., & Simmons, C. (1999). Arguments and deontic decisions. *Acta Psychologica, 101,* 27–47.

Griffin, D., & Tversky, A. (1992). The weighing of evidence and the determinants of confidence. *Cognitive Psychology, 24*, 411–435.

Habermas, J. (1984). *The theory of communciative action: Reason and the rationalization of society 1.* [T.McCarthy trans.] Boston: Beacon press.

Hogarth, R. M., & Kunreuther, H. (1995). Decision making under ignorance: arguing with yourself. *Journal of Risk and Uncertainty, 10*, 15-16.

Holyoak, K. J., & Simon, D. (1999). Bidirectional reasoning in decision making by constraint satisfaction. *Journal of Experimental Psychology: General, 128*, 3–31.

Johnson-Laird, P. N. (1983). *Mental models: Towards a Cognitive Science of Language, Inference and Consciousness.* Cambridge, MA: Harvard University Press.

Johnson-Laird, P. N. (1999). Deductive reasoning. *Annual Review of Psychology, 50*, 109–135.

Johnson-Laird, P. N. (2001). Mental models and deduction. *Trends in Cognitive Science, 5*, 434–442..

Johnson-Laird, P. N., & Byrne, R. M. J. (1991). *Deduction.* Lawrence Erlbaum Associates. Hove & London/Hillsdale.

Johnson-Laird, P. N., Legrenzi, P., Girotto, P., Legrenzi, M. S., & Caverni, J-P. (1999). Naïve probability: a mental model theory of extensional reasoning. *Psychological Review, 106*, 62–88.

Kahneman, D., & Tversky, A. (1982). The simulation heuristic. In D. Kahneman, P. Slovic, & A. Tversky (Eds.), *Judgment under uncertainty: Heuristics and biases* (pp. 201–208). New York: Cambridge University Press.

Kim, J., Allen, C. T., & Kardes, F. R. (1996). An investigation of the mediational mechanisms underlying attitudinal conditioning. *Journal of Marketing Research, 33*, 318–329.

Kuhn, D. (1991). *The skills of argument.* Cambridge: Cambridge University Press.

Kuhn, D., Weinstock, M., & Flaton, R. (1994). How well do jurors reason? Competence dimensions of individual variation in a juror reasoning task. *Psychological Science, 5*, 289–296.

Legrenzi, P., Girotto, V., & Johnson-Laird, P. N. (1993). Focusing, reasoning and decision-making. *Cognition, 49*, 37–66.

Legrenzi, M. S., Legrnezi, P., Girotto, V., & Johnson-Laird, P. N. (2000). Reasoning to consistency: a theory of naive nonmonotonic reasoning.

Lipshitz, R. (1993). Decision-making as argument-driven action. In G.A. Klein, J. Orasanu, & R. Calderwood (Eds.), *Decision-making in action: models and methods.* Norwood, N.J.: Ablex Publishing Corp.

Lord, C. G., Lepper, M. R., & Preston, E. (1984). Considering the opposite: A corrective strategy for social judgment. *Journal of Personality and Social Psychology, 47*, 1231–1241.

Mackie, D.M., & Worth, L.T. (1989). Processing deficits and the mediation of positive affect in persuasion. *Journal of Personality and Social Psychology, 57*, 27–40.

Macrae, C.N. (1992). A tale of two curries: counter-factual thinking and accident-related judgments. *Personality and Social Psychology Bulletin, 18*, 84–87.

Mason, R. O., & Mitroff, I. I. (1981). *Challenging strategic planning assumptions: theory, cases and techniques.*

McDonald, J., Samuels, M., & Rispoli, J. (1996). A hypothesis-assessment model of categorical argument strength. *Cognition, 59,* 199–217.

Moshman, D., & Geil, M. (1998). Collaborative reasoning: evidence for collective rationality. *Thinking and Reasoning, 4,* 231–248.

Oatley, K. K. G. (1996). Emotions, rationality and informal reasoning. In J. Oakhill & A. Garnham (Eds.), *Mental Models in Cognitive Science: A Festschrift for Philip Johnson-Laird* (pp. 175–196). Hove: Psychology Press.

Osherson, D., Smith, E. E., Wilkie, O., Lopez, A., & Shafir, E. (1990). Category-based induction. *Psychological Review, 97,* 185–200.

Oestermeier, U., & Hesse, F. W. (2000). Verbal and visual causal arguments. *Cognition, 75,* 65–104.

Pennington, N., & Hastie, R. (1993). Reasoning in explanation-based decision-making. *Cognition, 49,* 123–163.

Petty, R. E., & Cacioppo, J. T. (1984). The effects of involvement on responses to argument quantity and quality: Central and peripheral routes to persuasion. *Journal of Personality and Social Psychology, 46,* 69–81.

Petty, R. E., Priestner, J. R., & Wegener, D.T. (1994). Cognitive processes in attitudinal Change. In R.S. Wyer Jr & T.K. Srull (Eds.), *Handbook of social cognition (Vol. 2).* (pp 69–142). Hillsdale, N.J.: Lawrence Erlbaum Associates.

Rips, L. R. (1999). Reasoning and conversation. *Psychological Review, 105,* 411–441.

Shafir, E., Simonson, I., & Tversky, A. (1993). Reason-based choice. *Cognition, 49,* 11–36.

Shaw, V. (1996). The cognitive processes in informal reasoning. *Thinking & Reasoning, 2,* 51–80.

Slovic, P., Melissa Finucane, M., Ellen Peters, E., & MacGregor, D. G. (2001). The Affect Heuristic. In T. Gilovich, D. Griffin, & D. Kahneman, (Eds.), *Intuitive Judgment: Heuristics and Biases.* Cambridge University Press.

Stevenson, R., & Over, D. E. (1995). Deduction from uncertain premises. *Quarterly Journal of Experimental Psychology, 48A,* 613–643.

Toulmin, S. (1958). *The uses of argument.* Cambridge: Cambridge University Press.

Van Eemeren, F. H., Grootendorst, R., Henkemans, F. S. *et al.* (1996). *Fundamentals of argumentation theory.* Mahwah, NJ: Lawrence Erlbaum Associates.

Voss, J. F., & Means, M. L. (1991). Learning to reason via instruction in argumentation. *Learning and Instruction,1,* 337–350.

Wason, P. C. (1968). Reasoning about a rule. *Quarterly Journal of Experimental Psychology, 20,* 273–281.

Zajonc, R. B. (1980). Feeling and thinking: preferences need no inferences. *American Psychologist, 35,* 151–175.

11

Training Effects in Deductive Reasoning:
A Theory-Based Review

Karl Christoph Klauer
Thorsten Meiser

Human performance in tasks involving deductive reasoning frequently
falls short of the standards set forth by formal logic. Training in
deductive reasoning aims to reduce this discrepancy. According to major
theories of deductive reasoning, different kinds of training should be
most successful. A review of training approaches leaves little doubt that
deductive reasoning can be trained. The most successful kinds of
training improve the understanding of the linguistically complex
premises by using abstract semantic tools, such as truth tables or Euler
circles, or by providing concrete and helpful semantic contexts. Training
can also induce different and more efficient reasoning strategies than
those spontaneously employed by reasoners.

INTRODUCTION

Most empirical work in psychology aims at deriving or testing descriptive models.
Descriptive models give accurate specifications of human response patterns and
theoretical accounts of those observed response patterns in terms of psychological
mechanisms. Normative models in contrast derive standards for cognitive activity
that serve to optimize the accuracy of cognitive activity. For example, in research
on deductive reasoning, formal logic most often provides a normative model for
valid responses, whereas competing descriptive models are given by mental model
theory (Johnson-Laird, 1983; Johnson-Laird & Byrne, 1991; Johnson-Laird, Byrne,
& Schaeken, 1992), formal-rule theories (Braine et al., 1995; Braine, Reiser, &
Rumain, 1984; Braine & Rumain, 1983; Rips, 1994), pragmatic reasoning schemas
(Cheng & Holyoak, 1985), and others (e.g., Oaksford & Chater, 1994). These
theories acknowledge, and much research demonstrates that human reasoning
processes often deviate from the logical standards (Evans, 1989).

Limitations of cognitive resources are in part responsible for this
discrepancy between descriptive models and normative models. The evidence for
resource limitations stems from studies demonstrating that reasoning performance,
evaluated by means of the standards set forth by formal logic, deteriorates as mental

resources are taxed by additional processing loads (Logie & Gilhooly, 1998) and from studies demonstrating systematic interindividual differences in reasoning performance that covary with general analytic intelligence (Stanovich, 1999). Acknowledging cognitive resource limitations leads to the idea of replacing normative models by prescriptive models that explicitly incorporate limitations in mental resources and specify the optimum that can be achieved given human constraints in cognitive resources. Nevertheless, large deviations of descriptive models from prescriptive models frequently remain, as discussed, for example, in the vast literature on Wason's (1966) selection task, and different explanations have been offered to account for them. These explanations most often use one of the following basic ideas. First, reasoners may be irrational; that is, they systematically compute a nonprescriptive rule. Second, they may understand the task differently from what the experimenter intends, and, third, reasoners may follow another normative standard than that adopted by the experimenter.

Training in deductive reasoning aims to reduce the gap between the descriptive and normative models. As will be seen, understanding the conditions that lead to a successful training (i.e., one that reduces the gap between the descriptive and the normative models) contributes to understanding the causes of such gaps and has implications for the choice between competing descriptive models of deductive reasoning.

In the following sections, the major descriptive theories of deductive reasoning are sketched with a focus on the factors that contribute to the descriptive/normative gap according to each theory and that might be addressed by a suitable training regime. Then, training studies are reviewed, and a direct comparison of different training conditions is discussed.

THEORETICAL FOUNDATIONS OF TRAINING DEDUCTIVE REASONING

What are the factors that lead to the gap between descriptive and normative models of deductive reasoning? Different theories give different answers.

Formal Rule Theories

According to formal rule theories (e.g., Braine et al., 1995; Braine, Reiser, & Rumain, 1984; Braine & Rumain, 1983; Rips, 1994), reasoners avail of a universal repertory of inference rules that they use in deriving or proving conclusions. According to this account by mental logic, reasoners engage in three steps when they make an inference. First, they uncover the logical form of the premises. That is, the contents of the usually verbally provided premises are translated into the syntactic format to which inference rules apply. Second, reasoners access their mental repertory of inference rules to construct a mental derivation or proof of a conclusion. This involves reasoning strategies to combine inference rules to chains of derivations, to define intermediate goals, and to include newly derived premises into the chain of derivation. Third, reasoners have to translate the conclusion back into the content of the premises.

In this analysis, errors may occur first because the interpretative process maps the logical form of the premises incorrectly; second, the required derivation may surpass the reasoner's strategical competence or working memory capacity, or required rules may not be accessible. Finally, the reasoner may not be able to translate the conclusion back into the language in which the premises are phrased.

Training conditions might therefore improve reasoning performance by supporting the interpretative process, for example, by preventing wrong translations of premises. They might also enhance the accessibility of required inference rules or optimize strategies of their application in deriving or proving conclusions. Finally, the translation of derived conclusions into the language of the premises could be trained.

Mental Model Theory

According to mental model accounts of deductive reasoning (Johnson-Laird, 1983; Johnson-Laird & Byrne, 1991; Johnson-Laird et al., 1992), reasoners use the premises to construct a mental model of the situation described therein. Then they inspect the model to arrive at a tentative conclusion that is true in the initial model and that is informative, that is, goes above the information provided in the premises. Next, they engage in a search of counterexamples. This is done through the construction of alternative models of the premises and through checking whether the tentative conclusion also holds in these alternative models. If no counterexamples are encountered in this process, the tentative conclusion is considered valid.

Like the formal rule approach, the mental model approach comprises a comprehension phase and a deduction phase, and reasoners may fail either because they miscomprehend the premises and construct inappropriate models or because the required manipulations of models overtax their working memory. Mental model theory differs from the account by formal rules in that it is a semantic theory in which cognitive activity is guided by the meaning of the premises rather than their syntactical form. Training conditions might practise the construction of appropriate models of the premises, and they may aim at optimizing the required operations that must be performed on the constructed mental models.

Domain-Specific Accounts of Reasoning

Theories postulating domain-specific reasoning processes assume that there are qualitative differences in the reasoning process as a function of content domain (e.g., Cheng & Holyoak, 1985; Cosmides, 1989; Gigerenzer, 1996). The theory of pragmatic reasoning schemas (Cheng & Holyoak, 1985), for example, proposes that different contexts can evoke different schemas. The schemas are sets of production rules that facilitate inferences appropriate in the context. The permission schema, for example, is activated by the context if fulfilling a precondition is a necessary condition for obtaining the permission to perform a certain desired action or to receive a certain benefit. Once activated, the production rules will in general facilitate logically valid inferences in permission contexts and suppress invalid ones.

According to this analysis, reasoners may make errors because appropriate reasoning schemas are not available in a given situation or because the evoked production rules do not lead to formally correct inferences (Cheng, Holyoak, Nisbett, & Oliver, 1986). Training reasoning according to the account by pragmatic reasoning schemas would therefore involve

providing pragmatic contexts that activate appropriate pragmatic schemas and raising the accessibility of the production rules defining these schemas.

Dual-Process Theories

In recent years, research from different domains has increasingly encompassed dual-process frameworks in which two systems interact, and at times compete, for control (for an overview, see Stanovich, 1999; chap. 5). Although details differ, one of the systems is viewed as automatic, largely unconscious, and relatively undemanding of computational capacity. Thus, it embodies automatic and heuristic processing. The second system comprises the characteristics typifying deliberate, controlled processing and is guided by normative standards.

In the context of reasoning and decision making, Evans and Over (1996), for example, distinguish between tacit thought processes and explicit, controlled thought processes. The former focus our thinking on subjectively relevant features given by the task information and retrieved from memory. Such focusing serves subjective goals and is achieved by preconscious and tacit processes. Explicit reasoning on the other hand involves manipulation of explicit representations of the premises. Explicit thought processes underlie reasoners' deductive competence in reasoning and are guided by normative standards, such as formal logic.

Dual-process theories are relevant for training deductive reasoning because deviations from normative standards may result from the operation of tacit thought processes and heuristics that are not geared to fulfill the normative standards of formal logic. For example, in Wason's selection task, it has been argued (Evans, 1983) that the linguistic content of the four cards determines which cards are focused on by means of largely preconscious heuristics. Thus, errors may arise not because the explicit system computes a nonnormative rule but because tacit thought processes present normatively irrelevant kinds of information as subjectively relevant to the explicit thought processes or, conversely, because the normatively relevant kind of information is not presented as subjectively relevant by tacit thought processes.

Distinguishing heuristic from analytic processes thereby complements these theories of reasoning. The account by formal rules and the mental model theory can be understood as different models of explicit, analytic thought processes, but both classes of theories acknowledge the role of additional heuristic processes. For example, proponents of mental logic argue that heuristical processes can be applied when a logical chain of inferences cannot be constructed (Braine & O'Brien, 1998; Braine & Rumain, 1983). According to the account by mental models, representing premises in terms of mental models rests on selecting relevant information from the given premise, which in turn is guided by illogical heuristics. Pragmatic reasoning schemas in contrast can be seen as part of the system of tacit thought processes, and they admit the operation of additional heuristic processes in situations in which no pragmatic schema is activated.

Most reasoning tasks engage both systems and show evidence of a logical and illogical component of performance (Evans & Over, 1996, p. 144). For this reason, training deductive reasoning should also address the possibility that one error component is given by preconscious heuristic processes that, among other things, determine which information is selected for explicit thought processes.

A REVIEW OF TRAINING STUDIES

Lehman, Lempert, and Nisbett (1988) argued that instruction in abstract rule systems can affect reasoning about everyday life events. In fact, graduate training in psychology and medical training produced large transfer effects on statistical and methodological reasoning, and psychology, medical, and law training produced effects on students' ability to reason about conditionals in their field of study. The improvement of conditional reasoning by psychology training was replicated by Morris and Nisbett (1993), who also found that graduate training in philosophy did not benefit conditional reasoning. Lehman and Nisbett (1990) looked at the effects of formal undergraduate training on reasoning and found that natural science and humanities training had large effects on ability to reason about problems in conditional logic, whereas social science training did not. On the other hand, social science training had a substantial impact on statistical and methodological reasoning, whereas natural science and humanities training produced smaller, but still marginally significant, effects in these domains.

These field studies demonstrate that deductive reasoning can be improved by training. In addition, they show that the different kinds of undergraduate and graduate training have specific and different effects on statistical and methodological reasoning on the one hand and conditional reasoning on the other hand. The results thereby suggest that these different kinds of reasoning recruit different reasoning processes that are differentially practised by the different kinds of undergraduate and graduate training.

Because undergraduate and graduate training are very complex manipulations, little can be concluded, however, about which aspects of training were responsible for the effects and which cognitive processes underlie the improvements in reasoning. Experimental studies have realized simpler training conditions in the laboratory. Some of them aim at inducing better understanding of the linguistically complex premises. Others are motivated by the reasoning theories outlined earlier and aim to practice factors that limit reasoning performance according to the focused reasoning theory.

Comprehending the Premises

A so-called contradiction training of conditional reasoning proposed by O'Brien and Overton (1980, 1982) is of the first variety. O'Brien and Overton argue in a developmental context that improvement in performance with tasks requiring formal operations should occur only for those individuals who are competent, that is, for whom task failure is due to performance factors other than lack of competence. One such factor is a false interpretation of the conditional if-then as biconditional.

In their so-called contradiction training, reasoners infer a conditional rule of the "if p, then q" kind from a number of instances. Under the contradiction training, one of these instances makes particularly salient that the instance corresponding to $\neg p$ and q is admissible. The admissibility of an instance fulfilling q but not p distinguishes the conditional interpretation from the biconditional interpretation. If performance is limited by frequent misunderstanding of if-then rather than by more fundamental problems of reasoning competence, removing the misunderstanding through contradiction training should improve conditional reasoning performance.

This is in fact what O'Brien and Overton (1980, 1982) and Overton, Byrnes, and O'Brien (1985) found. Young adults profited from the contradiction training, as shown in improved performance on a number of subsequent conditional reasoning tasks. Younger children, however, did not exhibit training effects, which indicated to O'Brien and Overton that their performance was limited by more serious problems than misunderstanding if-then.

A number of other training conditions have also aimed to improve understanding of the premises in conditional and propositional reasoning as an important component of the training. Based on the account by mental models, Ziegler (1990) developed training conditions that were to benefit performance in Wason's (1966) selection task. In this task, reasoners are shown a rule of the form "if p, then q" along with four cards, representing instances of the rule. One side of each card shows information about whether p is fulfilled or not for the instance in question; the other side specifies q or $\neg q$. On the upper, visible sides of the four cards, information amounting to the cases p, q, $\neg p$, and $\neg q$ is written. Reasoners are asked to select those cards that would have to be turned to determine whether the rule is true or false. It is generally found that only a small percentage of participants, typically 10% or less, select the logically correct cards, that is the p card and the $\neg q$ card. The most frequent choices are to select the p card and the q card (Evans, 1989).

Ziegler's (1990) most successful training comprised two components:

(1) Participants were to generate all logically possible cards with

information about p or $\neg p$ on one side and information about q or $\neg q$ on the other side. They were then read one side of each of these cards and asked to imagine and name what was on the other side. This procedure was to facilitate imagining all relevant logical instances, to ensure that attention is equally distributed over all cards presented in the Wason selection task, and to allow explicit consideration of the "$\neg p$ and q" instance as an admissible case.

(2) Participants were given a rule and asked to construct the card that falsified the rule. This was to make salient that the "p and $\neg q$" case is the instance that is not consistent with the rule.

A training with Component 1 and Components 1 and 2 improved performance in the subsequently administered Wason selection task, the effect being more pronounced for the latter training. Only this training combining both components was successful in raising performance in a transfer task that administered the selection task with material that was not part of the training phase.

A similar approach to training Wason's selection task was taken by Houdé and Moutier (1996). Their training focused on reducing the so-called matching bias (Evans, 1983, 1989). Matching bias is the phenomenon that card selection is strongly influenced by a match in superficial linguistic features between the components mentioned in the rule and what is written on the cards. This leads participants to focus on matching cards and to disregard mismatching cards. In Houdé and Moutier's training, reasoners were explained the phenomenon of matching bias and were asked to consider all cards in their selection, including those that are not explicitly mentioned in the rule. In addition, the relevance of the p card and the $\neg q$ card for testing the rule in question was explained. This training improved performance in the selection task as shown both in a within-participants pretest-training-posttest comparison as well as in a between-participants comparison with respect to a control group without training.

The training conditions of O'Brien and Overton (1980) and Ziegler (1990) both clarify and emphasize the logical status of certain instances vis-à-vis a composite premise. That is, for a premise of the kind "if p, then q", it is made more salient that the case "$\neg p$ and q" is consistent with the premise (O'Brien & Overton, 1980; Ziegler, 1990), and that the case "p and $\neg q$" is inconsistent with the premise (Ziegler, 1990). Klauer, Stegmaier, and Meiser (1997) extended this rationale in a training of propositional reasoning. The training task consisted of a truth table evaluation task in which participants were shown a composite premise such as "if p, then q" along with the four cases considered in a truth table (i.e., p and q, p and $\neg q$, $\neg p$ and q, and $\neg p$ and $\neg q$). The reasoners' task is to evaluate for each case whether it is consistent with the premise or not. In the case of a wrong response, feedback about the error is provided, and the correct response is shown. Rather than focusing on particular cases, the training by Klauer et al. thus aims to explain the semantic definition of a given logical connective by means of the entire truth table.

Because Klauer et al. were interested in propositional reasoning with a number of different connectives, their training practiced comprehension not only of conditional premises but also of various biconditional and disjunctive premises in this manner. In a subsequent inference task, reasoners were presented composite premises along with minor premises in what are sometimes called propositional-syllogism tasks, and reasoners were required to draw a conclusion from composite and minor premises or to state that nothing follows. Substantial training effects were found both in a between-participants comparison with a no-training control group as well as in pretest-training-posttest comparisons within participants.

Trainings Based on Reasoning Theories

As already mentioned, Ziegler (1990) and Klauer et al. (1997) grounded their training in mental models theory. The account of mental models is a semantic one in which reasoning rests on the adequate representation of possible situations described by the given premises. It is therefore closely linked with the question of how reasoners understand the premises (Johnson-Laird, 1983). In propositional reasoning, mental models of composite premises have close connections to truth tables (Johnson-Laird et al., 1992). In fact, when mental models must be fully explicated according to that account, they correspond to those cases of the truth tables that are consistent with the premise. For these reasons, Klauer et al. expected their truth-table training to support the construction and explication of adequate mental models.

In a frequently cited study, Cheng et al. (1986) compared pragmatic and syntactic approaches to training Wason's selection task. Syntactic approaches were based on the idea of formal rule theories that reasoning proceeds according to syntactic inference rules. Pragmatic approaches were based on the theory of pragmatic reasoning schemas.

In Cheng et al.'s (1986) Experiment 1, four conditions realized an abstract rule training, an examples training, a rule-plus-examples training, and a control group without training. The rule training was focused on syntactic aspects of conditional reasoning. In particular, the equivalence between a conditional statement of the form "if p, then q" and its so-called contrapositive "if not q, then not p" was explained. Furthermore, the fallacies of affirming the consequent and denying the antecedent were explained. Affirming the consequent means wrongly inferring p from "if p then q"; denying the antecedent is to infer $\neg q$ from "if p then q" and $\neg q$. It is interesting to note, however, that the explanations did not take the form of a formal derivation, using appropriate inference rules, but employed semantic tools, such as truth tables, Euler circles, and an illustrative conditional statement. At the end of the rule training, participants went through an inference exercise in which they selected statements out of a given choice of statements that could be validly inferred from a given conditional. They received immediate feedback on correctness, followed by a brief explanation of the correct answer. One idea of this training was that making the contrapositive "if not q, then not p"

accessible should facilitate the choice of the ¬q card in Wason's selection task. Failure to select this card, and to select the q card instead, is the major source of errors in the standard selection task.

The examples training consisted of working through two selection tasks with immediate feedback about performance and explanation of the correct answer in terms specific to the particular problem. Rule plus examples training finally consisted of the rule training as well as the examples material. Importantly, the explanation of the correct answer for each example was now couched in terms of the abstract rules that had just been learned and, thus, focused on using the contrapositive of the given rule to select the ¬q card and on avoiding selection of the q card, which may result from committing the fallacy of affirming the consequent.

The effects of the different training conditions on performance in different selection problems were tested, and it was found that only rules plus examples training had an effect on performance in Wason's (1966) selection task compared with a no-training control group. This means that the formal-rule training was effective only when the application of the learned principles to concrete problems was explained.

In several studies, Klaczynski (1993; Klaczynski, Gelfand, & Reese, 1989; Klaczynski & Laipple, 1993) administered a training similar to the rule plus examples training and systematically varied the contents of the selection problems used in training and the contents of later test problems. Interestingly, there were larger transfer effects from practice with contents that initially led to poor selection performance (such as abstract content or causal rules) than from practice with contents that led to relatively good performance (such as permission contexts). These latter contexts tended to induce training gains only when practice and test problems shared the same general contents; for example, when both specified permission rules.

Cheng et al.'s (1986) Study 2 was a field study, in which selection tasks were administered before and after a one-semester course in formal logic taken by university students. Unlike in the field studies by Lehman et al. (1988), Lehman and Nisbett (1990), and Morris and Nisbett (1993), there were no beneficial effects on reasoning performance as a consequence of formal instruction.

In Study 3, finally, a schema-based training was compared to an analogous but more abstract training. The schema-based training referred to conditional statements on obligations. An obligation arises when certain circumstances or situations create an obligation to perform some action. The conditional statements were of the following general kind: "If situation I arises, then C must be done." The training explained the production rules defining the obligation schema in Cheng and Holyoak's (1985) theory and pointed out how to check for violations of an obligation. An analogous, more abstract training explained the same checking rules without reference to an obligation context. The obligation training had an effect on subsequent selection performance as compared to a no-training control group, whereas the abstract training did not. The effect was most pronounced when the selection task employed obligationary rules.

For a number of reasons, it is difficult to assess the implications of the Cheng et al. (1986) results. The effect of the rule plus examples training is difficult to interpret unambiguously. Due to the many semantic features of the rule training, it is difficult to tell whether reasoning by means of formal rules was facilitated or whether the comprehension of conditionals was improved. Similarly, with respect to the obligation training, it is difficult to tell whether providing a helpful semantic context improved comprehension of the conditional or activated context-specific production rules that supported selection performance, which is the interpretation favored by Cheng et al. In contrast, Thompson (1995) proposes in her contextual cueing theory that people's interpretation of the premises determines their representation or model of the premises and that this model directly mediates the inferences that are drawn (cf. Griggs, 1983; Johnson-Laird & Byrne, 1991; Pollard, 1982). According to Thompson, interpretational factors of major importance are the perceived necessity and sufficiency relationships induced by the availability of counterexamples as cued by the context. Similarly, the mental models theory predicts beneficial effects of appropriate semantic contexts due to the construction of more appropriate mental models (Johnson-Laird & Byrne, 1991).

Because Cheng et al.'s (1986) training conditions had different formats and were administered in different experiments, it is furthermore difficult to compare their efficiency. Finally, there is growing uneasiness with the interpretation of Wason's selection task as one of deductive reasoning (Evans & Clibbens, 1995; Markovits & Savary, 1992; Oaksford & Chater, 1994). Evans and Over (1996, chap. 8), for example, deplore the use of that task in the Cheng et al. study, arguing that the selection task is handled by preconscious heuristics and therefore elicits relevance judgments rather than deductive reasoning processes. Similarly, Sperber, Cara, and Girotto (1995) argued that the selection task relies on judgments of relevance, and the selection task has even been argued to elicit Bayesian decision making rather than deductive reasoning (Klauer, 1999; Oaksford & Chater, 1994).

Klauer, Meiser, and Naumer (2000) compared three theory-based training conditions in one study. Training effects were measured by means of an inference task, that is, by means of propositional syllogisms, rather than the selection task. The different kinds of training were of comparable format and length; they were realized within the same experiment so that their effectiveness could be directly compared, and there was a control training. Like in the Cheng et al. (1986) studies, there was a rule-oriented training as well as a domain-specific condition; these were supplemented by the abstract semantic training practicing truth tables described earlier. The abstract semantic training allows one to assess the separate influence of improved comprehension independently of any possible additional benefit stemming from the activation of helpful domain-specific reasoning mechanisms or from practicing inference rules.

In the control training, participants practice an inductive reasoning task adapted for computerized presentation from the Raven Advanced Progressive Matrices Test (Raven, 1962). The control training is to control for possible nonspecific training effects, such as motivational effects.

Different versions of a syntactic training were employed. The training used in Klauer et al.'s (2000) first study was based on the PSYCOP deduction system of mental logic (Rips, 1994). In Experiment 2, two kinds of syntactic training were based on another major rule-based theory, the natural-logic approach by Braine, O'Brien, and colleagues (e.g., Braine et al., 1984, 1995; Braine & Rumain, 1983). In each case, the syntactic training presented and explained derivations for simple inferences in a step-by-step fashion. Each step briefly explained the particular inference rule governing that step and how the given premises mapped on the inference rule and which conclusions resulted from the application of the inference rule. If subgoals were set up by an inference rule, the goal structure was discussed. The abstract semantic training was the truth-table training described previously, and the domain-specific semantic training simply embedded the propositions of the propositional reasoning task in helpful contexts. In Experiment 1, these helpful contexts were ecological rules that described interdependencies of a number of species living on a fictitious group of islands. In Experiment 2, the contexts described regulations that obtain in a large company, and they were designed to activate pragmatic reasoning schemas (Cheng & Holyoak, 1985, 1989; Cheng et al., 1986; Holyoak & Cheng, 1995).

The results of both studies were very similar. The two kinds of semantic training produced substantial training effects, whereas the syntactic conditions did not lead to training gains that exceeded those produced by the control training. Klauer et al. (2000) concluded that the training gains are likely to reflect improved understanding of the propositional premises and a beneficial effect on the construction of appropriate mental models. There was little evidence that the activation of domain-specific inference rules additionally contributed to the pattern of results because an abstract truth table training was just as successful as the domain-specific training.

Training and Working Memory

If comprehension of the premises employed in propositional and syllogistic reasoning tasks is a factor that limits performance, then removing misunderstandings should allow one to assess analytic reasoning processes and strategies more clearly and directly. This idea was followed by Klauer et al. (1997) and more systematically by Meiser, Klauer, and Naumer (2001), who argued that the impact of demanding reasoning strategies may be masked by frequent misunderstandings of premises. In a series of experiments, Meiser et al. employed the kinds of training used by Klauer et al. (2000). After training, participants worked on a propositional syllogism task and simultaneous secondary tasks designed to load, respectively, the phonological loop, the visuospatial sketch pad, and the central executive as conceptualized in Baddeley's (1986) model of working memory. In these experiments, the abstract semantic (i.e., training practicing truth tables) led to greater disruption of reasoning performance by concurrent loads of the phonological loop and the central executive than was found after other kinds of training (i.e., the control training, the rule training, and the domain-specific training). As argued by Meiser et al. and supported by their analyses, working memory involvement through demanding analytic reasoning strategies may have been present in all conditions. However, the impact of these strategies on reasoning performance, and consequently the detrimental impact of concurrent loads on the use of these strategies, is masked by frequent misrepresentations of the premises. Only after training the truth table definitions of the employed connectives do reasoners' interpretations and those implied by formal logic coincide, leading to a more direct relationship between performance and the investment of cognitive resources.

Another possibility is that the training induced different, and more demanding, reasoning strategies. This possibility is exemplified by results from a study of syllogistic reasoning conducted by Gilhooly, Logie, and Wynn (1999). Like Meiser et al. (2001), Gilhooly et al. (Experiment 2) assessed the impact of concurrent loads on reasoning performance after training. Unlike Klauer et al.'s (2000) truth table training, the focus of Gilhooly et al.'s training was not to improve comprehension of premises but to teach a method of solving syllogisms that involved reordering premises so that they conformed to a certain syllogistic figure and then to reason in terms of set membership. The training was highly efficient in improving performance in syllogistic reasoning, and it also improved comprehension of category relationships as found in pilot studies. After training, there were indications that the central executive, the phonological loop, and spatial subsystems of working memory were involved in syllogistic reasoning. However, in a previous study in the same series of experiments, reasoners exhibiting relatively high skill in syllogistic reasoning showed a somewhat different pattern of working memory involvement, indicating that their reasoning strategies loaded the central executive, the phonological loop, and visual rather than spatial subsystems of working memory. To the extent that such qualitative differences in the pattern of working memory involvement are significant, it is thereby suggested that the strategies induced by training were different from those employed spontaneously by highly skilled participants.

CONCLUSIONS

There is little doubt from the reviewed studies that deductive reasoning, as defined by diverse inference, selection, and evaluation tasks from conditional reasoning, propositional reasoning, and syllogistic reasoning, can be trained. Substantial training gains were obtained as a consequence of formal university training as well as by brief experimental training conditions administered in the laboratory.

A common thread running through the most successful kinds of training was that improving the comprehension of the linguistically complex premises led to substantial performance gains. Improving the understanding of premises means more precisely to make sure that the reasoners' representations are equivalent to what the experimenters intend them to be. For example, Klauer et al.'s (1997) abstract semantic training practiced the truth table definitions of logical connectives in propositional reasoning. This made sure that the truth table definitions of formal logic and the participants' definitions largely coincided. Apart from clarifying the meaning of composite premises, this training should also be helpful in constructing appropriate mental models of the premises. The same beneficial effects can be surmised to underlie the helpful effects of providing concrete semantic contexts that were found in several studies (Cheng et al., 1986; Klauer et al., 2000).

When syntactic approaches to training deductive reasoning were tested, there was in general less evidence for training gains. Klauer et al. (2000) found little evidence for effects of syntactic training conditions based on formal rule theories, whereas Cheng et al. (1986) obtained significant effects for what they called a syntactic, rule-plus-examples training. As discussed earlier, it is not clear, however, to what extent the comprehension of conditional premises was improved by this training rather than the application of appropriate inference rules. It should also be noted that the absence of training effects is an inherently weaker finding than their presence because there are many reasons why a training may be inefficient. For example, the training may have been presented in a didactically poor format, it may be too difficult to follow, and so on. These considerations notwithstanding, it seems fair to summarize that training grounded in formal-rule theories has so far not been found as successful as training based on the semantics of logical premises.

In dual-process theories, heuristic and tacit thought processes are argued to underlie frequent misrepresentations of the premises presented in deductive reasoning tasks. To the extent that improved comprehension of the premises underlies the training gains, a major impact of the training measures appears to be on the heuristic stage. On the other hand, training conditions can induce different, more efficient reasoning strategies than those spontaneously employed by reasoners (Gilhooly et al., 1999).

The effects of most of the training conditions reviewed in this chapter were tested by means of one particular reasoning task, and the training gain in that task was the crucial dependent variable to evaluate a given training and to compare different kinds of training. Another dimension on which training conditions are traditionally compared is the range of tasks to which transfer effects occur. From a practical point of view, it is desirable that a training has broad effects on a large number and diversity of different reasoning tasks rather than on only one task, such as Wason's (1966) selection task. Frequently, range of transfer and size of training effects are correlated negatively so that a training with broad effects produces relatively small effects on many tasks, whereas a narrower training may lead to large training gains in one particular task and have little or no effects on other tasks (Klauer, 1989). Future work might look at range of transfer over and above effect size, and it can be speculated that training grounded in semantics exhibits broader effects than training of task-specific solution strategies.

REFERENCES

Baddeley, A. D. (1986). *Working memory*. Oxford, UK: Clarendon.

Braine, M. D. S., & O'Brien, D. P. (1998). The theory of mental-propositional logic: Description and illustration. In M. D. S. Braine & D. P. O'Brien (Eds.), *Mental logic* (pp. 79– 89). Mahwah, NJ: Lawrence Erlbaum Associates.

Braine, M. D. S., O'Brien, D. P., Noveck, I. A., Samuels, M. C., Lea, R. B., Fisch, S. M., & Yang, Y. (1995). Predicting intermediate and multiple conclusions in propositional logic inference problems: Further evidence for a mental logic. *Journal of Experimental Psychology: General, 124,* 263–292.

Braine, M. D. S., Reiser, B. J., & Rumain, B. (1984). Some empirical justification for a theory of natural propositional logic. In G. H. Bower (Ed.), *The psychology of learning and motivation: Advances in research and thinking* (Vol. 18, pp. 313–371). San Diego, CA: Academic Press.

Braine, M. D. S., & Rumain, B. (1983). Logical reasoning. In J. H. Flavell & E. M. Markman (Eds.), *Handbook of child psychology: Vol. 3. Cognitive development* (pp. 263–340). New York: Wiley.

Cheng, P. W., & Holyoak, K. J. (1985). Pragmatic reasoning schemas. *Cognitive Psychology, 17,* 391–416.

Cheng, P. W., & Holyoak, K. J. (1989). On the natural selection of reasoning theories. *Cognition, 33,* 285–313.

Cheng, P. W., Holyoak, K. J., Nisbett, R. E., & Oliver, L. M. (1986). Pragmatic versus syntactic approaches to training deductive reasoning. *Cognitive Psychology, 18,* 293–328.

Cosmides, L. (1989). The logic of social exchange: Has natural selection shaped how humans reason? Studies with the Wason selection task. *Cognition, 31,* 187–276.

Evans, J. St. B. T. (1983). Linguistic determinants of bias in conditional reasoning. *Quarterly Journal of Experimental Psychology, 35A,* 635–644.

Evans, J. St. B. T. (1989). *Bias in human reasoning: Causes and consequences*. Hillsdale, NJ: Lawrence Erlbaum Associates.

Evans, J. St. B. T., & Clibbens, J. (1995). Perspective shifts on the selection task: Reasoning or relevance? *Thinking and Reasoning, 1,* 315–323.

Evans, J. St. B. T., & Over, D. E. (1996). *Rationality and reasoning*. Hove, UK: Psychology Press.

Gigerenzer, G. (1996). Rationality: Why social context matters. In P. Baltes & U. M. Staudinger (Eds.), *Interactive minds: Life-span perspectives on the social foundation of cognition* (pp. 319–346). Cambridge, UK: Cambridge University Press.

Gilhooly, K. J., Logie, R. H., & Wynn, V. (1999). Syllogistic reasoning tasks, working memory, and skill. *European Journal of Cognitive Psychology, 11,* 473–498.

Griggs, R. A. (1983). The role of problem content in the selection task and in the THOG problem. In J. St. B. T. Evans (Ed.), *Thinking and reasoning:*

Psychological approaches (pp. 16–43). London: Routledge and Kegan Paul.

Holyoak, K. J., & Cheng, P. W. (1995). Pragmatic reasoning with a point of view. *Thinking and Reasoning, 1,* 289–313.

Houdé, O., & Moutier, S. (1996). Deductive reasoning and experimental inhibition: The case of the matching bias. *Cahiers de Psychologie Cognitive, 15,* 409–434.

Johnson-Laird, P. N. (1983). *Mental models. Towards a cognitive science of language, inference, and consciousness.* Cambridge, UK: Cambridge University Press.

Johnson-Laird, P. N., & Byrne, R. M. J. (1991). *Deduction.* Hillsdale, NJ: Lawrence Erlbaum Associates.

Johnson-Laird, P. N., Byrne, R. M. J., & Schaeken, W. (1992). Propositional reasoning by model. *Psychological Review, 99,* 418–439.

Klaczynski, P. A. (1993). Reasoning schema effects on adolescent rule acquisition and transfer. *Journal of Educational Psychology, 85,* 679–692.

Klaczynski, P. A., Gelfand, H., & Reese, H. W. (1989). Transfer of conditional reasoning: Effects of explanations and initial problem types. *Memory and Cognition, 17,* 208-220.

Klaczynski, P. A., & Laipple, J. S. (1993). Role of content domain, logic training, and IQ in rule acquisition and transfer. *Journal of Experimental Psychology: Learning, Memory, and Cognition, 19,* 653–672.

Klauer, K. C. (1999). On the normative justification for information gain in Wason's selection task. *Psychological Review, 106,* 215–222.

Klauer, K. C., Meiser, T., & Naumer, B. (2000). Training propositional reasoning. *Quarterly Journal of Experimental Psychology, 53A,* 868–895.

Klauer, K. C., Stegmaier, R., & Meiser, T. (1997). Working memory involvement in propositional and spatial reasoning. *Thinking and Reasoning, 3,* 9–46.

Klauer, K. J. (1989). Die Messung von Transferdistanzen. Ein Verfahren zur Bestimmung der Unähnlichkeit von Aufgabenanforderungen [The measurement of transfer distance. A method for determining the dissimilarity of tasks]. *Zeitschrift für Entwicklungspsychologie und Pädagogische Psychologie, 21,* 146–166.

Lehman, D. R., Lempert, R. O., & Nisbett, R. E. (1988). The effects of graduate training on reasoning: Formal discipline and thinking about everyday-life events. *American Psychologist, 43,* 431–442.

Lehman, D. R., & Nisbett, R. E. (1990). A longitudinal study on the effects of undergraduate training on reasoning. *Developmental Psychology, 26,* 952–960.

Logie, R. H., & Gilhooly, K. J. (1998). *Working memory and thinking.* Hove, UK: Psychology Press.

Markovits, H., & Savary, F. (1992). Pragmatic schemas and the selection task: To reason or not to reason. *Quarterly Journal of Experimental Psychology, 45A,* 133–148.

Meiser, T., Klauer, K. C., & Naumer, B. (2001). Propositional reasoning and working memory: The role of prior training and pragmatic contents. *Acta Psychologica, 106,* 303–327.

Morris, M. W., & Nisbett, R. E. (1993). Tools of the trade: Deductive schemas taught in psychology and philosophy. In R. E. Nisbett (Ed.), *Rules for reasoning* (pp. 228–256). Hillsdale, NJ: Lawrence Erlbaum Associates.

Oaksford, M., & Chater, N. (1994). A rational analysis of the selection task as optimal data selection. *Psychological Review, 101,* 608–631.

O'Brien, D. P., & Overton, W. F. (1980). Conditional reasoning following contradictory evidence: A developmental analysis. *Journal of Experimental Child Psychology, 30,* 44–61.

O'Brien, D. P., & Overton, W. F. (1982). Conditional reasoning and the competence-performance issue: A developmental analysis of a training task. *Journal of Experimental Child Psychology, 34,* 274–290.

Overton, W., Byrnes, J. P., & O'Brien, D. P. (1985). Developmental and individual differences in conditional reasoning: The role of contradiction training and cognitive style. *Developmental Psychology, 21,* 692–701.

Pollard, P. (1982). Human reasoning: Some possible effects of availability. *Cognition, 12,* 65–96.

Raven, J. C. (1962). *Advanced progressive matrices, Set II.* London: H. K. Lewis.

Rips, L. J. (1994) .*The psychology of proof.* Cambridge, MA: MIT Press.

Sperber, D., Cara, F., & Girotto, V. (1995). Relevance theory explains the selection task. *Cognition, 57,* 31–95.

Stanovich, K. E. (1999). *Who is rational? Studies of individual differences in reasoning.* Mahwah, NJ: Lawrence Erlbaum Associates.

Thompson, V. A. (1995). Conditional reasoning: The necessary and sufficient conditions. *Canadian Journal of Experimental Psychology, 49,* 1–58.

Wason, P. C. (1966). Reasoning. In B. M. Foss (Ed.), *New horizons in psychology 1* (pp. 135–151). Harmondsworth, UK: Penguin.

Ziegler, A. (1990). Deduktives Schließen mit mentalen Modellen [Deductive reasoning with mental models]. *Sprache and Kognition, 9,* 82–91.

Author Index

Subject Index